Widows of Japan

JAPANESE SOCIETY SERIES
General Editor: Yoshio Sugimoto

Lives of Young Koreans in Japan
Yasunori Fukuoka

Globalization and Social Change in Contemporary Japan
J.S. Eades, Tom Gill and Harumi Befu

Coming Out in Japan: The Story of Satoru and Ryuta
Satoru Ito and Ryuta Yanase

Japan and Its Others:
Globalization, Difference and the Critique of Modernity
John Clammer

Hegemony of Homogeneity: An Anthropological Analysis of Nihonjinron
Harumi Befu

Foreign Migrants in Contemporary Japan
Hiroshi Komai

A Social History of Science and Technology in Contempory Japan, Volume 1
Shigeru Nakayama

Farewell to Nippon: Japanese Lifestyle Migrants in Australia
Machiko Sato

The Peripheral Centre:
Essays on Japanese History and Civilization
Johann P. Arnason

A Genealogy of 'Japanese' Self-images
Eiji Oguma

Class Structure in Contemporary Japan
Kenji Hashimoto

An Ecological View of History
Tadao Umesao

Nationalism and Gender
Chizuko Ueno

Native Anthropology: The Japanese Challenge to Western Academic Hegemony
Takami Kuwayama

Youth Deviance in Japan: Class Reproduction of Non-Conformity
Robert Stuart Yoder

Japanese Companies: Theories and Realities
Masami Nomura and Yoshihiko Kamii

From Salvation to Spirituality: Popular Religious Movements in Modern Japan
Susumu Shimazono

The 'Big Bang' in Japanese Higher Education:
The 2004 Reforms and the Dynamics of Change
J.S. Eades, Roger Goodman and Yumiko Hada

Japanese Politics: An Introduction
Takashi Inoguchi

A Social History of Science and Technology in Contempory Japan, Volume 2
Shigeru Nakayama

Gender and Japanese Management
Kimiko Kimoto

Philosophy of Agricultural Science: A Japanese Perspective
Osamu Soda

A Social History of Science and Technology in Contempory Japan, Volume 3
Shigeru Nakayama and Kunio Goto

Japan's Underclass: Day Laborers and the Homeless
Hideo Aoki

A Social History of Science and Technology in Contemporary Japan, Volume 4
Shigeru Nakayama and Hitoshi Yoshioka

Scams and Sweeteners: A Sociology of Fraud
Masahiro Ogino

Toyota's Assembly Line: A View from the Factory Floor
Ryoji Ihara

Village Life in Modern Japan: An Environmental Perspective
Akira Furukawa

Social Welfare in Japan: Principles and Applications
Kojun Furukawa

Escape from Work: Freelancing Youth and the Challenge to Corporate Japan
Reiko Kosugi

Japan's Whaling: The Politics of Culture in Historical Perspective
Hiroyuki Watanabe

Gender Gymnastics: Performing and Consuming Japan's Takarazuka Revue
Leonie R. Stickland

Poverty and Social Welfare in Japan
Masami Iwata and Akihiko Nishizawa

The Modern Japanese Family: Its Rise and Fall
Chizuko Ueno

Widows of Japan: An Anthropological Perspective
Deborah McDowell Aoki

Social Stratification and Inequality Series

Inequality amid Affluence: Social Stratification in Japan
Junsuke Hara and Kazuo Seiyama

Intentional Social Change: A Rational Choice Theory
Yoshimichi Sato

Constructing Civil Society in Japan: Voices of Environmental Movements
Koichi Hasegawa

Deciphering Stratification and Inequality: Japan and beyond
Yoshimichi Sato

Social Justice in Japan: Concepts, Theories and Paradigms
Ken-ichi Ohbuchi

Gender and Career in Japan
Atsuko Suzuki

Status and Stratification: Cultural Forms in East and Southeast Asia
Mutsuhiko Shima

Globalization, Minorities and Civil Society:
Perspectives from Asian and Western Cities
Koichi Hasegawa and Naoki Yoshihara

Fluidity of Place: Globalization and the Transformation of Urban Space
Naoki Yoshihara

Advanced Social Research Series

A Sociology of Happiness
Kenji Kosaka

Frontiers of Social Research: Japan and beyond
Akira Furukawa

A Quest for Alternative Sociology
Kenji Kosaka and Masahiro Ogino

MODERNITY AND IDENTITY IN ASIA SERIES

Globalization, Culture and Inequality in Asia
Timothy S. Scrase, Todd Miles Joseph Holden and Scott Baum

Looking for Money:
Capitalism and Modernity in an Orang Asli Village
Alberto Gomes

Governance and Democracy in Asia
Takashi Inoguchi and Matthew Carlson

Liberalism: Its Achievements and Failures
Kazuo Seiyama

Health Inequalities in Japan: An Empirical Study of Older People
Katsunori Kondo

Widows of Japan
An Anthropological Perspective

Deborah McDowell Aoki

Trans Pacific Press

Melbourne

First published in 2010 by
Trans Pacific Press, PO Box 164, Balwyn North, Victoria 3104, Australia
Telephone: +61 (0)3 9859 1112 Fax: +61 (0)3 9589 4110
Email: tpp.mail@gmail.com
Web: http://www.transpacificpress.com

Copyright © Trans Pacific Press 2011

Designed and set by Digital Environs, Melbourne, Australia. www.digitalenvirons.com

Distributors

Australia and New Zealand
DA Information Services/Central Book Services
648 Whitehorse Road
Mitcham, Victoria 3132
Australia
Telephone: +61-3-9210-7777
Fax: + 61-3-9210-7788
Email: books@dadirect.com
Web: www.dadirect.com

USA and Canada
International Specialized Book Services (ISBS)
920 NE 58th Avenue, Suite 300
Portland, Oregon 97213-3786
USA
Telephone: 1-800-944-6190
Fax: 1-503-280-8832
Email: orders@isbs.com
Web: http://www.isbs.com

Asia and the Pacific
Kinokuniya Company Ltd.

Head office:
3-7-10 Shimomeguro
Meguro-ku
Tokyo 153-8504
Japan
Telephone: +81-3-6910-0531
Fax: +81-3-6420-1362
Email: bkimp@kinokuniya.co.jp
Web: www.kinokuniya.co.jp

Asia-Pacific office:
Kinokuniya Book Stores of Singapore Pte., Ltd.
391B Orchard Road #13-06/07/08
Ngee Ann City Tower B
Singapore 238874
Telephone: +65-6276-5558
Fax: +65-6276-5570
Email: SSO@kinokuniya.co.jp

All rights reserved. No production of any part of this book may take place without the written permission of Trans Pacific Press.

ISSN   1443–9670 (Japanese Society Series)

ISBN   978–1–920901–28–8 (Paperback)

The National Library of Australia Cataloguing-in-Publication entry

Aoki, Deborah McDowell.
  Widows of Japan: an anthropological perspective / Deborah McDowell Aoki.
  ISBN: 978 1 920901 28 8 (pbk.).
  Japanese society series.
  Includes bibliographical references and index.
  Widows – Japan – History.
  Women – Japan – Social conditions.
306.8830952

Cover illustration: War widow praying with her infant and child at Yasukuni Shrine during World War II. The widow in this picture is represented as a teacher who dedicated her husband to the war and gave birth to a boy.

Contents

Photographs	viii
Tables	ix
Note on Japanese Translations, Names and Places	xi
Acknowledgements	xii
1. Introduction	1
2. Cross-Cultural and Historical Perspectives	16
3. History of Widows in Japan	32
4. War Widows: Poverty, Activism and Identity	49
5. At the Crossroads of Life and Death: Ethnography of ritual and ceremony	83
6. Life as a Widow	104
7. Conclusion – The 'New Widows' – Free at Last	131
Endnotes	139
References	152
Index	168

Photographs

4.1: War widow praying with her infant and child
at Yasukuni Shrine.   55
4.2: A widow portrayed as an eroticized figure.   66
4.3: Two older brothers going off to war and
Katsumi-san.   77
4.4: Tokiko-san right before marriage.   79
4.5: War widows paying their respects to the war
dead at Yasukuni Shrine.   81
5.1: In front of the Butsudan.   93
7.1: Two widows: Katsumi-san and Tokiko-san.   132

Tables

6.1: Percent of irregular employees by sex in the
      labor force   109
6.2: Total number of widows in Japan   113

Note on Japanese Translations, Names and Places

Following anthropological practice and with respect for the privacy requests of individuals who contributed to this book, all names of places and informants have been changed except for those of major cities such as: Tokyo, Nagoya and Sapporo. The names of these larger cities have been written without macrons in the following text. Japanese individuals who have published works in English and have expressed their preference are cited with personal names first, while other names are written in accordance with the Japanese practice of writing surnames before given names. All translations are the work of Drs. Deborah McDowell Aoki and Osamu Aoki.

Acknowledgements

The groundwork for the idea to devote a book exclusively to widows in Japan originated while conducting dissertation research in Japan almost 15 years ago. At that time, I was examining the problem of gender and the household division of labor and in the process of carrying-out these interviews became interested in the issues of widows. The stories of loss, societal discrimination, surveillance, new challenges and finally freedom greatly shaped the resulting research and solidified my view that widows have experiences which are often different than those of married women. Additionally, I was initiated into the laws regarding widows which existed in the Meiji Civil Code, as well as the cultural customs based on these laws which still silently but pervasively exist even today.

The challenges and learning experiences involved in the research were abundant, and I am grateful for the participation of the widows who donated their voices, time and personal experiences to facilitate the work. There is no way to repay them for their many kindnesses, and I will always be indebted; some of these women have passed away before the completion of this book for which I am deeply saddened. I would like to acknowledge Suzuki Itsuko, a tireless activist for women's rights and a fair pension for widows. I thank her for her support and insight regarding war widows, as well as her kindness in freely sharing precious photographs and accounts of widow's political activism. She remains my most important and ardent supporter.

I wish to express my additional thanks to all of those supporters who helped make this work a completed reality. From the beginning, my husband and collaborator, Osamu Aoki, Professor at Hokkaido National University, patiently read and re-read this book in order to make salient and insightful revisions greatly contributing to its final form and content. His assistance in the translations of Japanese to English enhanced this work beyond measure. Many of the connections to informants were based on a close affiliation with a research group at Hokkaido University and various volunteer/

Acknowledgements

service groups associated with the university. A special thank you goes to Professor Hiroshi Sugimura (Hōsei University) and Dr. Mika Iwata (Hōsei University) for their help and suggestions. My warmest appreciation goes to Chiaki Ono who helped me with the translation (English version). I also acknowledge my long-time advisor and friend, Dr. Richard H. Moore of The Ohio State University, for his gracious assistance and detailed comments. Dr. Keith Kilty, also of The Ohio State University, patiently read the manuscript offering his positive encouragement. Professor Evelyn Christner greatly contributed to the final editing of the manuscript. Professor Kayoko Yoshida, Hokusei Gakuen University, supported and encouraged me to take a one year sabbatical in order to complete the manuscript. Participant observation of the memorial ceremony and accompanying rituals carried out in Honshū (Aichi Prefecture) was made possible through friends and family members enhanced by my many years of residence in Japan. Interviews in Tokyo and Aichi Prefecture were also facilitated through friends who arranged interviews with willing participants.

A special thank you goes to Machiko Yoshikawa for her help in facilitating interviews in a small mining town in northern Japan. Another note of acknowledgement goes to the individuals who generously allowed me to use copies of pictures, letters and other materials. My thanks to *U.S.-Japan's Women's Journal* for their permission to use parts of an article upon which a slightly different and expanded Part 4 of this book is based.

I appreciate the financial support of Hokusei Gakuen University of Sapporo, Japan for generously funding a one-year sabbatical leave in Tokyo at Ochanomizu Women's University and providing a publication grant for the Japanese version of this book by Akashi Shoten. Lastly, I want to send a thank you to my fellow researchers who are studying the problems and issues regarding widows. I was greatly inspired and encouraged at the GENCAS Conference on widows in July 2007 at the University of Wales, Swansea. Many of the ideas contained in this book were formulated and shaped through the interaction with other scholars who attended this conference.

1 Introduction

This book presents a wide-ranging and intimate study of widows in Japan filtered through the dramatic and complex intersection of women with death as intensely personal and yet foreshadowing momentous societal ramifications. The work represents eight years of ongoing research and fifty-eight personal interviews conducted throughout the country. It situates widowed women in the arena of Japan's political economy, but also presents the voices of widows who participated in the research. Why write a book about widows? Widows provide a point of focus for a multi-level analysis through the exploration of the inner-workings of the state, the family and the social relations of gender.[1]

Placing widows at the core of the study provides an opportunity to integrate and address important themes addressed throughout the book. These themes include: the fetishism of female bodies to protect and embody family honor, the historical role of state formation in creating family and kinship systems, and the integrative functions provided by women. The issues collectively establish a platform for a cross-cultural comparison to establish common ground in the historical interaction between women and the developing state (McGinn, 2008). However, to situate widows as a particular group for research is hardly a new idea as reflected at an international conference at the University of Wales – GENCAS 2007. Specific laws, cultural customs, issues of sexuality, land ownership, custody of children, gender ideologies and most dramatically the influences of war, all may come into play when a woman becomes a widow (Owen, 1996). All of these dimensions are detailed and linked using extensive documentation, life histories and interviews with a view to reclaiming the history of widows of Japan.

Japan, considered the most rapidly aging society in the world, can be positioned as a weather vane heralding the future direction of the winds that will shape advanced industrialized nations throughout the 21st century. To provide a further perspective, according to the 2000 population census figures released by the Japanese

Government, widows comprised thirteen percent of the total number of women in Japan (Population Census of Japan 2000, pp.100–101). More recently in 2004, the average life-span of Japanese women rocketed to 85.5 years making them the longest living group in the world; they now outlive their Japanese male counter-parts by eight years with projections for an even greater gap in longevity between women and men expected by the year 2020 (*http://www.mhlw.go.jp/toukei/saikin* [Accessed 12 August 2005]). The figures represent a steadily increasing group of widowed women who face numerous problems as they negotiate economic and social realities.

The research includes women from diverse social, educational, and economic strata ranging from a highly educated middle-upper-class tea ceremony teacher to women working as part-time cooks, day laborers, fish packers, egg factory workers, vegetable pickers and maids. Political activists are represented, as well as widows who lost husbands in New Guinea, the Philippines or Manchuria during the Pacific War and in coal-mining accidents in northern Japan. By portraying widows engaged in disparate work reflecting class differences, the book avoids the facile construction of one particular 'blueprint' of widows; however, to balance this point of view, common experiences which affect all women are explicated through focusing upon the synergistic effects of history, family structure and the development of the state. More clearly, it is not a simple dichotomy of presenting a picture of 'difference' versus one reflecting commonalities but rather, there are areas of overlap and convergence which are detailed. The book is informed by these dimensions and the connections among them illustrating that political and economic structures are interlocked and serve to reinforce each other. These points of intersection create legal and societal constraints on the rights and opportunities of widows; even so, as the following pages reveal, women actively make the most of hard-won niches carved out of these challenging and sometimes tragic situations.

Historically, most cultures examined in anthropological research clearly delineated the roles of wives and husbands, widows and widowers, concentrating on functional aspects of family life, and the hierarchical transmission of property and assets through men. There have been notable exceptions in English involving such research in other countries (e.g., Potash, 1986; Owen, 1996; Lopata, 1996; Kerns, 1997), where the multifaceted roles of widows were examined in detail. There are a few comprehensive English references in recent academic discourse, which acknowledge the crucial roles that women play in funeral and mortuary rituals in Japan (Sered, 1999; Bremmer & Van Den Bosch, 1995; Martinez, 1995; Traphagan, 2004). Along with detailed interviews, studies and references in Japanese are translated and used extensively as an indispensable basis for this work making these materials available for the first time in English.

Recently, poverty and more specifically the feminization of poverty have been 'discovered' in Japan. A distinctive feature of this research is the examination of the accelerating problem of impoverishment among single women and the elderly; the work highlights the disjuncture between the lives of low-income widows with those of more affluent widows. Although the annual income of widows varies, a government cabinet report states that 39.6 percent of women over 65 years old (for men the percentage is 21.5), who are living alone have an income of less than $12,000 per year. Additionally, the average annual income of all single mother families is $21,200 per year (Nationwide Report on the Survey of Single Mothers, *Zenkoku Boshi Setai tō Chōsa Kekka Hōkoku*, 2005). The National Pension System provides a minimum public assistance base of approximately $8,000 per year even though the poverty line (loosely set by welfare policy) is approximately $10,000 to $13,000 per person per year (variation in payment is based on community). The research reflects the little known fact that of the approximately 7,660,000 million widows in Japan, about forty percent live at or below the poverty line (Population Census of Japan, 2005; Government Cabinet Report, 2003).

Far from the common stereotype, which arose during the 1980s expansive economic bubble-period, that all Japanese are wealthy and that most widows are assisted and provided for by family members, this study interrogates these presumptions through the narratives of widows who struggle just to make ends meet.[2] Japan has been undergoing a severe recession and class bipolarization due to the effects of corporate downsizing, outsourcing of jobs, and a relentless restructuring of the labor market into a dual-track (featuring regular well-paid employees and part-time low-wage workers) system, which has created ripples of uncertainty and anxiety among Japanese people (OECD, 2005; Aoki and Aoki 2005, pp. 1–21).

Even though most individuals have national health insurance and a pension, there is a substantial gap among persons who receive medical and/or social support services (Hiraoka, 2001; Kondō, 2005). The research documents how this gap is particularly played out in the lives of widows and shows that not only is the problem of poverty worsening, but the growing bipolarization of rich and poor is now clearly manifested (Tachibanaki, 1998; Satō, 2000). Among widows, the respective job statuses of deceased husbands represent a major point of economic disjuncture due to the overall low pension payments by the state. Women "alone" are confronting their own aging, and under the current economic conditions, many of them are frequently living on meager pensions, caring for an elderly parent or attempting to turn to their own children (usually with little success) for financial assistance; these situations reflect the escalating trend of poverty throughout the country.

Research method and context

This book is based on a long-term study beginning in 1996 and is the result of qualitative research including participant observation, personal interviews, informal conversations and questionnaire distribution. Thirteen of the fifty-eight interviews involved multiple visits and detailed life histories taken over several years. In order to reflect as many different localities as possible, questionnaires were disseminated and interviews were conducted with widows in a small rural city outside Nagoya in Aichi Prefecture and from large urban cities such as Tokyo and Sapporo (in Hokkaido Prefecture, the second largest and northernmost island). Attention given to the regional differences and the many overlapping similarities throughout the country enables the construction of a complex and nuanced picture of Japanese culture and history (Bailey 1991, pp. 5–6; Rosenberger, 2001). The majority of the women (forty of the fifty-eight), who contributed to this research through personal interviews were solidly in the very low household income range (defined as near or below poverty levels) of $10,000 to $20,000 or less per year with the remaining participants in the middle-upper-class range from $40,000 to $120,000 and above per annum. Thus the discontinuities, which exist throughout Japan, represented by lower, middle, and higher income groups are reflected, along with other axes of difference delineated among women of different ages and rural and urban area distinctions.

Aichi Prefecture located in the central area of Honshū, the main island of Japan, provides the ethnographic context for the Buddhist memorial ritual presented in this book, as well as a major source of additional informants. Hokkaido Prefecture remains one of the most impoverished areas of present-day Japan, and there continues to be a low percentage of manufacturing jobs available in the local economy compared to the heavily industrialized core regions such as Aichi Prefecture (the home base of the well-known automobile manufacturer Toyota). Manufacturing employment provides higher salaries, stable employment and liberal benefits, but such jobs currently account for only 8.4 percent of total employment in the Hokkaido region. In marked contrast to the security provided by employment in manufacturing, one of the largest employment sectors in Hokkaido involves unstable manual and day labor, construction work, and jobs related to seasonal public investment projects, e.g., highway maintenance and road repair (Population Census of Japan, 2005). The juxtaposition of these two areas of Aichi and Hokkaido Prefectures dovetails neatly with the current problem of the economic bipolarization throughout the country.

Without the infusion of government funds via various public work projects, Hokkaido would sink even further into a serious economic depression fueled by rampant unemployment and unabated deflation. In a determined effort to stimulate the flagging economy, local people are promoting sight-seeing tours to residents of other Asian countries, such as Taiwan, Korea, and China and heavily advertising Hokkaido as a resort area offering luxurious hotels and hot springs, along with the natural beauty of the island. One of the important results of Hokkaido's continued stagnant economic situation and absence of job opportunities providing adequate salaries and benefits is that significant out-migration to large cities like Tokyo is occurring. This trend is contributing to a serious depopulation of the province with the exception of its largest city, Sapporo.[3] Approximately seventy percent of the population of Hokkaido is concentrated in urbanized areas such as Sapporo, Asahikawa and Hakodate with a total population of 5,660,000 accounting for 4.4 percent of Japan's total population. The average size of a household in Hokkaido has steadily contracted and stands at 2.36 people representing a continuous downward spiral from the 2000 average of 2.42 and the 1980 average of 3.0 people. Within this demographic picture of the Hokkaido Region, there are approximately 366,805 widows and about 70,870 widowers (Population Census, 2005).

In contrast, Aichi Prefecture has a total population of 7,250,000 representing approximately 15.7 percent of Japan's total population. Even in Japan's depressed economy, manufacturing jobs still make up about 26.4 percent of employment in Aichi Province, which is significantly greater than Hokkaido's 8.4 percent and considerably higher than the national average of Japan at 17.3 percent. Aichi Prefecture has a large urban city, Nagoya, where the average size of a household stands at 2.63. Thus the Aichi area, even in Japan's present economic situation, is considered one of the wealthiest regions of the country.

Among the older residents in small villages outside of Nagoya remain tightly knit rural communities where the traditional family system (*ie seido*)[4] still operates. Families expect to keep land and assets intact for the (usually) eldest son of the next generation. Even in recent times, women complain that they are dominated and controlled while living in the countryside where a father's word remains law, and an elder brother is considered to hold a position above that of any other child in the family. For many rural families, the *ie* system continues to exert an abiding influence rooted in strong, frequently idealized, attachments to farming and land with accompanying rhetoric embedded in a discourse of ancestral duty, nationalism and reciprocity. In the case of some upper-class families (e.g., in the ethnography presented in this book), the *ie* may be connected to and situated within the distinctive cultural milieu of *ikebana* (flower arrangement) and the *chanoyu* (tea ceremony) traditions. Research in this small rural city shows that the residents continue their traditions and the village represents a conservative area; it is located a mere fifteen kilometers from Nagoya and only two hours from Tokyo via the *shinkansen* (bullet train). Thus the town actually has two distinct and discordant faces including that of an historical and traditionally conservative rural village and a new, rapidly expanding bed-town with younger people settling in who frequently do not have the same traditional values as older residents.

In conducting the research, community centers and city offices throughout Japan were used as bases of operations for interviews and to establish contact with others who might be interested in becoming research participants. Interviews were then carried-out at the community center and/or at the homes of participants. Problematically, as in the translation of any language into another, meanings of words are not always equivalent. Therefore, some editing is essential and at times a particular meaning or nuance was chosen depending upon the context of the situation. After every interview, translations of narratives in Japanese and English were prepared and compared for clarity, accuracy and context. Although this process naturally presupposes the somewhat arbitrary nature of translating one language into another, I assert that the final English narratives expressed in this study reflect the basic thoughts, feelings and words of the Japanese women interviewed.

The narratives I have chosen to present are, and perhaps this is axiomatic for researchers, from those widows who were the most talkative and cooperative. The narrative style was carefully selected because, as Tamanoi (1998) has argued, it is essential in understanding a group which has been muted and rendered invisible in the official records and history of their country. Furthermore, topics relating to death and personal family relationships are usually not interrogated in Japanese culture. The inclusion of personal narratives helps mediate objectifying descriptions by softening the contradiction between the personal and sometimes emotional stories of the informants and the authoritarian voice of social science (Pratt, 1986); the narratives give life to the sometimes dry pages of academic discourse. Self-conscious attention has been given to the presentation of the voices of informants in detail, while carefully locating events in historical contexts and exposing the differences in individual experiences. However, within these differences there are overlapping constraints placed upon women through structural impediments enforced by the state, community and the codification of laws (e.g., the law regarding waiting 6 months until remarriage still remains intact as a relic of the Meiji Code). The informants included in this work reflect a multitude of experiences and gleaning the variations, as well as the similarities encompassed in women's narratives, represents a definitive research theme throughout the book.

Within socially constructed landscapes, resistance, negotiation and empowerment are discordantly expressed; thus there is no portrayal of widows in a unilateral way as passive victims. The many strategies and formations of political organizations that widows initiated after the Pacific War to obtain desperately needed governmental assistance to ensure their future and that of their children are documented. These powerful political movements provide a positive counter-point to stereotypical images of widows as powerless. Although women's movements in Japan have been characterized as being localized, fragmented and based on a single issue (Gelb, 2003), widow's political organizations formed to regain their pension and dignity encompassed not only local communities but eventually embraced other supporters nationally. During these national meetings, widows passionately articulated their views regarding the merits of diverse political strategies (Suzuki, 1983). However, while recognizing the ability of women to work positively and accomplish much, widows operated within areas of constraint and structural impediments, as will be detailed throughout the book.

The research indicates that throughout the country, communities have historically attempted to control the behavior of widows, through both covert and overt methods, employing a variety of disciplinary mechanisms including: physical coercion, exclusionary tactics, neighborhood and police enforced observation, targeted gossip, societal condemnation and even isolation of the offending individual. While these basic methods have been practiced in many societies, they are particularly effective in Japan (Foucault, 1979). Widow surveillance, i.e., "widow-watching" emerged as a predominant theme of societal coercion particularly during wartime, but the practice continues in a covert fashion in present-day Japan.

The examination of the lives of these women provides a critical elucidation of the nature of hidden politics deeply entrenched in the social site of the family. The book also presents a response to inquiries regarding the necessity to clarify the differences and hierarchies among women, as well as those between women and men (Moore, 1989; Brown, Subbaiah, Sarah, 1998; Lamphere, 2001). The rupture among women depending upon marital status is not only economic, as shown in the study but is also reflected in the realities and social constraints within which widows live. Widowed women may actively discriminate against divorced women constituting a pervasive practice in many Japanese communities; however, the research will also show that widows in turn are discriminated against by married women fearful of the 'eroticized widow' stealing 'innocent' husbands.

The analysis makes the argument that while the individual expressions of women's experiences of widowhood are specific and diverse, there are general underlying causes and effects of transformations, which can be directly traced to the influences of history, family and state development. Through the explication of these large-scale processes on widows, families and communities, the specific nature of local and individual responses is revealed. By examining the 'bigger picture' but also thoroughly analyzing the details, the book illustrates the necessity for ethnography, as well as theoretical and analytical rigor, through the presentation of a multi-layered analysis at the individual, local, national and cross-cultural levels.

Organization of the Book

There is no argument advanced within these pages for an all-encompassing archetypal widow; however, it is also axiomatic that some widows have shared experiences, and many of these historical developments and experiences have been and continue to be reflected cross-culturally as will be shown in Part 2. While a woman becomes a widow through the intersection of events and circumstances arising at a particular time and place, gendered and structural impediments affect women in very real and concrete ways. Approximately thirty years ago it was noted (and the argument is no less relevant today), that the institutionalization of sexual inequality is widespread throughout the world and deeply embedded in a long and complex history (Reiter, 1975). To better understand the current permutations of inequality, it is necessary to 'dig out' the roots of these inequalities and trace them through their origins and various manifestations. Therefore, Part 2 exposes the connections between the cultures of China, Korea and Japan highlighting cross-cultural similarities in the processes of family development and state hierarchies of power, as well as teasing out the differences.

The concept of patriarchies[5] facilitates analysis of the historical and societal aspects of women's positions; this enables the analysis to be centered in cultural and spatial dimensions circumventing biologically reductionist points of view. Throughout Part 2, the concept of patriarchy will be reinvigorated and specifically utilized to explicate the different strands of dominance, resistance and negotiation interwoven in history, family and society on a cross-cultural basis (McGinn, 2008). The chapter focuses on linking the individual to the past and present carefully maintaining cultural contexts while making comparisons. Within this purview, we can adapt various models under the rubric of 'particularized patriarchies' to combine the analytical power of the concept with the flexibility necessary to analyze diversity among cultures.

The underpinning theme throughout the book is that as states developed, there was systemic bias toward patriarchal interests through policies and actions. Although the government may act to protect the rights of women (e.g., the recent prosecution of sexual harassment suits that women have successfully pursued in Japan), their reasons for doing so are frequently based on preserving and protecting the societal status quo. How patriarchal and nation-state frameworks were specifically constructed, implemented and maintained is an important focus of the study, and the analysis seeks to clarify the impact of larger economic and political forces shaping the family in cross-cultural terms[6] (Lamphere, 2001; Mc Ginn. 2008).

In Part 3, the paths of widows from ancient historical periods to post-war Japan is both elucidating and didactic. While noting the transformational processes and the dynamics in the distribution of power occurring in society, the origins of gendered images and practices are revealed. The purpose of this in-depth examination is pragmatic in terms of the development of historical accounts and ramifications that are connected to specific legal and political impediments resonating in the everyday lives of widows even today. Furthermore, the chapter explores the complicated relationship between women, the family and the state reflecting the view that history has immanent meaning and that cultural and historical processes are linked to the events that follow.[7] The research demonstrates the structural and individual effects of historical legacies.

The dynamic interaction between the state and family is specifically analyzed by exploring how discriminatory practices against women originated and evolved in tandem with a developing patriarchal social order by tracing diverse influences from the ancient Heian Period (794–1191 C.E.) extending to present-day Japan. Beginning with one of these influences, Confucian ethics, Part 3 documents how these ethics were imported to Japan from

China initially in the Heian Era and transplanted onto indigenous social structures. The result of this superimposition was that Confucian morals, particularly filial piety, became an integrated part of Japanese culture and family through the initial adoption of particular aspects of the ideology by the feudal warrior (*buke*) class. The adoption of Confucianism led to the creation of a 'family-state' structure with the emperor at its apex and precipitated the transformation in roles and positions of women in the family and throughout society.

The resulting ramifications in inheritance and marital laws, government policies and institutionalized gender inequalities were eventually solidified in the Meiji Civil Code of 1898 (Ueno, 1994; Bernstein, 1991). For example, divorce was made more stigmatizing and more difficult to obtain for upper-class women. However, the law allowed a man to divorce his wife at any time; for ordinary people, however, as has often been noted, divorce was relatively common for both men and women (Fuess, 2004; Smith and Wiswell, 1982). These historical developments are connected to and reflected via language; thus Part 3 carefully documents linguistic shifts in terminology used for widows and links these changes to cultural and ideological transformations in society. The chapter crystallizes the 'power of naming,' as Bourdieu (1991, pp. 239–240) states, as a struggle over legitimacy regarding official views of the social world. Through the historical analysis presented, the positions of widows in society are explored by examining the interaction between ideology and state processes.

Part 4 documents how nationalistic sentiment fueled by the military government's support of Japan's imperial wars created conditions within which the options of widows were particularly limited. So-called 'choices' were sometimes enforced physically and rigorously through the power of the state and the tacit cooperation of individuals in the community; fetishisms were created and centered on the chastity of war widows maintained through coerced abortion. Through this state-sponsored violence, the alleged honor of men embodied by 'virtuous widows' was protected and promulgated. The documentation of the role of the state in perpetuating patrilineal kinship systems reflects how the institutionalization of inequality was solidified through law. Of course, the state does not operate monolithically. Thus this book follows the specific trajectory of how structural processes and historical legacies are translated into the everyday lives of women.

Part 4 also demonstrates that as Japan embarked upon a course of colonial conquest, widows were caught up in the turmoil of the country's militaristic regime; while soldiers declared their fidelity to emperor and country, wives and widows, particularly of high-ranking officers, were asked to support and even to promote the wars. The controversial issue of war widows as victims of the vicissitudes of war, co-conspirators in Japanese war propaganda or somewhere in-between is examined with references to recent discourse among scholars such as Ueno (2004, pp. 59–62) and Kawaguchi (2003). The treatment and history of war widows is a particularly urgent aspect of the research, since these women have experiences to share and stories that should be heard. However, most of the widows involved have now reached the ages of seventy, eighty and even ninety; the information that they can share will soon be lost to researchers. These stories of war or 'blood memories,' as Green (1999, p.170) has termed the war stories of widows, have created in widows a dual existence as both victims and survivors of wars. Their experiences also include the 'collateral' violence of war brought into the homes and everyday lives of women and children. In centering Part 4 on the subject of state sponsored violence, it is possible to connect gendered ideologies of women and masculinity and how these images were linked and put into the service of the wartime state.

In Part 5, the role of religious ritual in the lives of widows and its present-day, as well as historical, importance in the structure of the family is examined through an ethnographic study set in an upper-class family in Aichi Prefecture. The family represents a site of shifting values and challenges where once taken-for-granted relationships are undergoing rapid transformation in Japan. Issues involving widows in the family and society are frequently ignored, in part, because their roles and work are rendered invisible, and it is facilely assumed they are always taken care of and supported within the family (Aoki, 2000). This myth-making is perpetuated by the inadequate attention devoted to research focusing on widows, since most current studies pertain to questions relating to the provision of appropriate social services for aging women without consideration of the historical, cultural and social meanings of widowhood.

Considering the family as a political site leads to the exposure of kinship politics and economically based strategies through the analysis of how widows effectively use niches carefully sculpted out of the dominant structures in their everyday lives; these strategies illustrate how women both accommodate and subvert gender, family and class ideologies. The 'weapons' that widows may effectively use reflect this same theme of subversion and accommodation, as shown in the ethnography of a Buddhist memorial ceremony. The interpretation of ritual framed by the works of Van Gennep (1960){1908} and Turner (1969) has been adapted to Japanese ceremonies. The memorial rite is positioned in a seamless world of the living and dead where it is believed the deceased roam back and forth at will. The mediation of these worlds through ritual is the focus of the ethnographic study and includes participant-observation and conversations followed by a separate analysis addressing the implications of ritualized practices. It depicts the articulation between the widow's invisible work and the grounding of the memorial ceremony within the situated narrative. The chapter seeks to impart the liveliness of the conversations and the ritual experience itself with a feeling of being 'on the ground' and inside the activities taking place.

Widows may be viewed as mediating the 'corridor' between the living and the dead; they are symbolically feeding and appeasing hungry ghosts who are viewed as close-by watching and able to act in benign or malevolent ways with significant ramifications for the family and community (Namihira, 2004; Hori, 1986). Researchers studying Japan have devoted very little analysis to this critical role of women and their connection to symbolism and ceremony; existing studies focus on how women are excluded from, rather than involved in, this ostensibly male-dominated world as Martinez (1995, pp. 183–200) has noted. However, within the broader academic arena, scholars have long used rituals and rites of passage as classic vehicles for analyzing and understanding cultural meanings and as a reflection of social customs (Douglas, 1966; Lincoln, 1991). This rich field of exposition and the specific analysis of ritual in the lives of Japanese widows illustrated through this ethnographic case study will hopefully represent an important addition to the body of literature on religious rites and women in Japan.

In Part 6, widowhood is used as a vector through which investigation into the multiple causes of poverty, and its devastating effects on women and children in general and widows in particular, combine to form a critique of Japan's post-welfare state. The study contributes to the overall body of academic knowledge on the lives of impoverished women through opening a window to shed light on the realities of poverty. In analyzing pivotal issues including kinship and family networks, the influence of the state, retrenchment of social welfare programs, effects of restructuring and outsourcing of jobs, and the historical construction of images which stereotype women as *natural* care givers, the book addresses quintessential themes within the larger arena of studies of Japan. As one widow stated, "I've spent my entire life caring for other people, now I only have to care for myself. It's the best time in my life," and this widow's sentiments were resoundingly echoed from Aichi Prefecture to Hokkaido.

Throughout Part 6, cultural practices and conventions, which situate present-day widows in socially constructed roles, are reflected through narratives of resistance, accommodation and negotiation. This study necessarily engages other broadly based historical and societal issues such as the ongoing transition of women's roles in families and society, as well as widows living on government assistance, in rural farm areas and 'just getting by' in the workplace.

The book concludes with Part 7 and a discussion of the 'new widows.' These women did not passively accept definitions of roles or images assigned to them, but eventually found and constructed their own cultural and individual meanings with many of them declaring themselves 'free at last' after the death of a husband. This declaration represents a challenge to the Japanese family which is already in crisis. With widows in this research posing the question, 'what is marriage,' the very foundation of society is called into question. Furthermore, elderly widows who reject care giving roles send ripples of anxiety throughout the halls of the Japanese government, as it is still deeply dependent (although this is not acknowledged) upon women as care givers to absorb the social costs of its aging population.

The problem of rising poverty is also analyzed in the conclusion in Part 7 with a focus on widows, children and the elderly who are suffering the most. The conclusion will present the argument that widows and other female headed households historically have been impoverished with rates of poverty now accelerating in contemporary Japan. However, most widows greatly value their freedoms and are taking the power to define themselves and their own lives into their respective hands as they traverse the gendered terrain of widowhood in 21st century Japan.

2 Cross-Cultural and Historical Perspectives

Historical and cross-cultural positioning of widows within the framework of emerging state formation and changing family and kinship structures leads to a wide range of variation as well as similarities. Through an examination of the past, this chapter will show that common ground can be established while still elucidating variation, since these two foci of analysis are not mutually exclusive. In many cases (e.g., Japan), biological differences between women and men are not only reified through gender roles, but are solidified through structural implementation including inheritance laws, residence practices, state manipulation and transformations in family form. By focusing on widows as a group (as illustrated through the University of Wales GENCAS 'Merry Widow' International Conference in 2007) and following them through time and space, the ongoing changes in present-day society and the linkages of women's status in the family and state to historical events may be traced (McGinn, 2008). The strands of common ground which will specifically be traced in the following section include: 1) the integrative role of widows in early state formation and creation of kinship systems; 2) the role of widows through self-sacrifice; 3) structural violence targeted at widows and implemented through laws and codification of customs; and 4) the fetishism of women's bodies to protect male and family honor particularly with respect to widows.

Death, gender and widows in anthropological studies

Contemporary studies suggest that anthropologists can make meaningful cross-cultural and historically-based comparisons with the important caveat that attention must be given to teasing out cultural differences, for example, in focusing on the creation of laws with respect to inheritance and marriage structures not only on descent patterns per se (Goody 1990). In particular, kinship systems are intricately linked to descent and residence patterns which affect community networks and life (Goody, 1983; Parkin, 2004; Stone, 2001). Situating widows in this cross-cultural context mirrors the assertion that anthropologists have generally held that not only can concepts be 'culturally translated,' but after subjective meanings have been ascertained, these terms and ideas can be compared even across radically different societies (Goodman, 2002). History also shows that widows throughout the world may be forced through economic or by other means to re-marry or conversely prevented from re-marriage, and women may or may not inherit all (or even a portion) of the possessions and assets of deceased husbands (McGinn, 2008). Variations in customs and social practices regarding acceptable and non-acceptable behavior for widows can be linked to family ideology as well as the construction and maintenance of existing power structures within specific cultures.

Anthropological research has clearly illustrated the gendered aspects of bereavement and kinship roles when widows, but not widowers, are encouraged to assume greater responsibility for displaying extreme suffering and other ritualized behaviors. Cross-culturally family-based responsibilities including arranging burials, caring for the souls of dead family members and ritualized mourning are commonly left to widows, and these societal expectations and integrative practices are mirrored throughout the world (Owen, 1996; Weiner, 1988; Potash, 1986). Widows frequently have additional integrative functions and spiritual roles as bridges between the world of the living and that of the dead (a theme which will be explored in detail in Part 5).

Cultural expectations and ideologies *appear* to fuse naturally as part of the construction and socialization of gender roles and to define appropriate expressions of grief, ritualized practices and the obligations of mourning (Metcalf and Huntington, 1991; Maynes, Waltner, Soland and Strasser, 1996; Martin and Doka, 2000). However, as the following section will show, cultural norms and gender greatly affect rituals and accepted customs regarding the display of grief and who should and should not express sorrow, as well as the timing and duration of acceptable mourning behavior (Liu, 2000; Kerns, 1997).

The roles of widows in a global perspective

A brief exploration of historical contexts and a survey of customs in various cultures illustrate how the lives of widowed women are shaped by the four themes cited at the beginning of this chapter; major anthropological contributions have also reflected these linkages even seventy years ago. New Guinea has been a favorite area for study by anthropologists as many of the indigenous groups were not discovered by Western researchers until the 1930s. This reality led anthropologists to argue that the area was less contaminated by European contact (Faithorn, 1975; Dahlberg, 1981). Anthropologist Margaret Mead's classic 1935 work in New Guinea argued that Arapesh widows were frequently encouraged to re-marry preferably to one of the dead husband's relatives. There was strong pressure for widows to remain within the husband's kinship group because she was considered a family member, but no particular duration of mourning or special clothing was required for a widow nor was she expected to remain celibate for the remainder of her life. Mead (1935, pp.100–106) stated that among Arapesh widows, seventy-five percent of them re-married through the levirate custom by entering the home of the deceased husband's younger brother. Later, Evans-Pritchard (1956, pp. 162–164) stated that widows among the Nuer of Africa neither re-married nor did they inherit kinship assets but continued to be married to their respective husbands until the widow herself died. The Nuer people historically practiced the varied customs of the levirate (marriage to a brother of the deceased husband), widow-concubinage and ghost marriage (when a man dies without leaving a male heir); the important issue was the cultural insistence that widows keep the name of their deceased husband in perpetuity, and the children that she bears, as a widow-concubine or by the practice of levirate marriage, will have the name of the former husband. In this way, a widow solidified the children within the family and kinship group.

Another one of the most intensely studied groups in anthropological literature, the !Kung people of Africa, have been described by Draper (1975, pp. 77–109) and Lee and DeVore (1968) as gatherer-hunters who gradually adopted a settled way of life and exhibited a relatively egalitarian lifestyle based mostly on foraging and some hunting.. Both younger and older widows were encouraged to re-marry and build a new family life. If an older woman could not find a new husband on her own, then she had the option of joining a sister (sororate marriage) or another close female relative as a co-wife; other older women who chose not to re-marry lived in separate huts located in the same village as their married children. Shostak (1981, p. 203) has argued that widows had important roles to calm and unify the village, and were frequently encouraged to marry as soon as possible in order to prevent fights among competing males residing in the village (Shostak, 2000).

Self-sacrifice is another common strand shared by widows in many cultures, but this theme is particularly applicable to India and the ritual of women who immolate themselves after the death of a husband; suttee is the anglicized orthography for the act itself (Weinberger-Thomas, 1999). The practice was formally abolished in India in 1829 by the British Government, although it is seldom acknowledged that it was actually native Indians who initiated the political movement to ban it. Many Indians argued that the burning of widows was not sanctioned by the Vedic religion as scriptural authority for the rite did not exist. It was believed that Brahmin priests distorted the meaning of the Vedic texts through later insertions in order to fit societal and cultural customs of the time (Agnes, 1999). Even if a widow continued to exist, a life of severe hardship was prescribed as follows, "Let her be patient of hardships, self-controlled and chaste...let her emaciate her body by living on pure flours, roots and fruits; but she must never mention the name of another man after her husband has died"[1] (Basu, 2004; Chandra, 2004; Agnes, 1999; Tambiah, 1973).

From early in the nineteenth century, reform movements began in India and focused on widows by targeting the practice of suttee, the prohibition on widow remarriage and promoting property rights for widows (Basu, 2004 pp. 67–84; Forbes, 1996). The goal of most reformers was not to liberate women but to make the family structure stronger and more acceptable for women of middle and upper-classes (Jayawardena, 1986). Thus these important pieces of legislation were implemented as critical points of legal reforms.

Basu (2004, pp. 1–10) notes that the Hindu Widow-Remarriage Act (1856) and the Hindu Succession Act (1956) were two reform landmarks in the history of social legislation and were enacted to bring about major changes in the status of Hindu women. The Hindu Widow-Remarriage Act was proposed to allow widows to remarry and work; the Hindu Succession Act represented a significant step forward for widows because it gave them the right to full ownership of property like male successors. A widow previously had no freedom in either economic or personal terms because women in Hindu society had no right of succession to property. Hindu widows inherited nothing on either side of the families and were only entitled to a bare maintenance support from in-laws.[2] This was why the legislation to allow widows to remarry was enacted, but it failed to serve its purpose and the attempt to encourage the remarriage of Hindu widows did not make any progress in Indian society. As a result, it was reported that in the 1850s ninety percent of the prostitutes in India were widows.

Weinberger-Thomas (1999, pp. 20–21) asserts that widow-burning is only one form of a variety of funeral ceremonies that involves the voluntary sacrificial death of individuals who follow a higher-ranking person (ruler, master or husband) into death. She argues that it is actually this settling of a debt of obligation and love that lies at the heart of the practice of sacrificing oneself for another and from this standpoint, the act is not indigenous only to India and is not solely enacted by widows. However, this argument, which frames widow sacrifice in romanticized terms of love and devotion (in practice, often applied to women only), ignores the gendered reality embedded in the act and dodges the question regarding why widows were obligated to sacrifice themselves based on devotion and duty, while widowers were never compelled to do so on behalf of their wives.

While India has been the historical target of research on widow's rituals, it is far from existing as the only country with a custom of sacrifice of widowed women.[3] While it is only supposition to assume the actual motives of these widows, there are commonly recurring patterns in the theme of 'sacrifice' for women in other countries discussed throughout this chapter. Archaic views of women reflected in Greek, Roman, Hebrew and German customs illustrate that the actions of wives brought honor or dishonor to a husband and his family particularly through their sexual behavior. Members of society expected that the dutiful, chaste and obedient behavior of widows would continue long after the husband's death. A widow protected her honor and reputation by exhibiting her modesty, chastity and acceptance of the authority of men (Anderson and Zinsser, 1988). In many European countries influenced by ancient Roman and customary law, widows usually had rights to claim any assets she may have brought with her to the marriage (dowry) or other assets to which she could legally show ownership. Personal items such as clothes, jewels, furniture and anything the husband had given to her as a gift could be legitimately claimed and represented a common acceptance of widow's rights.

Upon remarriage, Roman law was constructed to protect heirs in terms of assets and property, and motherhood was not perceived as an important consideration in determining inheritance. A common legality in wills was that any decision to remarry by the widow would render null and void all claims she might assert regarding property or assets held jointly with her husband. As a result, the poor relief lists of seventeenth and eighteenth-century towns make clear the predicament of impoverished widows who accounted for a third or more of the recipients with the highest levels of widows living in poverty (approximately half) found in Spain (Hufton, 1995).

The fourth strand of the common ground outlined in this section, the fetishism of the female body, featured chastity as a key component of a woman's virtue and this concept was applied with particular rigor to widows. Widows specifically were not to engage in excessive talking, wearing fancy clothes designed to enhance their bodies and certainly older widows should forgo any public displays of flesh (Thomasset, 1992). During the Middle Ages in Europe, leaving the confines of the house alone could be dangerous, and women were often admonished that even on the way to church they could unwittingly arouse a man's lust. In public sermons and moral tracts, women who left the so-called safety of the home by themselves were risking the prestige and honor of their respective families. An uncontrolled act or untoward glance could compromise a woman's honorable status and therefore that of her kinfolk. Women played important roles as family representatives in communities and her public behavior should be modest, composed and respectful (Thomasset, 1992). Seemingly innocent actions such as standing in a doorway or leaning out of the window might be enough to establish contact with the outside world and could lead a woman to abandon her cloistered place as noted by Casagrande (1991, pp. 70–104). Justification for keeping women inside the home was predicated upon the patriarchal dogma that women must be submissive to men as part of the social hierarchy that ruled relations between God, Christ and all of humanity (McGinn, 2008). The necessity of fostering protection underpinned through the control of women by men was particularly applicable to widows, who were clearly exposed to 'dangerous freedoms,' since they were no longer under the custody of husbands.

Thus the individual cases of widows varied greatly based on class and societal status, and this point of disjuncture was the basis of Janus-faced myths and stereotypes regarding widows as 'merry' (spendthrifts) or 'poor' (as portrayed in the religious parable of the widow's mite). In the first case, upper-class widows freed from the constraints of marriage and left in charge of marital assets could represent a real financial threat to members of the husband's family as to how she would administer that wealth. On the other hand, lower-class widows, who inherited a husband's debts and had little or no dowry or other assets, could be left dependent upon her own work to support herself and her children; the names of such widows were found in great abundance on the lists of paupers.

State instituted changes in English law after 1670, witnessed the decline of the widow's financial position and the rise of the advantage of the oldest male heir (primogeniture). A childless widow's right to her husband's assets was cut in half, and the courts enforced more restrictive laws governing widows' total inheritance reducing it to one-third. While at the time of marriage, an upper-class woman's dowry or settlement appeared to be protected, relatives and sons often colluded to break settlements; male heirs, including a widow's own son, could make life exceedingly difficult (Mendelson and Crawford, 1998). As wives, women were expected to be dependent, but as widows they were suddenly on their own; thus the financial ramifications of a husband's death were often catastrophic which led to the economic necessity of a speedy remarriage for some widows. If widows with little or no property/assets did not remarry, they worked at various low-paying jobs or lived meagerly relying on the assistance of community alms and public support.[4]

Widows shared commonalities with other widows because their collective position in society was considered to be one entailing self-sacrifice and often deprivation; the fetishism of widow's bodies as representing male and family honor was particularly clear because their sexuality was in question and they were watched with ongoing suspicion. The gradual implementation of specific laws which made inheritance of land and assets problematic for widows, and the integrative role of widows in the consolidation and formation of states have been traced as threads of common ground for widows cross-culturally. The next section will deal with East Asia specifically but follows these same shared issues as experienced historically and presently in China and Korea.

Widowhood in East Asia – China and Korea

Scholars usually designate China, Korea and Japan as 'East Asia' largely because of the common influence of Buddhism and Confucianism. Buddhist logic (*inmyō*) came to Japan by way of China and Korea in the 6th century. It was to China that ancient Japanese scholars went to study Buddhist doctrines, and these early Buddhist monks would eventually introduce these concepts to Japan (Goody, 1996). Japan imported the Chinese writing system and many other artistic and cultural conceptualizations which will be discussed in the next chapter.

However, it would be through Confucian ideology that the connection between these three ancient cultures would eventually be cemented. In China, during the Sung Dynasty (roughly estimated as beginning in 961 C.E. and extending to 1279 C.E.), the developing ideology regarding family and kinship inculcated through Confucianism was reflected by the new cultural focus on the importance of widows maintaining their chastity. The transformations in kinship structure and society were based on the belief that civilization and the patrilineal kinship system represented the 'natural' and original mode of family organization (Waltner, 1996). According to a study by Fuma (1993), the custom whereby widows were expected to reject remarriage and remain single eventually permeated all levels of Chinese society during the Ming (1368 C.E. to 1644 C.E.) and Quing (1644 C.E. to 1912 C.E.) Dynasties; this ideological shift facilitated a new cultural and kinship based code of morality. Conversely, there were many cases of 'forced marriage' during the later Chinese dynasties creating significant instability for widows throughout these historical periods. Forced marriage involved the selling of widows, who were viewed as possessions, by the family of the deceased husband; this custom was often practiced by lower-class families so that they could receive additional betrothal monies. Although widows in upper-class families could exercise power within kinship groups based on the position of their deceased husbands, society generally praised individual widows who did not remarry and looked askance at widows who did. After the collapse of the Quing Dynasty, the cultural approbation and economic considerations regarding widow remarriage continued through the establishment of the Republic of China in 1912.

Shirōzu (2001) has shown that even after a half-century since the founding of The Peoples' Republic of China in 1949, societal taboos enforced through cultural expectations regarding kinship roles and women's place in the family still remain. The remarriage of a widow in present-day rural Chinese society is considered shocking and represents a serious breach of Confucian-based ethical norms regarding family, kinship, and village due to the fact that remarriage is viewed as disgraceful and denigrates family honor. Even so, the government is attempting to promote and popularize remarriage in old age because of high rates of widowhood throughout the Chinese countryside (Ikels, 2003).

However, in other areas of China such as Shaanxi Province located south of Beijing, remarriage is no longer a moral problem but one of practicality. Men are still believed to be incapable of managing a house on their own, and most men argue that household chores must be done by women. Women in rural areas also believe that it's difficult to survive without a man due to the necessity of physical work including carrying water home from wells and performing manual labor (Liu, 2000).

As Hong (1996, pp. 17–42) summarizes, the adoption of Confucianism eventually resulted in the unequal treatment of women; the ideology imposed a double-standard which viewed women's sexuality as belonging to her husband and his family, but men were under no such restraints. Hong further argues that the roots of Confucianism emerged out of an agrarian way of life in China which promulgated and enforced patriarchal power. In its earlier stages of existence, Confucian tradition fostered the creation of positive social values which maintained stability and aided in the development of the country. However, the well-known Confucian concepts involving loyalty and obedience from ministers to kings, from son to father, and from wife to husband (defined as the three bonds) were eventually adopted in order to enforce conformity, unify the nation and ensure the status quo for absolute rulers. The system based on these values was underpinned by the most important of Confucian ethics, i.e., filial piety, upon which the ruling regime as well as the family was modeled. The ruler was represented as the father of all of the people, and the 'filial' obligation was fulfilled when individuals were unreservedly loyal to the designated leader; in the same way, a wife must necessarily display loyalty to her husband and his family. Historically, the remarriage of widows entailed the violation of this gendered 'bond' of loyalty and would bring forth shame and loss of honor (face) to the husband's family within the local community. Based on Confucian concepts of chastity, a woman whose husband dies should remain a chaste and self-sacrificing widow throughout the remainder of her life. This important ideology incorporated the bodies of women as the embodiment of the honor of a kinship group; thus widows came to be living symbols of their husband's honor.

In the case of Korea, until approximately 2,000 years ago, the area now designated as Korea was comprised of an assortment of tribal-based groups, who had a complex shamanistic belief system and practiced the veneration of family ancestors. Women had important roles, particularly as shamans, actively practicing healing, divination and functioning as priestesses. However, as aggression from their powerful neighbor China grew, the tribal groups began to organize themselves into kingdoms resulting in the formation of three states: Silla, Paekche and Koguryo. Eventually, the kingdom of Silla succeeded in establishing its hegemony over the Korean peninsula in the 7th century A.D. (Jayawardena, 1986). Buddhism was introduced into the region in the 4th century originally in the state of Paekche but eventually encompassing all of the other kingdoms. The ruling authorities believed that the adoption of Buddhism would unite the diverse tribes in order to resist the impending threat from invasion by China. During this period, women enjoyed equal status with men in Buddhist ceremonies, but no longer had roles of leadership in the same way they functioned under shamanism; however, many widows became nuns (particularly wealthy women) and donated substantial tracts of land to the developing Buddhist temples that were being established throughout the country (Jayawardena 1986). As will be demonstrated in the next chapter, the same trend occurred in Japan with upper-class widows of aristocrats and samurai (warriors) frequently donating family assets to temples upon the death of a husband.

Kinship and family lineage remained a dominant factor in social relationships as queens were chosen to rule over the Kingdom of

Silla after the male line of the royal family died out. Hence, female rulers were able to succeed to the throne. However, by the 6th century, Confucian values were seeping into Korea, and government leaders discovered that its system of strict moral and ethical values was more utilitarian than those of Buddhism in unifying, organizing and controlling a stratified and highly authoritarian society; thus Buddhist temples and monasteries began to decay without the support of the ruling authorities. Confucian ideologies and morals eventually held sway and dominated the development of the Korean state. Society became more rigid and stratified but for a time women continued to maintain equality in inheritance rights, both patrilineal and matrilineal descent was recognized, and widow remarriage was not forbidden (Kim, 1976).

Eventually, as Korean leaders predicted, the Mongols (known in China as the Yuan Dynasty), invaded the peninsula in 1231 and exerted a considerable measure of control over the country; after the fall of the Yuan regime, the dominance of China in Korea also waned. In 1392, a Korean general founded the Yi dynasty which ruled until 1912. Under this dynasty, there was a stronger emphasis on Confucian values, particularly as applied to women's morality. Accordingly in 1432, 'The Three Principles of Virtuous Conduct,' (*Samgang haengsil-to*) was published by the government (Kim, 1976). This tract spelled out guidelines for appropriate female behavior through illustrations using stories of virtuous women and detailed new restrictions including a prohibition upon the remarriage of widows.

A woman who lives independently and successfully presents a challenge to the core foundation of patriarchal-based family-centered societies. However, in a paradoxical sense, a widow who asserts her desire to re-marry also challenges traditional kinship practices and customs involving the grieving widow who remains chaste and perpetually devoted to the memory of the deceased husband (Aoki, 2000; Kim, 1976). As state formation proceeded in Korea, the introduction of Confucian family ideology dramatically altered the social standing and position of women. Before this time, under the Koryŏ dynasty (918–1392), women had relatively more social and economic freedom. For example, women could share with brothers in the inheritance of ancestral assets, and divorce was readily accepted without negative impact from society if a husband was deemed incompatible. Widows, too, could remarry with no social stigma and were considered attractive marriage partners (Deuchler, 2003).

Upper-class widows in Korea, before the commencement of the Chosŏn Dynasty (1392–1910), seldom remained single after their husband's death. Women preferred to take a new husband as soon as possible, but the government gradually attempted to discourage women from re-marriage by offering widows special awards and citations if they remained unmarried. However, these societal inducements proved to be inadequate in dissuading women from marrying again. By 1485 CE, the Korean dynastic powers, under the influence of an ongoing Confucian morality based state, determined that upper-class widows should be forbidden by law to remarry and implemented grave consequences for any widows who dared challenge the new edicts. If a widow violated the state decree, her sons and grandsons would be disqualified from taking any kind of governmental service exam, thereby excluding them from high-status positions. However, these legal prohibitions applied only to women of the upper classes. For commoners and women of lower classes, re-marriage was not initially forbidden, but eventually Confucian societal taboos filtered down to encompass all classes of women. Even young women without children were coerced into living alone after the death of their husbands with many widows choosing suicide rather than lead a solitary, isolated life. As was previously discussed with respect to India, the cross-cultural theme of widow-suicide arises again, as widows who sacrificed themselves were admired and revered in both China and Korea. Kim (1976, pp. 97–99) states that Confucian scholars and governmental figures publicly praised these suicidal actions interpreting the tragic cases, not as an escape from a state-enforced unendurable existence but as the 'noble conduct of a chaste widow.' Of course, praise from state officials functioned in self-serving ways, masking the role of government and focusing upon individual conduct and the 'choice' of a widow.

Chastity, as a key aspect of the fetishism of the bodies of women, was one of the defining moral concepts of Confucian ideology. Similar to the previously cited cases of India and Europe, female chastity came to be equated with family honor embodied by women. Widows had a particularly important role in displaying continued faithfulness to deceased husbands through devoting themselves to prayers at their husbands' graves or more dramatically through committing suicide after the husband's death. Although this custom was initially practiced only by upper-class widows in the Chosŏn Period of Korea, in later times even commoners and slave women sacrificed their lives to honor deceased husbands (Deuchler, 2003). Thus the custom of widow-sacrifice resonates with societal morals and Confucian ideologies regarding women's chastity embodied as family honor and can be treated as a significant cross-cultural theme.

The concept of chastity for women served patriarchal interests well in several dimensions at the nexus of economic and family politics and made the codification of law regarding natal and affinal inheritance problematic for women. Women in Korea were absorbed into the structural patrilineage of the husband's family forfeiting natal ancestral kinship inheritance rights, which rendered women dependent upon the economic provisions of more fragile affinal kinship ties. Sejiyama (1996, pp. 216–218) comparing Korea to Japan with respect to the adoption of Confucian-based family values, argues that the ideology took root more deeply in Korea. With the core of Confucianism based on filial piety, ancestor worship and the patrilineal system, the position of women was firmly cemented. Okada (2007) also notes that the Confucian image of widows became stronger in both Japan and Korea in the colonial period during the Japanese occupation. The particular dynamic of widows in the crucible of war is detailed in Part 3.

Conclusion: Cross-cultural perspectives and common ground

To shed light on the history of forgotten groups is the first step in taking up the struggle on behalf of women (Ehrenreich and English 1973), and out of this cross-cultural and historical analysis, this chapter has focused on four specific themes. One of these themes is that widow-sacrifice or suicide in diverse forms was not uncommon in some ancient cultures, and thus provides the basis for historical common ground among widows. There are tantalizing sources for this possibility including archaeological, anthropological and literary references. The practice of widow sacrifice or suicide has been noted as an ancient custom even among Scandinavian people with ancient Norse legends enshrining Brynhild[5]; therefore, scholars argue that the possible origin of the rite was rooted in ancient Indo-Germanic customs (Puckle 1926). Additionally, according to Thompson (1928, pp. 2–27), the custom also appears in Greek legend through the work *Seven Against Thebes* in which the wife of one of the heroes in the story was immolated with her deceased husband.[6] Thompson further argues the rite has an archaeological and folk history basis in Thrace, Scythia, ancient Egypt and that widow-sacrifice, the suicide of widows and/or sisters of tribal chiefs has been practiced in Tonga, among the Maori people and in many African tribes.

Self-sacrifice was *not* just as important for men as for women because the context and ultimate societal meaning of the sacrifice is radically different. Of course, men may sacrifice themselves for nationalistic purposes or for fellow soldiers, rulers, or friends, but there is no overall pattern of men sacrificing themselves at the time of a wife's death. To be sure, men do battle on behalf of women's honor but these so-called selfless actions are not really about dying for the sake of women; these actions are self-serving to enhance the personal honor of men and the collective honor of their respective families. The bodies of women and widows continue to provide ongoing and timely testimony to the collective honor or shame of families, and this theme of embodiment permeates the research.

Reviewing the above cross-cultural examples spanning time and geographical locations, it is evident that different societies exercised control over women for a multitude of reasons, and this control is expressed in diverse ways (Palazzi, 1996). If a specific disjuncture in historical development is isolated, it is at the point of emerging states. As regions consolidated into states, widows performed various integrative functions for emerging states and kinship groups. This was accomplished through actions which served to unite family members, and by the power of the state through legally reinforcing tradition and custom.

In cases where widows are encouraged or forced to re-marry quickly, they may be removing the perceived community threat of a single independent woman living on her own or reducing the possibility of community break-down and violence between males competing over the attentions of widows (Metcalf and Huntington, 1991; Mead, 1935). Widows (particularly when they are younger) often remain in the patrilineage of the husband's kinship group through the common custom of levirate marriage, which integrates control of family assets, land and reproductive labor. Divergence in the practice of the levirate is expressed based on age and economic considerations, as poor widows may be sold in order to provide income for the deceased husband's impoverished household. Women of higher classes may wield considerable power and influence within the husband's kin-group proper.

Levirate marriage preserves the patriarchal claims to women and the selling of widows also benefited the husband's kinship group financially. Although the manifestation of control is exercised quite differently and resistance through the circumvention of societal rules is illustrated in this chapter, the underpinning legal and cultural right to the *use* of women is asserted. State intervention to control the behavior of widows specifically included legal restraints on inheritance rights, remarriage, control of children and reflected cultural expectations regarding proper behavior.

It has long been argued, and the fact remains, that throughout the vast majority of cultures men have exercised authority over women, and this power was asserted and maintained through culturally legitimated and institutionalized subordination (Rosaldo, 1974; Bourdieu, 2001; Hong, 1997). At the same time, women were far from passive and at times wielded a great deal of influence within hierarchies of power, especially for women of the nobility; however, in many societies this power was carefully exercised 'behind the scenes' in a covert manner, frequently masking the origin of the influence.

As detailed above, state development and the incorporation of morals with its locus rooted in the patriarchal family affected diverse societies in India, Europe, China and Korea, which were eventually organized based on gendered inequalities. In Japan too, we will see the organization of society based on the reification of gendered roles. Although there are cultural differences between Japanese families and those in other societies, Muta (1996) argues that this fact does not mean that the Japanese family is 'so different' or unique that it cannot be compared to those in other countries. Japan, like countries in Asia and Europe, went through a feudal transformation, built a centralized government and experienced industrialization and urbanization. By the end of the Meiji Era, the domestic nuclear family in Japan was regarded as ideal and due to similar changes in other countries, including those of Western Europe, we may consider similarities and differences with various societies.

One of the most important strands of common ground illustrated by this chapter is that gender inequalities did not spontaneously 'grow' or 'develop' magically out of these diverse societies due to biological necessity or some supernatural predestination. Inequality was initially incorporated as part of the basic building blocks of nascent social orders tied to and necessitated by nation building and state formation. The patriarchal family became the organizing model of how society *should* be (even though there were exceptions).[7] This model was interpreted as a reflection of a moral order based on male dominance over women, adults over children, the state over individuals (Bourdieu, 2001) and worked to unify and stabilize developing nations.

Finally, as this chapter illustrates, societal expectations, the role of the state and kinship practices cannot be analyzed in isolation but represent an integrated part of social formation and organization in a nexus of culture, gender, politics and specific periods of history. By speaking through these specificities, as Strathern (2005, pp. xvi–xvii) has noted, we are able to consider generalities and vice versa while looking across epochs. It is to these multifaceted connections within diverse historical periods in Japan and to tracing the details of the linkages between state development, linguistic change and family transformations to which we will now turn.

3 History of Widows in Japan

Until recently in Japan, widows were usually expected to remain in their deceased husband's family and devote themselves to the continued care of in-laws, but this has not always been the case. In the Heian Period (794–1191 C.E.) of Japan, divorced and widowed women were permitted new love affairs or even re-marriage. Considerable evidence exists which indicates that Japanese women of the eighth century could choose freely to participate in a sexual relationship or not. Ancient texts such as the *Chronicle of Ancient Matters* (*kojiki*) document stories of women who freely chose their preferred mates while rejecting others. Sekiguchi (2003, pp. 27–46) states that women could refuse marriage proposals and most importantly, a woman's sexuality was not viewed as the property of the husband and his kin group. Women of wealth inherited land and family residences, as well as agricultural property, from their parents and these valuable assets were frequently bequeathed to daughters.

It was common during this period for matrilocal marriage residences to be established (Bingham and Gross, 1987). If a husband died or in the case of divorce, a woman was protected and supported by the financial assets of her natal family and over time could effectively control these resources. Women's power and status is dramatically affected by post-marital residence and enhanced by matrilocal residence. Stone (2000) argues that family organizational patterns, as key indicators of the status of women, are frequently employed as critical markers of female prestige and power (Brown, Subbaiah, and Sarah, 1998). It has been repeatedly shown that matrilocal residence greatly increases a woman's overall support network, and she may draw on these kinship affiliations as necessary. However, with the acceptance and promulgation of Confucian familial ideology imported from China, matrilocal residence patterns gradually faded and the custom of patrilocal residence, embedded in the patriarchal family system, slowly but steadily became the rule. The resulting change from matrilocal to patrilocal residence patterns affected the structure and texture of life in villages and communities (Stone, 2000). Establishment of the 'patriarchal family paradigm' was linked to the embodiment of the centralized authority of the Emperor system (*tennō seido*) and the organization of Japanese society along the same lines as Chinese-based patriarchal households (Sekiguchi, 2003). This point marks a watershed for women's status and inheritance rights which gradually diminished.

Loyalty to the family patriarch and by extension to the Emperor thus became the basis of legitimizing state rule. The family may be situated as the basic unit of the state; thus it is not separate from history or social forces and constitutes a political site as stated by Ueno (1994, pp. 69–74), Nishikawa (1996, 2000, pp. 1–17), Koyama (1999, pp. 1–27) and Muta (1996). In analyzing the development of the family in Japan, the family should be viewed as a system of political strategy connecting society and the individual; this construction was viewed as essential for the building of a modern state. Japan developed a system based not on democracy but with the Emperor as the symbolic head of the state. There was additionally another transformation that occurred which stressed the importance of emotional ties within the family, and this point is critical in understanding the intersection of the family and state or a 'family-state view' (*kazoku kokka kan*).

Ascertaining and understanding the details regarding how these transformations in societal organizations and ideologies occurred as well as how these changes affected Japanese women, particularly widows, is the focus of this chapter. Pursuing these questions involves a complicated historical, legalistic and linguistic quest to seek out the turning points that precipitated these developments. While scholars continue to research the earliest words used in reference to widows (some of them rooted in the Chinese language), the basic evolution of these terms can be traced and connected to historical events, the formation of the Japanese state, wartime ideologies and changing cultural practices.[1] The tracking of language metamorphoses through the terms used to designate widows, especially in diachronic terms, is developed as an explanatory tool to explore the process whereby language is actually involved in the construction of gender and inequality as Christie (2001, pp. 110–111) has noted. The role of language in establishing gender identity and the political process and implications involved in these constructions are also reflected in recent studies, such as Gal (2001) and Duranti (2001, pp. 29–30). Through the study of the meanings of words used to 'name' widows, the historical and political axes of power involved are drawn and linked.

Studies of the connection between language and culture have been within the explicit purview of anthropology since its inception as manifested in enduring and classic works (e.g., Boas, 1911; Sapir, 1933; Goodenough, 1957; Hymes, 1959), as well as in more contemporary studies representing a diversity of cultural interests and theoretical orientations (Kulick, 1992; Duranti, 2001; Gottlieb, 2005). The explication of changes in the Japanese language is pursued due to the fact that such an analysis offers tantalizing clues regarding the way gendered meanings are constituted and re-constituted through history. More specifically, the exploration of language explains and reflects much, e.g., the 'fall from grace' in society that Japanese widows suffered at the close of Japan's imperial wars. The following section demonstrates that the study of language and gender is enhanced through the analysis of the particular social contexts, historical periods, and the development of social institutions.

The formation of the patriarchal family system

The analytical focus of this section is the relationship of gender and language beginning with how particular words participate in or help create and maintain cultural constructions like family systems (Duranti, 2001). Linguistic change in terminology for widows is traced throughout the study of several different words (*kafu, yamome,* and *goke*) used to designate widows, including the most recent term, *mibōjin,* which increased in usage during the Meiji era (1868–1912). Although historical sources are scarce regarding the emergence of the latter term, it initially appeared at the same time that Japan engaged in two imperialistic wars: the Japan–Quing War in 1894–1895 and the war with Russia in 1904–1905 (Fukuta, 1903, 1906). Sōgō and Hida (1986, pp. 485–486) state that the word originated as an ancient Chinese idiom used to refer to oneself meaning, 'one who should have died with her husband, but has not yet died' (Sōgō and Hida 1986: 485–486). The term implies that a woman should be willing to sacrifice her own life and follow her husband into the grave. However, war widows much preferred other terms, such as 'white lilies,' 'blue orchids' or 'beautiful reeds' to describe themselves rather than the word *mibōjin* due to the discrimination conveyed by the term. The ensuing research shows that while there are overwhelming difficulties in challenging words in the arena of the symbolic order, widows did exactly that by defining themselves in terms that reflected their own interpretations of widowhood framed by their experiences. This struggle, as informants often stated, is ongoing; the search for a more acceptable word for widows continues even now.

In English, there are no separate words for widows that may be used as indicators of differential status and meaning, but in Japanese there are four basic words that have historically designated widows: *kafu, yamome, goke* and *mibōjin*. Each one of these words has a specific history and has encompassed divergent meanings depending on the era and context; we can define the context as a constantly changing frame within which language itself is one of its constitutive elements (Gal, 2001). Among the four terms listed above, two of the oldest words for widows, *yamome* and *kafu,* were used as far back as the Nara (701–788 C.E.) and Heian (794–1191 C.E.) Eras at the end of the historical period delineated as ancient Japan. However, *yamome* was more commonly used in literature and everyday language, but is not found in important village documents with reference to widows.[2] Embedded in the meaning of the term *yamome* was the idea that males or females needed to be protected or helped by society, and this category of 'needy' individuals also included single women. Persons called *yamome* were frequently without family or relatives and were sometimes exempted from the duties of ordinary citizens, such as: paying taxes to the government, working on the repairs of roads and irrigation systems (Kurushima, 1989). Therefore, the term was not one based on gender but grounded in the neediness of a person who was alone or weaker than other individuals in society.

On the other hand, the word *kafu* which was absorbed directly from Chinese has mainly been used in formal documents designating widows throughout Japanese history, but the term gained prominence in legal usage especially after World War II. Currently, the term *kafu* is used to legally designate a woman who does not have a spouse and has children over the age of twenty. For example, it is present in legal writings regarding welfare laws pertaining to fatherless families and widows (*Boshi oyobi kafu fukushi hō*).

The third word used for widows, *goke,* is a completely indigenous word to Japan. The roots of the word are not found in Chinese, and do not reflect influence from China in the same way as *yamome* and *kafu.* The word initially came into use in the late Heian and early Kamakara Periods (1192–1333 C.E.) with respect to naming a successor of land rights; it did not apply only to widows during these eras but referred generically to bereaved family members. At this same point in time, the influence of Confucianism was gaining momentum along with the concomitant development of the warrior (*buke*) class and the patrilocal based family system; thus the term *goke* developed in tandem with the acceptance of Confucian ideology, the restructuring of the kinship system and to indicate a successor to the family estate of the deceased, i.e., a legally designated person who has the right to inherit (*sōzoku)* the deceased's assets (Nomura, 1992; Īnuma, 1992; Kurushima, 1989).

By the end of the eleventh century, during the transitional period to the Middle Ages (*chūsei*), *goke* took on another legal meaning of a word used to refer to a woman who had lost her husband. This usage is represented in official documents, but the word was rarely used in literature. We can clearly contrast the term *yamome,* used as a general term referring to a weak person, with the image that the word *goke* evokes of power, authority and sacrifice. Kurushima (1989) additionally argues that one of the distinctive points reflecting the difference in nuance between *yamome* and *goke* was that the latter term was deeply connected to the *ie* system illustrating an even clearer difference between the two words. This connotation, which became common in use along with the construction of the new patriarchal family system, reflects the establishment of patrilocal residence patterns and the permeating cultural influence of Confucianism. Confucian ideology spread throughout village societies from the *buke* (warrior) class to ordinary farm families (especially in the case of middle-class farm families known as *honbyakushō*) by the Edo Period (1603–1867 C.E.) (Saku, 1962). As part of this transformation in kinship structure, terminology and women's position in the family was the awareness that wives legally inherited their husband's rights, obligations and debts as part of her pivotal role in the newly formed familial system. A widow in an upper-class *buke* family was expected by society to carry out all the duties that such a position entailed; for example, she was charged with the responsibility of collecting land taxes and rent from tenant farmers.

The image of widows as *goke* during the Kamakura Period was one that evoked duty and power because women became de facto representatives of their deceased husbands in order to facilitate and manage his assets; more importantly, a widow became the legal head of the family. Widows in upper-class families controlled extensive assets but also inherited a serious obligation to protect and preserve all of the wealth and influence of the family which would be passed on to the children. According to the will of the husband, she could decide the apportioning of assets to children and administer the assets for them until they attained a certain age. Even if the husband died intestate, the widow could decide the apportionment of assets and could claim her own inheritance called *goke-bun* (a widow's legal portion). At this time, the authority of parents in Japanese village society was absolute, and maternal rights (*boken*), not only paternal rights, were still an integral part of an authoritarian parental view held in Japan. Even an oldest son could be controlled by a powerful widow with the extent of her influence extending well into his adult life (Nomura, 1992; Inuma, 1992).

In the late Kamakura Period, the word *goke* began to frequently appear in legal village documents concerning inheritance and land ownership. Important information is contained in these ancient records, which substantiates the fact that women often received valuable assets directly from parents. There was an established legal precedent for this practice called a woman's portion (*joshi-bun*). Additionally, in accordance with the cultural conventions of the time, most women kept their natal family name and did not change it to that of the husband's family at marriage; perhaps, even more significant in terms of economic independence was the common practice of keeping assets from her natal family (*jikka*) separate from those of her affines.[3] Using these family assets, wealthy widows could and did make extensive contributions in their own right bequeathing land and money to Buddhist temples. These actions facilitated their societal duties to arrange the many Buddhist memorials and events required for salvation of souls and status maintenance of respective families within local communities (Takagi, 1982).

At this juncture, the reconstituted patriarchal family system was well on its way to establishment, and the role of the *goke* continued to be important. However, as the new kinship system crystallized throughout the country, the assets and property of the family were gradually inherited by the eldest son signaling that the once formidable *goke* was beginning to lose her power. More clearly, this waning of influence and position of widows within the family marks a critical turning point in fourteenth century Japan; it illustrates an ideological transformation in that a widow was no longer a legally recognized representative of the husband and family. Thus the once powerful *goke* had become only the necessary biological link between the family lineage and the eldest son (Nomura, 1992). New cultural practices mandated that if a widow inherited the land of her husband, she was now expected to quietly devote herself to prayer and mourning on his behalf for her entire life and to perform Buddhist memorial services at regular intervals for the repose of his soul. These duties were not mere expectations by society but involved strong admonitions by government officials as well as from family members. In this context and under these circumstances, widows in upper-class families usually did not re-marry but remained faithful based on the then reigning societal ideology of *teijo* (a woman should have only one husband in her lifetime remaining faithful and chaste); widows were expected to keep busy with prayers and protecting family assets for children (Takagi, 1982).

If a widow chose to remarry in contravention of these ideological and legal requirements, she would lose everything including the land she inherited from her husband and would be forced to return all assets to the children. Specifically, according to Article 24 of an early codified compilation of laws written in the year 1232 C.E. by the *buke* class consisting of a total of fifty-one articles (*goseibai shikimoku*), it is clearly stated that a widow must forfeit all inheritance received from her deceased husband upon remarriage. If a woman decided to remarry, she could legally do so. However, there was also an intervivos gift custom (land that was transferred as a gift at the time of marriage), which tended to keep widows in the same family and deter them from remarriage lest they would be forced to forfeit these additional lands too.

The custom of upper class widows becoming Buddhist Nuns, informally and sometimes formally, initially developed in the early Middle-Ages of Japan. Sugano (2003, p. 187) argues that women may have chosen to take Buddhist vows in order to remain single for the sake of parents (to devote themselves to offerings and prayers on behalf of their souls) or to avoid marriage altogether. However, in the case of most widows, they did not actually enter a religious order located in a convent or take specific vows but became what is called a *goke-ni*. This term denotes the informal practice in Japan of becoming a 'secular nun,' even though these widows shaved their heads, practiced celibacy and lived a monastic kind of life, *albeit* in their own homes. Most of these informal nuns continued to live in their respective villages though others formally took vows, left their homes, and eventually entered convents (Takagi, 1982).[4]

As Confucianism steadily consolidated its grip in towns and villages, even more stringent social sanctions applied if upper-class widows remarried. In addition to forfeiting inheritance rights, her status, good name and honor would be held in disrepute. However, in the case of impoverished widows, the sanctions would not apply, as these families had little to lose financially because there were few assets involved. Destitute widows frequently had to remarry to survive and to ensure an adequate means of support. Although the influence of the patriarchal family and underlying Confucian ideology was pervasive, it was pragmatically tempered by class realities. If poor widows didn't marry again, they would become dependent upon relatives or left to the scant provisions of the local community through charitable, but rather miserly, practices such as the ancient codified custom known as, 'gleaning rights,'[5] of rice fields after harvesting (Takagi, 1982).

During the Edo Period (1603–1867),[6] the ruling shogunate government (*bakufu*), shaped by Confucian-based concepts of morality, values, and family ideology, increasingly developed stricter expectations regarding women in general as Bingham and Gross (1987, pp. 31–35) have noted. Widows were admonished by custom to wear mourning attire for thirteen months approximately four times as long as the requirement for widowers. Frequently, women expressed their continuing faithfulness to their deceased husbands by arranging their hair in the ponytail style (*kirisage*) common to widows at that time (Cherry, 1987). Being chaste and remaining steadfastly devoted to a deceased husband was part of newly-fashioned cultural expectations which encouraged the sacrifice of widows for the sake of men and mandated unquestioning obedience to societal mandates for women.

Additionally, as meanings and images were once again undergoing change with respect to widows, the historical meanings of *goke* and *yamome* were lost and the terms started to overlap in usage. General images of widows that had once evoked power and authority were diluted and debased reflecting the downward spiraling trend evidenced in women's overall lower position and status in society. Widows began to gradually appear in pornographic pictures and in risqué stories, entertainment, and jokes; these negative, frequently sexualized, images were well known and bantered around as a form of ridicule (*yayu*) in the closely-knit, strictly controlled society of Edo Japan (Nagano 2006; Kurushima 1989). Kitahara (1995, p. 211) notes the plummeting status of widows in urban lower classes in Edo (Tokyo) who worked at piece rate jobs and as day laborers accounting for about ten percent of the total households.

During this same time period, although women had been excluded from inheritance rights in general, there were still some women who succeeded to the assets of kinship groups particularly in upper-class farming families in rural districts as well as in urban merchant families as Wakita, Hayashi and Nagahara (1987, pp. 113–128) detail. Talented women frequently ran family businesses as it was incumbent upon merchants to consider the success and continuity of the enterprise with savvy widows successfully taking over breweries after the death of owner-husbands (Lebra, 1984, pp. 134–137). Thus the argument made by some scholars, e.g., Tocca (2003, p. 194) that most literature regarding the Tokugawa period reflects the 'nadir in the status of Japanese women' (Tocca 2003,p. 194) is not really accurate; the majority of historical and anthropological works, particularly in Japanese, situate the lowest point of women's status legally and within the family in the Meiji Period (Kondo, 1990; Nishikawa, 2000; Muta, 1996; Bernstein, 1991).[7]

The spatial and environmental context during the Edo Period was such that there was well over one million people living in the city of Edo (Tokyo), and there were already many urban nuclear families. It was at this time that the often quoted Japanese saying originated which states that if a man lost his wife, he could not look after himself or keep the house clean. The basis for the saying was rooted in a developing urban reality that extended family members continued to dwell in rural areas far from Tokyo; thus widowers, with no family members to help and possessing neither the ability nor the will to clean, were forced to live in filthy surroundings like a maggot. On the other hand, if a woman lost her husband, it was often said that she bloomed like a flower, '*Otoko yamome ni uji ga waki, onna yamome ni hana ga saku*,' (Terai, 1982). In this proverb, the same word is used to designate both widows and widowers (*yamome*) indicating that the word had become established in ordinary conversation and generally referred to both women and men. This saying also reflects a recurring theme in this book's research that without the burden of caring for a household and resident husband, a woman would finally be free of care giving and other family services.

The debasing of the status and images of widows in the family mirrored the descending position of women throughout Japanese society during the Edo Period; however, the positions of and cultural expectations for widows was contoured by class variation. While the samurai class was dominated by the emphasis on loyalty interpreted as a commitment to maintaining the lord's house, for commoners the most important moral concept was filial piety (Sugano, 2003). It was through the Confucian ideology of filial piety, which linked generation to generation, that the family household system (*ie seido*) was established and became a key social institution in Japan.

Institutionalized inequalities and widows (*mibōjin*)

As Japanese government officials sought to forge a modern state, the family became a critical part of the political strategy to cement the tie between individuals and society itself, and women were an integral part of this formation. The patriarchal family system (*ie seido*) norm was legally superimposed upon the Japanese in the Meiji Era through the implementation of civil law (*minpō kazoku seido*). Actually, the *ie* system has a 'double-structure' with the father symbolizing the authority of the family and also embodying the connection to the outside world as he controls the external environment. However, the mother and child relationship is central to the familial inner-world and facilitated the development of the modern family in Japan. Paradoxically, these aspects of the family (particularly the mother/child tie) worked as a structural unit to support the national organization of patriarchal families in Japan (Uno, 1999). Thus the transformations during the Meiji Period heavily relied on women in decisive roles as leaders of new moral norms. During the modern period of Japan, women have autonomous responsibility in the family centered on the mother–child relationship under culturally-based sex role norms. Women also secured niches of power within the family sharpening their 'weapons of the weak' (*jyakusha no buki*) and cementing important roles in kinship groups and within the community (Scott, 1985; Muta, 1996).

On the other hand, indicative of just how far women had fallen in Japanese society, all of the historical trends signaling a lowering of women's overall status initiated during the Kamakura to Edo Periods culminated in the Meiji Era (1868–1911) state supported institutionalization of the patriarchal family system (*ie seido*). This resulted in the total loss of property rights for women although they had held these legal rights for over one-thousand years. In 1871, the Family Registration Law (*koseki hō*) was enacted and with the enactment of this law, formalized marriage was introduced in 1883 as documented by Wakita, Hayashi and Nagahara (1987, pp. 199–200). Within this background, women were completely barred from politics and the right to serve as family heads even though they had maintained these rights and participated in political activities throughout Japanese history (Uno, 1991; Nolte and Hastings, 1991). During this period, if a widow wanted to remarry, it was customary and obligatory to obtain permission of the head of the family (i.e., the family of her deceased husband). This principle was expressed in specific legal terms in the Meiji Civil Code of 1869 (Article 750), which stated that if a family member married in contravention of the wishes of the family head, that person, within one year from the date of such a marriage, could be expelled from the family or forbidden to ever return to the family house, even to see her own children (Gubbins, 1897). Additionally, the actions of women were further regulated legally by prohibitions against any remarriage before six months had elapsed after divorce or becoming a widow (Article 767); this legal prohibition continues to this day.

Patriarchal rigidity and the legal dominance of male family household heads reached its zenith during the Meiji Period, and the ideology of men as providers and heads of families was solidified and promoted through the power of the state (Muta, 1996; Nolte and Hastings, 1991, pp. 151–174; Sievers, 1983). Koyama (1999, pp. 29–37) argues that the importance of this family system and women's so-called 'proper place in the home' was specifically inculcated throughout Meiji society. Many women lived lives of repressed sexuality and a controlled existence, and it was often asserted that women could only obtain true freedom if they totally separated themselves from the family system. Husbands, more often than not, were considered a burden to be cared for, and yet ironically, they had to be carefully obeyed.

Most of the ideology and rhetoric of women being miserable under the Japanese family system originated during the Meiji Era. Toward the end of this period, a new term for widows emerged, i.e., *mibōjin*. Although the usage of the word actually exploded in tandem with the appearance of war widows after World War II, the word *mibōjin* gained a certain acceptance and usage during the Meiji Period. The term originated as an ancient Chinese idiom initially used only to designate oneself as shown by Ōtsuki and Ōtsuki (1935) and Sōgō and Hida (1986), but it remains unclear as to exactly why and how the term gained acceptance and usage at this time. The word *goke* continued to be used in the Meiji and Taishō Periods and even in the Showa Era but is seldom heard nowadays and younger Japanese rarely know the meaning of the word.

Although historical sources are scarce regarding the sudden emergence of the term *mibōjin*, it seems to have initially appeared at the same time that Japan, imitating Western colonial powers, engaged in imperialistic wars with the word *mibōjin* growing in usage particularly during the period of war with Russia in 1904–05 (Ōkubo, 1999; Kanō, 1983; Futaba, 1906). The increased use of the term may have been connected to the position of war widows, and the status of professional soldiers who supported the ideological foundations of the *tennōsei* (the emperor system) which was the pillar of Japan's modern state (*tennōsei kokka*). While additional proof needs to be obtained in the future, the spirits of dead soldiers began to be called '*eirei*' in this time of war with Russia. Tanakamaru (2002, p. 18) suggests that it is probably not a coincidence that the appearance and use of these terms, i.e., *mibōjin* and *eirei*, by the media and the military establishment helped to facilitate nationalism and support of the war. Allegiance to the emperor embodied the belief that a soldier sacrifices himself not only for the emperor but for his country. The Meiji State and military authorities placed the bodies of dead soldiers under their control by burying them in the national memorial Yasukuni Shrine (Namihira, 2004). The Shrine symbolized the belief that even though the body may be destroyed, the spirit of soldiers will live on embedded in the memories of faithful, chaste wives and through state-supported rituals glorifying war, duty and sacrifice.

In the same way, within the microcosmic society of the family, a woman should be willing to sacrifice herself as the wife of the living spirit of a physically deceased soldier (*eirei no tsuma*). By this time, most widows (not only women of upper-class aristocratic families) were morally and culturally expected to live as spiritual wives (*seishin-teki na tsuma* or *kokoro no tsuma*) of the deceased and to spend most of their time praying for husbands. The use of the term *mibōjin* expresses a blended nuance of meaning conveying duty, sacrifice, youth and sexuality which reflects this positioning of women within militaristic Japan. Women were called on to support men, the state, imperialistic war efforts abroad, and the emperor; this message was disseminated and enhanced by the media and press building on wartime propaganda (Ōkubo, 1999; Kitamura, 2005).

The societal foundation underlying this subsuming of women in the family system was established at marriage. A bride (*hanayome*) during the Meiji Period *legally* entered her husband's family and fell under the control of not only her husband but also that of her husband's parents. A woman who resisted marriage or lived without a man was considered dangerous since she was free from the well-established Confucian framework of the overlapping triple obedience to father, husband and sons (Robertson, 1991: 94). While some women were undoubtedly protected and nurtured within the family, others simply moved from the control of a father to that of her new husband and his parents. However, in lower-class families after the death of the husband, many women faced the problem of ongoing poverty and outright destitution with little financial support, much less protection, from family members (Ōhama, 2003; Gunji, 2003).

Women legally belonged to her husband's family and for widows who were submerged in this complex familial system from the time of marriage, the death of their husbands did not break the linkage to the family. Although a wife had no legal rights of inheritance, as women had been stripped of these legal rights, her connection to the family system was much stronger and more pervasive than that which dying could dissolve. She had, for all intent and purposes, become the legal property of not only the husband but of his family in perpetuity. These societal and familial realities dovetail with the negative meaning of the word *mibōjin*, which sometimes overlapped in usage with *kafu* and *goke* during the Meiji Era and implied that a widow is 'a person waiting to die' or 'one who is not dead yet but should have died.' More importantly, as Endo (1995, p. 29) has noted, the term conveys the ideological message that a woman should be willing to sacrifice her own life and follow her husband into the grave. This meaning and its cultural resonance functioned to reassure professional soldiers and reluctant draftees going off to foreign countries to conduct wars and possibly die. Thus in the analysis of the origination of the word *mibōjin*, there were quite likely militaristic forces working behind the scenes in Japan seeking to raise the position and status of widows through the coinage of the new terminology. Paradoxically, the term and its youthful evocation implied not only the sacrifice and fidelity of widows, but a dangerous sexuality (Ōkubo, 1999); however, this sexuality had to be controlled lest soldiers should worry more about wives left at home than fighting battles and securing victories on behalf of emperor and country. As one 78-year old informant, Ms. Sasaki, comments,

> A lot of war widows really hated the word 'mibōjin' because it conveys a dark sexual view of widows. However, it also reflected the imagery of the honor and pride of being a widow of a fallen soldier. Once the war was lost, it seemed that the term had no meaning except for the negative sexual one. The honor and pride widows once enjoyed as 'yasukuni no haha' (Yasukuni Shrine Mothers) was taken away.

The older term of *goke* evoked images of an elderly woman and did not suit the abundance of youthful widows who were being created on a daily basis through the deaths of soldiers. In this way, the relationship between gender, the state, nationalistic politics and language is clearly drawn.

A widow's chastity was also considered a husband's property which was why re-marriage entailed the loss of honor and status in the community. Even at her death, a wife would be buried in a common grave with her husband, her husband's parents and the ancestral members of her husband's family. This family unit extends through time and space, and therefore a widow is expected to 'sleep together' with her husband and in-laws throughout eternity. She was a member of the family not only in body but also in spirit, remaining with the deceased and all the generations of his family perpetually in both life and death; the family was a microcosm of the State, so women were inevitably embedded in both systems simultaneously.

Miyake (1920) has argued that even though the term *mibōjin* is a word which engenders images of a dependent weak woman, society continued to practice constant surveillance of widows as if they needed to be controlled. Why, she argued, if women are so weak, do they have to be constantly surveilled? However, there was another face to the multi-faceted meanings of the newly minted word for widows; this new meaning also implied the idealization of romantic love for the individual as developed during the brief Taishō Era (1914–1925). The family system (*ie seido*), as established in the Meiji Period in tandem with the development of capitalism and industrialization, was influenced by these new ideologies and the family system changed to accommodate these images of 'home' (*katei*). Thus, we can see that Japanese families consisted of a dual structure of the old *ie* system along with the new feelings of home. The term *mibōjin* started to appear in literature and was reflected in the ideologies of 'Taishō liberalism' and love based on the individual feelings of partners not on the relationships between families.[8]

Along with these new ideas and stimulating debates, the dark sexuality and sense of danger started to be conveyed by the term *mibōjin* blended with the nuance of liberalism. This nuance specifically reflected the idea of the freedom to experience romantic love on one's own terms. Individualized love was a revolutionary idea in Japan particularly because the socially constructed form of marriage itself was challenged. Women were expected to perform the duties of wives and to serve her husband's family; this had been the pillar of Japanese society from the implementation of the family system as previously discussed in this chapter. Young middle-class women were carefully socialized to cultivate traits of gentleness, self-control, and modesty (Sato 2003). Thus the very act of women debating and challenging long held views regarding these expectations was revolutionary.

The historical transformation of widow's status and roles

As Nakamura (1966) would later write in *Women and the Sword (Onna to katana)*, widows had been too long prohibited from enjoying a rich, full life (*namami*). Women were subjected to the control of deceased husbands who seemed to reach out from the grave to embrace widows. This, then, was another part of the negative meaning embedded in the term *mibōjin*. It can be well understood why widows in this research objected to the term. In this chapter, it has been demonstrated how social practices and customs regarding the position and proper conduct for widows vary widely depending on the historical period and the contextualized cultural milieu. By the time of the Meiji Period, the relatively better conditions and freedoms that Japanese women (at least upper class women since the circumstances of ordinary widows is not well-known) had in the early Nara and Heian Periods slipped away due to the influence of Confucianism and patriarchal family ideology. The samurai class initial adoption and endorsement of this ideology signaled ominous ramifications for all women.

The lives of women are dramatically transformed upon the death of husbands. However, these transformations were historically shaped along complicated and interconnected fault lines of the emergence of a militaristic regime in Japan supporting the emperor, changes in family structure, divisions of class, rural–urban distinctions and the influence of gendered images of widowed women regarding conduct and behavior. As Gottlieb (2005, p. 3) suggests, no language is monolithic, unique or unchanging but language is a multifaceted and constantly developing entity which has different meanings for diverse users, and the manipulation of language has played an important role in Japan's social and cultural policies. Particularly, this chapter has illustrated the power of the state in using what appears to be objective language to mask and promulgate basic social assumptions regarding what it is really trying to change; in this fashion, the state purports to simply be presenting what is natural (Goodman, 2002). The analysis in this chapter of language and words used for widows demonstrated that what is defined as 'proper' behavior and acceptable conventions for women constantly shift with the passing tides of historical eras and reflect the current customs and societal whims of that particular age.

Poor widows have diverse experiences from those of wealthy and middle-class women after a husband's death. Impoverished women may become totally destitute; they might lose most or all of what few possessions they have, and may or may not be aided by their own natal family much less by relatives of the deceased.

Many lower-class widows hoped to re-marry as a survival option or if re-marriage was impossible, they were summarily left to meager societal provisions of gleaning fields, farming small plots of land or eking out a subsistence living as best they could. For these women, Confucian ideology and the culturally contoured demands of gendered roles were secondary considerations compared to the unrelenting necessities of having adequate food on the table and decent shelter for themselves and their children.

Not all widows are elderly with grown children, and in the specific case of war widows many of them were quite young; thus age represents another disjuncture in the developing images and treatment of widows. The necessities of survival in a crisis situation and the further exploration of the intersection of war, nationalism and gender as women are differentially and collectively affected is a theme which will be addressed in the following chapter.

4 War Widows: Poverty, Activism and Identity

In Tokyo and other large urban areas, once bustling marketplaces were transformed into bombed-out charred areas which echoed hauntingly with the refrains of women calling out, 'Give us rice,'(*kome yokose*). The desperation in these voices was indicative of the main problem for most Japanese after the war, i.e., there simply wasn't enough to eat in the major cities. One widow recalls her wartime experiences, and how it changed her life forever.

> Well, I was the youngest of six children, and I only graduated from elementary school. My mother died, and I was taking care of my sister's family; we lived in Osaka. I got a job as a maid during the war and worked in the house of a judge. After the war was over, I decided to move away from the city because there was no food and no housing, so my brother recommended that I leave the city. I left for the country, and after that I decided to marry a farmer.

By 1945, Japan had been at war for years (since 1931 with the beginning of the Sino–Japanese War as a result of the Manchurian Incident,[1] although war was not formally declared until 1937), and the losses due to continuous warfare and the effects of the subsequent military defeat were staggering. It has been estimated that the number of Pacific War dead alone (from 1941–1945) reached over 3,500,000, but there are no absolutely precise figures of persons wounded or injured. War always creates not only the well-known tragic casualties among soldiers, but invariably wrecks havoc and loss on civilians as well, particularly upon women and children. The Pacific War devastated the country of Japan from the explosions of atomic bombs in Hiroshima and Nagasaki[2] to the fire bombings of large cities, and the fierce battles that raged on the islands of Okinawa at the close of the fighting.

For people living in rural areas with access to farmland, it was usually possible to secure a few sweet potatoes, vegetables, and sometimes wild rabbits hunted down providing extra food for the fortunate few. During the war, farmers were closely monitored, since most agricultural produce, especially rice, was confiscated by the government for general distribution. As one informant, Ms. Gondō, explains.

> I was in Tokyo working as a telephone operator during the war and there was nothing in the city after the war. Houses were gone, and there was no food. I met my husband during the war and we got married. I was from a good family, a bushi (samurai) family, but after the war, my husband and I went to Hokkaido in 1949. I worked on farms as a day laborer, and then we would go to sell food in the city. My husband was never the same after the war though. He started to gamble and drink. Then, one day he just ran away and never came back. I found out that he had lost our house gambling, so they took the house away. I got a job at an egg company, and I worked there for the rest of my life. The police came to my door about 20 years ago and told me that my husband was dead. The only thing I thought when I heard the news was that finally he was gone for good. Then, I thought, why was it that I never had good luck with men or money?

The brutality of the war and its aftermath plunged ordinary Japanese people into an unforgettable nightmare, which still lives vividly in older people's memories. The war had drained the spirit, as well as the life-blood of Japan. Ensnared in a doomed militaristic and political vision to compete with, as well as imitate, the imperialistic practices of European powers and the United States (Johnson, 2004), Japan had committed itself to the path of war. The wartime slogan of 'Asia for the Asians,' representing one of the most cherished Japanese dreams of 'freedom from the white man' was partially achieved (in an economic sense) only after World War II according to Toland (1970, p. 876), although Japan continues to serve as a quasi-militarized U.S. colony housing an estimated minimum of thirty-two military bases and approximately 50,000 soldiers.

Most of the war dead consisted of men who supported households, so that widows, children and older people were virtually left on their own with little in the way of economic support (Cook and Cook 1992). While conditions were steadily deteriorating in Japan, there were also over 6,600,000 Japanese living or stationed overseas and these individuals were caught-up in the process of returning to Japan with little prospect of welcome or comfort waiting at the end of their journey (Sasaki 2000). Additionally, women were sent to foreign countries to marry soldiers stationed there; the stories of young women sent to the wartime colonies (e.g., Manchuria) of Japan as "continental brides" *(tairiku no hanayome)* are occasionally the subject of novels, but one 78-year old informant, Yoshida-san, relates her personal experiences.

> I was born in Nīgata, and I got married at 22. It was an arranged marriage (omiai), but actually another girl was supposed to marry my husband. When I saw the picture of him though, I persuaded the girl to let me marry him. I traveled to Manchuria to marry because my husband was one of the pioneer farmers trying to get some land. When the war started to go bad, we came to Hokkaido, and we were farmers for 20 years together until my husband died.

When these 'continental brides' and their soldier husbands stationed overseas returned, the economy was completely unprepared to accommodate the large influx of soldiers returning from foreign countries, since unemployment was endemic throughout the country; farming was one of the few available ways to earn a living. Japan lost all of its assets in foreign countries and as the military industry ceased to function and imports stopped, the economy collapsed. Thus ordinary living standards continued to deteriorate, especially in the areas of housing and food.[3]

When the Japanese military was defeated, the government could no longer effectively control farmers to supply adequate provisions to the general populace and the resulting food shortages led to a booming black market trade in food. Cohen (1948, p. 173) documented that while the average calorie intake for most adults is about 2,100 or 2,400 per day, in 1946, the average intake for a Japanese adult was only 1,000 calories supplied by the state.[4] Obtaining enough food to survive through the black market or other means was the main preoccupation of not only widows, but of all people living in urban areas. People in the cities adopted a survival lifestyle maintained only by selling personal belongings one by one *(takenoko seikatsu)*.[5] The essential conundrum as to why Japan could not get international aid immediately to alleviate the starvation and suffering of the general population was connected to political maneuverings and agreements which occurred after the war. It was argued in international circles that since Japan had been an invading country, the Japanese people should not be provided with better standards of living than people residing in those invaded countries (Sasaki, 2000). This basic agreement at the level of international relations prevented the United States government from supplying food due to intense criticism. Thus the supply of provisions during the years of 1945–1946 amounted to significantly less than it had been during actual wartime, and even though the U.S. government could have relieved much of the endemic mass starvation of Japanese people, relief was stymied by complex geopolitical considerations.

Another major consideration in explaining conditions in post-war Japan was the critical housing shortage. Due to the American military strategy of intense bombing of urban industrial areas, most Japanese homes in large cities were destroyed although information varies regarding the exact number of houses incinerated. However, it has been estimated that more than 2,210,000 houses were burned and over 9,210,000 people suffered from the effects of the intense bombings (Nakamura and Miyazaki, 1995).[6] Women and children, who had run away from the cities to escape the conflagrations, returned to urban areas but were essentially homeless. Children, some orphaned and others separated from their families, were forced to live in shacks, train/subway stations or in bombed out houses. Under these conditions, it was axiomatic that there was a severe housing shortage.[7]

This information helps to portray the conditions in which widows were living at the end of the war. Widows, like everyone else, were caught up in this nightmarish landscape, which makes their individual and collective stories all the more remarkable in that they were able to overcome this legacy and free themselves from years of 'ultra-nationalistic indoctrination' as Dower (1999, p. 124) has commented. While there was initial resistance from feminists and socialists to Japanese imperialism, such resistance gradually faded as women were called upon to support the war effort by having additional children, volunteering for self-defense duty, working in neighborhood associations and seeing off sons and husbands at railway stations throughout the country (Mackie, 2003; Sievers, 1983). With this contextual background of the conditions in wartime and post-war Japan established, the problems of survival, political activism, personal experiences of widows and societal transformations in their images, which arose in the context and aftermath of war, will be detailed.

Wives of the spirits of dead soldiers

War widows, many under the age of thirty and most under forty, were initially protected during the war as the 'wives of the spirits of dead soldiers' (*eirei no tsuma*) or sometimes referred to as the 'wives of the spirits of the war dead at Yasukuni Shrine' (*yasukuni no tsuma*). As one war widow living in Aichi Prefecture relates,

> After my husband died in New Guinea, there was talk that I would be married to the youngest brother in my husband's family, but unfortunately he was also killed in the war before the marriage could take place. After the war, there were hard times for everyone in Japan, especially for widows. I stayed in the country because if you lived on a farm, you could get food for yourself and your children. Some poor widows worked as street vendors and peddlers. They would fill their bags with vegetables early at sunrise lifting the heavy bags on their back. Then, they would walk to the city to sell the produce, and sometimes their young children would be trailing behind as the women trudged away.
>
> You see, it was part of the black market trade; it was illegal. It didn't matter though because without a husband you had to think about taking care of yourself. During those days there was no safe place to run, and we didn't have many choices. The one choice we could make was survival; we chose to survive. People have forgotten now, but in those days, widows were called the "white lilies," the "beautiful reeds" or the "blue orchids;" we were the wives of the spirits of dead soldiers.

Like Ms. Someya states above, widows were expected to pray for the souls of their husbands at Yasukuni Shrine and remain faithful to the memory of men who were culturally and politically positioned as sacrificing their lives on behalf of the country. However, at the end of the war the 'widow's problem,' exploded into the consciousness of Japanese society, along with the full realization of the poverty and suffering that existed. This problem was due to the fact that at the close of the war there was little in the way of a safety net (the family system not-with-standing) or social security available to women when their husbands died (Iwao, 1993). If women were trained in skills connected to teaching or nursing, they could adequately support themselves and their children even though they were living as single mothers; however, among widows suffering from poverty, it was not uncommon to arrange to re-marry simply in order to survive. Women living on their own, including single women, divorcees and widows, occupied a tenuous position in male-dominated Japanese society. In fact, 'women alone,' between the ages of twelve and forty were conscripted during the war for compulsory work in the munitions industry (Miyake, 1991). They were deemed as unnecessary in the family and society at large, but they could make themselves useful through contributing to the war effort; thus single women were called upon to justify their basic right to exist in a solitary state.

The ongoing situation of widows who were unable to provide for their children prompted the imperial government in June of 1939 to implement educational programs designated as, 'Special Teachers' Training Schools for War Widows,' and these vocational schools were subsequently established by the State. Yamataka (2001, p. 99) and Ichinose (2005, pp. 109–115) both state that these schools were initiated in order to prepare widows for jobs as midwives, nurses, dressmakers and teachers in junior, elementary and pre-schools. The importance that the government placed upon the training and education of widows was far from altruistic. Widows were to be trained so that they could support themselves without government assistance, and this economic independence would also protect the honor of the fallen soldiers; it would not be necessary for women to resort to remarriage or other means to secure adequate financial support. The schools were tuition free with the government bearing the cost of fees, dormitories, and even nursery facilities (Henmi, 2003; Kawaguchi, 2003).

In May of 1940, the students (widows) were notified by the government that they were required to travel to the Yasukuni and Meiji Shrines before they finished their schooling. It was considered particularly essential that the widows make a pilgrimage to Yasukuni Shrine and formally pledge to serve the honor of fallen husbands and the nation through their work as teachers. For the imperial government authorities, the mandated trip to the famous Shrine represented considerably more than the collective promises of widows to serve as teachers; it was an official ceremony which

Photo 4.1: War widow praying with her infant and child at Yasukuni Shrine. This picture is by Nabezō Kito. The widow in the picture is represented as a teacher who dedicated her husband to the war and gave birth to a boy.

demonstrated to the nation that these women were dedicated not only to the country but to their deceased husbands and the overall war efforts (see Photo 4.1). As the students visited the Shrine, pictures were taken by local newspapers, and images were constructed to reinforce the roles of women on the home-front as loyal supporters of the Japanese military government (Henmi, 2003).

Yasukuni Shrine was an important ideological symbol controlled by the State, since most deceased soldiers were interred there. Thus war widows were intrinsically connected to the memorial shrine through the placement of the physical remains of husbands, and this is why widows, as a group, were compelled by the government to visit the Shrine (Namihira, 2004). There were no exceptions to this official requirement for all widows reflecting the intersecting power of educational systems, the media and politics as, 'ideological state apparatuses' (Althusser, 2001), which create and reify images of women while tightly controlling them through the institutionalization of activities and the use of state resources. Kawaguchi (2003, pp. 75–76) and Kitagawa (2005, p. 159) note that governmental actions were tightly underpinned by the overall political strategy of a general prohibition of remarriage because the remarriage of widows would negatively affect soldiers at the front line.

The military government focused particular attention on the behavior of widows and these targets (widows of soldiers) were observed, bullied and confronted by neighbors as well as by the police. While the Ministry of Justice (Office of Criminal Affairs) argued that widows were proud of sacrifices made, officials also argued that widows faced problems of inheritance and inadequate financial provisions. Widows were seen as corrupting public morals and causing dissatisfaction in the community because they complained about government treatment of the families of deceased soldiers. This is also an ambiguous, albeit a polite way to refer to the fact that widows were considered a source of temptation to men living in the same community. There was also the serious problem for the government of who would receive a survivor's pension and who could claim public assistance on behalf of the bereaved family, i.e., the war widow or the head of the family (Yamataka, 2001; Kawaguchi, 2003; Ichinose, 2005).

Furthermore, more direct methods were used during the war years to constrain and enforce culturally sanctioned behavior for women. Local police officers routinely monitored war widows throughout the country. For example, in Akita Prefecture (in northern Honshū), the police requested surrounding neighbors to carefully watch and report on the actions and behavior of these women. Testifying to this common practice, detailed records were maintained regarding any woman who became pregnant during her husband's absence or had 'dishonorable' extramarital relationships. In some cases, mental coercion and forced abortions were employed by authorities to properly 'guide' women, so that they would, at the very least, *appear* to remain faithful to husbands and properly honor the soldiers fighting and dying on the battlefield. Women literally and physically embodied the honor of men and their families so much so that when consensual sexual relationships were discovered, these cases were often officially (but falsely) documented as forcible rape. In this same prefecture (Akita) in Showa 13 (1938), soldiers in battle heard the disturbing news that there were breaches of chastity committed by wives. It was subsequently reported that war widows had become a particular target of rapists with two-hundred sixty-six cases occurring in Akita Prefecture alone; however, the Ministry of Justice additionally recorded that many of these cases were *actually* acts of consensual sex (Henmi, 2003). Of course, soldiers engaged in life and death battles on the frontlines could hardly be told the truth about the reality of the situation at home.

The Japanese government responded to these 'breaches' of chastity by sponsoring a 'Home Front Support Week' from October 5th to the 11th in 1938, requiring various industries and business to give preferential treatment to the employment of widows. Again, rather than altruistic motives regarding widows and their families, the military government was motivated by an interest in demonstrating to society that the state would support and respect the memory of fallen soldiers. Without this demonstration of support, it was felt that the general populace might rise up against the war or even against government officials. Additionally, Gunji (2003, pp. 156–223) states that the government tried to assist the bereaved family under the slogan, 'Rinpo Sōfu,' which meant that people should help each other within the neighborhood.

The Japanese government manipulated meanings regarding widows in both ideological and economic spheres promoting respect for war widows due to their state constructed status as 'wives of the spirits of dead soldiers.' During this time, widows had collectively received a small amount of assistance money in support from the Japanese war-regime through public funds. However, change was about to occur for widows and their elevated status in society in tandem with two significant events that severely impacted the lives of these women economically. First, the government sponsored special schools for training widows as teachers were completely abolished in June, 1946; second, in the same year, the General Headquarters (GHQ) of the U.S. Occupation Forces curtailed all public assistance payments to widows of soldiers and separated Yasukuni Shrine (a long time financial supporter of war widows and families of soldiers) from its inter-connected relationship to the Japanese government.

The separation of the military government from Yasukuni Shrine represents a critical turning point, as the economic and social situation constructed by the state on behalf of war widows changed drastically. War widows were no longer looked upon as honorable wives of the spirits of war heroes; whispers and rumors commenced which accused these once respected cultural icons of being 'war collaborators,' and widows were no longer viewed as victims but as active perpetrators of war propaganda (Kawaguchi, 2003). This argument regarding widow's participation in war propaganda wages on today. However, as Ueno (2004, pp. 59–65) pointedly argues, in order for countries to wage total wars the nationalization of women is a requirement, i.e., it is a given necessity. Women residing in countries of the Allied Powers and those of the Axis Alliance were mobilized in order to prosecute war; thus when the question is posed regarding the responsibility of women as war perpetrators, what is the reflexive school of women's history actually reflecting upon? In other words, Ueno suggests that if the waging of war itself is not the point of critique, then it must follow that it is only the fact that Japanese women supported a 'bad war,' as opposed to women from the Allied Countries who supported a 'good war.' However, it is impossible to determine what war is good or bad until after the war has ended, and the winners and losers declared. The nationalization of women as an integral part of the mobilization of the state in waging war simply reflects the fact that women share a common fate with the state while at the same time, they are not actually considered equal citizens no matter which side they support during war.

As for war widows themselves, one informant, a leader and activist in the Hokkaido Welfare for Single Mothers and Children Federation, related the following salient insight;

> During the war, widows came into the city of Sapporo (in Hokkaido) from the surrounding countryside, and some came from northern Honshū, Tokyo and even from Kyūshū. Life was hard, but we could

get sweet potatoes, dried crackers and bread but not rice. Rice was considered the most precious commodity, and any buying or selling of it was strictly controlled by the Japanese government although sometimes there were rumors about the black market. Women were expected to be independent during the war and to support husbands and support the war; however, after the war, with the power of Yasukuni Shine broken by the GHQ, the status of widows really changed in society. There was a lot of prostitution (*panpan*) where women sold themselves along the streets, down by the river, and particularly near the airport because that's where a lot of American soldiers were stationed. When the occupation began, we had to endure a lot. American soldiers could invade our homes as they liked; they could just walk into our homes at any time! They said things to us, but we didn't know what they were sayings, so finally they would leave. Anyway, after the connection of widows to Yasukuni Shrine was broken, widows lost their honor and pride as wives of soldiers.

Thus widows who supported the war through mandated institutionalized activities and received state financial support were stripped of all benefits after the war and felt deeply betrayed and cast aside. While widows had been positioned by the state during the war as symbols of virtue and sacrifice, when the war concluded, these meanings were challenged and deconstructed by the incoming power of the new ruling regime, the American GHQ. In suspending the pensions for widows and bereaved families of soldiers, the American military leadership inflicted punishment on Japanese citizens for support of the war of aggression waged against the Allied Powers. Thus widows were sacrificed by the Japanese government during the war and by the Americans after the war. The time had come for women to re-group and resist.

Fighting back: widows and children – Strong like weeds

A clear wake-up call to the Japanese people came just a few months after Japan's momentous surrender on August 15, 1945 and the Allied Forces Occupation commencing a couple of weeks later. In November of 1945, Makino Shūji, a leader of the Musahino dormitory (*Musahino boshi ryō*) for single mothers and their children, gave a speech on NHK radio in which he stated that he wanted to send a postcard to all widows to support them during these desperate times. He undoubtedly recognized the seriousness of the situation considering the fact that at the end of the war it was estimated there were 1,880,000 widows (including 570,000 war widows) in Japan. Of this number, widows with children numbered 1,560,000 with many of these women widowed through the loss of husbands in the intense fire bombings of Japan as documented by Ichibangase (1978, p. 537), Kitagawa (2005, p. 156) and personal interview (2004).[8] In 1946 in Tokyo alone, it was estimated that forty-seven percent of all widows in the city were unemployed without adequate means of support placing these destitute women in the position of actively seeking any available employment as a means of survival. By September 1948, the total number of single mothers receiving public assistance skyrocketed to sixty percent. It's hardly surprising that many young urban widows in Tokyo were desperate to re-marry stating that they wept 'tears of hardship,' and lived on nothing else but the simple hope that they could adequately raise their children (Ichibangase, 1978).

Tarukawa (2002, pp. 1–20) states that according to the largest research focusing on widows implemented by the Japanese government in 1949, widows with children numbered 610,208, while widows receiving public assistance numbered 173,284 (28.4 percent of the total number of widows). Destitute widows receiving no public assistance numbered 108,529 (17.8 percent of the total) and the number of relatively poor widows not receiving any public assistance was estimated at 224,271 (36.8 percent). Widows with enough resources to meet minimal family needs were listed at 104,127 (17.1 percent). Even as late as 1950, poverty continued to be endemic throughout the country with large numbers of homeless people crowded together in underground causeways near railway stations in Tokyo and other large urban cities (Tanaka, 2002). Poverty and widespread economic instability in the destitute country took on a life of its own creating terrors of survival and constituting daily assaults on ordinary civilian life.

Women did not passively accept defeat or impoverishment due to the cessation of their pensions without an intensely fought battle. There are many examples of Japanese widows successfully empowering themselves in the midst of the poverty engulfing Japan in the aftermath of war. As the masses of indigent people struggled to piece together a daily living, widows were able to integrate their various abilities and strengths to achieve economic independence.

In Niigata Prefecture in 1948, a Peace Market managed and staffed entirely by widows was initiated; women involved argued that they could no longer rely on men to support them and had learned the hard way that they must be independent. At these markets, they sold sweets, fish, fruits, vegetables, used clothing, pans, charcoal, salt, oil, and an assortment of other articles. In another example of creativity and tenacity in the face of extreme hardship, forty widows combined their talents and resources establishing a doll factory in Yamanashi Prefecture in 1948 (Ichibangase, 1978).

A famous example of the activities of war widows was a group called '*Miashi-kai*' (Beautiful Reeds Association) in Ibaraki Prefecture. It was started by a woman returning to her hometown after her husband's death and beginning a new life working in the office at a local school; eventually she decided to initiate the formation of a widow's group in the small city and christened the newly formed group 'Beautiful Reeds' (*miashi*). Widows formed networks and raised money in innovative ways by selling homemade ice cream and candy during the summer months. In the winter, they prepared and sold noodle-soup dishes (*rāmen*) out of a small restaurant. The determined widows called the new restaurant '*ikoino-mise*' (relaxation place) where people could visit and partake of hot soup and a little local conversation, as well as warm up on a cold, wintry day. Also, they initiated the publication of the famous bulletin called '*Boshisō*' (Widows – Strong Like Weeds) in 1950. This bulletin continued its publications without interruption for an amazing twenty-five years (Suzuki, 1983). Other groups were rapidly established by widows throughout the country, as additional women were encouraged and stimulated by the activism and formation of each new organization (Koibuchi, 2000; Ichibangase, 1978).

According to a report from the Ministry of Welfare, the number of widow's groups had reached 2000 in Japan by January 1949. The political synergism created had led to the formation of the national organization known as the Japan Widow's Group Association (*Zenkoku Mibōjin Dantai Kyōgikai*) in 1950. The Director General of this organization, Kaneko Koibuchi, was one of the leaders of the 'Beautiful Reeds Association' in Ibaraki Prefecture. At the local level, many of the widow's groups were simply called 'Widow's Association' (*Mibōjin Kai*), but some groups also had original names represented by 'White Plum' (*shira ume*). Widows continued to be actively resistant to the misogynistic connotation of *mibōjin*, although this word was used at the national organizational level. The women involved in these groups consciously evoked the symbols of nature, as a counter-point to the word *mibōjin,* because they wanted to emphasize that they remained proud of their deceased husbands and wished to convey, as well as protect, the name and honor of their families. The message was conveyed to society that war widows were living moral lives symbolized by fresh flowers through drawing on and invoking the same nuance of natural beauty. Women preferred to be called white lilies (*shira yuri*), blue orchids (*seiran*) or white plums (*shira ume*) depending upon the region. These images can be juxtaposed against the all-encompassing aftermath of war and growing post-war demands for a more positive image. Taking the names of flowers represents a symbolic and critical point of departure for war widows who wished to separate themselves from the frequently pornographic sexual meanings rampant, continuing even now, conjured up by the Japanese word for widow. Widowed women were reacting in a public and substantive way against the superimposition of meanings that Japanese culture had constructed and imposed upon them by taking a clear, yet subtle line of resistance. As one 55-year old widow emphatically stated,

> I really hate the name of "mibōjin" because only women have such a name – men do not. So, why do we have to use that name? I say clearly, I don't want people to call me that.

Claiming one's own name and calling attention to the injustice of society's sexist perceptions of widows can be situated in a clear cross-cultural pattern of resistance frequently practiced by women within historically male-dominated and agriculturally based systems. The resistance may be informal or even covert, but is usually concerned with some specific immediate issue (Scott, 1985). The issue in this case was the assertion of the right to reject society's anachronistic name for widows and to create their own name and identity representing an act of symbolic reclamation; this reclamation was based on a more accurate expression of the unrecognized societal reality experienced by these women. More clearly, while widows suffered and endured hard times, they were not waiting to die nor willing to follow their husbands into death even though this fact contradicted cultural and state constructed gender expectations of female sacrifice.

Widows continued to form networks across the country and in September of 1949, nine prefectures (Ibaraki, Gunma, Saitama, Tochigi, Kanagawa, Nagano, Yamanashi, Niigata, and Tokyo) formally combined to initiate a broader-based organization to regain governmental economic assistance for widows and children, which had been abruptly curtailed by the GHQ. By this time, the situation had reached calamitous proportions with jobless rates among widows climbing to over fifty percent. Thus in 1950, the All Japan Widow's Group Association was created, and it was at this time that the word *mibōjin,* as part of the name of the organization, was hotly debated. It was decided at one of the first meetings that if they took the time to debate the name, the momentum of the movement to gain financial support that widows desperately needed might be delayed or even lost. This reasoning prevailed and explains the decision to eventually table the debate regarding the detested term. Women wanted to focus on the practical aspects of government assistance with as much haste as possible stating that it was their deepest wish to be independent and to decide their individual futures on their own (Yamataka, 2001; Ichibangase, 1978). Group members were painfully aware that any loss of time could well mean the difference between survival and complete financial collapse for destitute women and children.

The political activism of these women was initially part of another movement to obtain compensation on behalf of bereaved families through Japan's League of War Bereaved (*Nihon Izoku Kōsei Renmei*) formed in 1949. However, the organization of war bereaved families, which had started as a victim's alliance group in 1949, was replaced by a male-centered organization. This organization focused on public funerals and formal visitations to honor the war dead at Yasukuni Shrine as the most fundamental way of showing respect for the soldiers that died in the war. Implicit within this view was the critical point of departure from other organizations, i.e., soldiers were viewed as victims of the state and were idealized as sons, brothers and fathers who unselfishly sacrificed themselves on behalf of the nation of Japan. This perspective regarding soldiers who died in Japan's imperial wars still resonates in Japan manifested through regular visits to Yasukuni Shrine by elected government officials, including former Prime Ministers of the country.[10]

However, within the League of Bereaved Families, widows were dissatisfied because they wanted to focus on obtaining financial security through the implementation of a lifelong widow's pension, and the passage of legislation to help support and raise children in these families. Thus the focus of the widows was economic rather than ceremonial visits to the Shrine, and this focus became the basic objective of the widow's movement.

The situation of widows and their families continued to grow more critical day by day contributing to the intense activism of the widow's organization. According to Japan's Child Welfare Ministry Report on Single Mothers in 1952, approximately fifty percent of single mother households were created from right before the Pacific war ended to right after the war ended reflecting the heavy casualties, many scholars argue needlessly, inflicted upon Japan at the close of the war (Johnson, 2004). Since widows were not receiving government assistance during the time period from 1946 until 1954, it was necessary for most of them to perform some kind of revenue producing labor. Only ten percent of the total number of widows were in the privileged 'no need to work category,' while approximately thirty percent worked as day laborers/peddlers or doing piecework at home (*naishoku*) with the largest percentage (sixty percent) self-employed or working full-time. Many widows worked in agriculture, sewing kimonos (*wasai*), as school-teachers or making handicrafts (*shugei*). However, most widows were untrained and had never expected or even imagined that they would become the sole financial support of their family. Kitagawa (2000, p. 171) notes that widows worked in whatever jobs they could get, such as waitresses, bar hostesses, charwomen, cooks, maids, insurance saleswomen and food stall-keepers. As day laborers, women performed back-breaking work carrying various goods and vegetables to sell directly to customers through a free-lance peddling/vending system as Suzuki details (1983, pp. 11–12, 103–106).

Society frequently sends contradictory messages to widows regarding marriage and codes of acceptable behavior arbitrated along lines of age and class. Most middle and upper-class women were confined to a world of gentility and within this enclosed society they were closely scrutinized. These widows, who remained singularly dedicated to the memory of deceased husbands, were symbolized through the purity of white lilies or beautiful reeds based on cultural idealizations of sacrifice and family honor. However, younger women were pressured to re-marry within acceptable frameworks dictated by society. Many war widows were quite young with seventy-three percent under the age of thirty and ninety-one percent of all widowed families had children. Poor urban widows either worked or were encouraged to re-marry (*saikon*) after the war. As one LDP (Liberal Democratic Party) politician speaking to women activists, who were advocating a government pension for widows, unabashedly put it, 'just tell those women to get married again' (interview with Suzuki, 2004).

Transformations in the images of widows

As widows fell from their formerly exalted positions of wives of the spirits of war heroes, societal changes in the constructions of images and norms for war widows that began to occur in tandem with the GHQ cutoff of monetary support were reflected in the print media. Widows, particularly those who were young, were no longer viewed as white lilies or beautiful reeds, but were now transformed into eroticized sex symbols reflecting the cultural awareness that some impoverished widows resorted to prostitution in order to support themselves. Though most widows did not work in the sex industry nor did they have any connection to it, this biased perception was reflected and promoted in junk magazines (*kasutori zasshi*).[11] Eroticized images of war widows (see illustration of the 'dangerous war widow' in a *kasutori* magazine) were pervasive in this genre of magazines promoted in the general *kasutori* culture, which celebrated a post-war movement of self-indulgence and commercialized sex as suggested by Dower (1999, p. 122). The pages of these magazines were filled with sinister images of widows portrayed as predatory seductresses eagerly seeking out sexual partners and tempting men with their beauty, haunting loneliness and youth (Yamamoto, 1976). These grotesque images reflected the assumed sexual experience of widows mingled with the titillating cultural taboo of a liaison with a once married (though widowed) woman.

Most of the magazines were nothing more than barely disguised coarse pornography specifically addressing topics such as: how to kiss, how to strip, bizarre and macabre sexual escapades, pictures of women's underwear, obsessions with virgins and their seduction, prostitution, women castrating men and incest between sisters and brothers. The magazines were sold through the underground market as part of the male oriented escapist culture (Dower, 1999), and

Photo 4.2: *According to the 'kasutori' magazines, widows were portrayed as eroticized figures: sometimes this eroticism was considered dangerous as well as evoking the haunting sadness of war widows.*

out of this seamy side of publishing came that most famous of all the symbols of eroticism that emerged from the sleazy genre, the erotic and lonely war widow. Stories of war widows became prolific best-sellers for the pulp magazines with the young vulnerable widows, appearing in its yellowed pages, eternally seeking love and a sexual encounter. They appeared with such regularity in the publications that widows became the main characters in most of the stories because of the appeal of a sure-fire success in terms of sales (Yamamoto, 1976).

Younger women, who had never been married, were considered by society as chaste or at least that was the basic expectation. They, along with married housewives, were situated as an integral part of ordinary life and accordingly placed on pedestals as mothers and wives or potential mothers and wives. On the other hand, young war widows could be portrayed as knowledgeable about sex due to the fact that they had once been married reflecting the cultural reality that actual knowledge about sex was hidden in Japanese society (Yamamoto, 1976). Dancers, entertainers, geishas, and widows were expected to know about sexual desire and passion leaving these human emotions and desires to experts or to those who ostensibly had special 'skills' in this eroticized world. It was not considered suitable or polite to express these deepest of feelings in everyday life and society.

That person never came home: Impoverished rural women

In another world, far from the distorted portrayals of sexy, lonely widows in pornographic magazines were the books and publications which illustrated and catered to refined images of middle-upper-class widows. Magazines like 'Housewife's Friend' (*shufu no tomo*) and 'Public Opinions of Women' (*fujin kōron*) reflected opinions of women who were literate and usually impeccably educated. These women had the means, abilities and opportunities to express themselves in literature and in the press, but other widows had little chance to give voice to their concerns in such a profound and meaningful way. Within this literary and cultural context, Kikuchi and Ōmura's 1964 book, 'That Person Never Came Home,' (*Ano hito wa kaette konakatta*) made a substantial impact in Japan. The two researchers conducted extensive interviews and were among the first to record narratives from poor rural women regarding individual experiences of war widows, as well as collecting and documenting the letters of deceased soldiers to wives and family members.

Widows in rural areas faced an assortment of divergent issues from those of their urban widowed contemporaries, since many poor women living in the country could neither read nor write. Kikuchi and Ōmura (1964) in their research for *That Person Never Came Home* related stories from interviews with nine women who lived in Iwate Province, one of the most rural and secluded areas of Japan. The women resided in a heavily mountainous area, all married oldest sons, and subsequently all nine husbands were killed in the war. The difficulty encountered in managing and handling the events which arose as a result of these deaths is expressed by one widow who recounts her experience when she received the letter informing her of the death of her husband. She related that she didn't even know the exact details of what had happened because she was unable to clearly read the notification. These kinds of experiences represent the situation of the majority of impoverished, rural women who were unable to express themselves in a literate way and lived in remote areas where educated women (and sometimes men) were a rarity.

One widow in the research tells her detailed story as follows:

> I only lived with my husband for five months before he was drafted. I came to his house in the spring of 1942, and I was only 18 years old. When he finally left home, I was already pregnant. My husband's family made charcoal for a living, and I remember the last morning my husband and I walked to the mountain. We always left early in the morning with his mother and father; the four of us walked to the kiln at dawn every day. When we were resting, the ceiling of the oven fell-in. I thought maybe it's a sign of something, and I looked at my husband's face. When we finally stopped working and went home, the draft notice was already waiting there. So, he entered the army and was sent to China. I went to see him off at the station, but the train had already gone; I just missed seeing him. I was pregnant then, and I was looking for my husband's name to match the letters with his name written on the paper I had brought with me. I ran from window to window with the paper in my hand looking, and then they told me he was just here, but you missed him. Someone told me my husband asked about me...
>
> After that, my husband's brother was drafted and my father-in-law started to change. It was about two years later on the first day it snowed that year, when I received the letter informing me of my husband's death. My mother-in-law became sick, depressed and later died of grief. I eventually heard the details that he had been sent to New Guinea and died of malaria after four days of suffering. I had

sent him a picture of our daughter when she was born; I guess I'll always wonder if he saw it before he died.

Anyway, life was hard because making charcoal involves very difficult physical labor. I had to do it though, and I'd take my daughter on my back and leave in the dark long before the sun came up in the early morning hours, although it seemed like the middle of the night. Everything had changed at home because my father-in-law had lost both sons, and he was like a crazy man. People taunted me, and I think people will say almost anything about widows. They laughed and told me I should take up with my father-in-law; people said it was only a joke, but what a cruel and terrible joke! I thought so many times I would leave, but what could I do with my daughter, Tomi. We needed money, so during the off-season from making charcoal, I worked as a day-laborer. I did any job I could get. I'd come home late at night sometimes, so my father-in-law would be angry and say that I was the wife of the war-dead, a noble soldier that sacrificed his life for his country, and I should not be out late at night; such behavior was just not respectable. Sometimes when I was late, he would refuse to let me in the house, but I kept telling myself over and over, I'll hang in there until my daughter grows up; then I'll leave.

However, my father-in-law became sick with cancer, and we had to buy a lot of medicine even though we had practically no money. That was the lowest point in my life; I was miserable. I went into debt to buy the medicine. My daughter and I had no decent clothes, the roof was leaking and the house was broken-down. Suddenly, I got the news that widows would receive a survivor's pension, and I was so happy.

One day my father-in-law said to me he was going to see my husband, please take care of my house he said and with that he passed away. With just my daughter and me to look after, my life became easier, but I worried about my reputation after my father-in-law was gone. I was a woman living alone and widowed, so I knew there was talk about me and people watched me constantly. I was still only in my twenties, and when I went to community meetings sometimes we all went drinking afterwards. I wanted to sometimes enjoy myself and forget everything if only for a short time. After I returned home, I'd hear noises outside, and I was afraid that maybe a man or several men would come. Other widows told me that drunken men had come to their houses and wanted to have sex with them.

It wasn't just the men that we had problems with though. Women also had prejudice against widows. If we asked a man to do some manual labor for us, people would start gossiping and say we always asked the same man. If we changed and asked a different man, then people would say we were using men one after another. No matter what we did, we couldn't win. Married women talked about us like that because they were worrying about their husbands. Gradually, I became stronger and understood about people's prejudice. Even when I received a plaque for our house that said it was the house of the war dead, I really didn't feel anything. My own parent said to me that I was alone, and I'd be without a man for my whole life. You're pitiful they said. For the most part, war widows lived for the children and the husband's honor, and I think it is better that way. No one understands about it but war widows. Nowadays, I always remember when we made charcoal we would leave the firewood in the kiln, and the wood becomes charcoal. However, sometimes the wood doesn't become charcoal; it just rots. I was like that too. I couldn't become charcoal, but I became like rotten wood and then dirt. That's how I feel about my life.

Widows in Kikuchi and Ōmura's research (1964) reported that they often slept with a sickle to protect themselves against men who came in the night to 'visit' women living alone. These incidents became so frequent that one widow reportedly said to her four children, 'I think that we should die together.' However, her oldest son said he didn't want to die, even if he had to work hard to support the family. Women were ridiculed by men who said they were too young to be left without a virile husband. Most of these widows endured daily harassment in silence for the sake of their children and survival, but there was another reason women were silent. Widows couldn't accept the death of their husbands; someday he'll come home they believed and spent their lives clinging to that hope. More pragmatically, there were few chances for re-marriage due to the heavy casualties of young men in the war. The resulting loneliness fueled the illusions that many war widows had about their husbands perhaps facilitated by the fact that they were married only a short time. As Kikuchi and Ōmura (1964, pp. 161–163) noted, widows could keep their spirits up by holding on to those faded memories.

However, for the most part rural women were silent as a result of unrelenting societal surveillance practiced in small villages and towns. Watching widows and gossiping about them was an effective form of social control; it functioned to silence women, keep them distracted and of course, obedient. Even if widows did speak up, their basic credibility might be subjected to derision resulting in additional gossip as the only tangible and bitter result.

Levirate marriage

Hendry (1982, p. 112) has argued that the revival of levirate marriage (the marriage of a widow to a brother of the deceased husband), which had been prohibited during the Edo Period, was due to the mounting casualties incurred as Japan carried out its imperialistic conquests, and the custom was practiced particularly after the Pacific War. Levirate marriage (*gyakuen-kon*), an ancient custom practiced in many cultures, was actually common throughout various periods of Japan's history. The form of marriage was not unusual among widows, particularly among war widows. The practice particularly fit the ideology and militaristic climate pervasive in the late Meiji era; widows still belonged to the family of their husbands, so it seemed natural that brothers could replace the deceased husband in order to claim the widow and any children produced in the marriage. Even ghost marriages (where a woman is married to a deceased man) on behalf of unmarried sons who had died in the war were not uncommon during this time.

In order to understand the more pragmatic reasons for the revival of levirate marriage, particularly in rural areas after the Pacific War, it is again necessary to consult the Meiji Civil Code of 1898. As mentioned previously, under the code, widows had no recourse to inheritance (*katoku*), but upon the death of the husband, assets were passed directly on to children, and children were legally incorporated into the family system. This legal practice was closely followed throughout post-war Japan and confirmed by research conducted in 1949 in four different prefectures. The research indicates that eighty percent of all widows inherited no assets from the husband's estate (Kitagawa, 2000). However, after the war, widows were protected in terms of inheritance with apportionment clearly spelled out in Article 900 of the *Civil Code of Japan*. The law states that if there are two or more successors in the same rank (i.e., spouse and children) shares in the inheritance shall be determined in accordance with the following provision: 'Where children and the spouse are successors, the shares in the succession of the children and that of the spouse shall respectively be one-half' (Gubbins, 1897).

This legal change was an important underlying reason for the resurgence of the custom of levirate marriage and illustrates the ongoing connection between the family and the state. After the new Civil Code was instituted in Japan, if a widow married her deceased husband's brother thus staying within the same family register (*koseki*), it would not be necessary to divide the land or assets in order to provide the widow with her lawfully allotted inheritance. This is a critical factor since the family household system was fundamentally connected to an agrarian based lifestyle. Land is a scarce commodity in Japan and dividing the already small amount of farmland into even smaller plots would have seriously disrupted Japanese farming practices and traditional rural communities; it is within these communities where the feudal family system was strongly entrenched, and although weakened, still exists even today.

Levirate marriage was commonly accepted in rural areas, but there were few opportunities since many families had lost all their sons. Anzai (1993, pp. 147–159) carried out studies of levirate marriage in the 1960s. Although the data was collected in the 1960s, the research was not published until thirty years later. The research was extensive and far reaching encompassing 284 municipalities throughout Japan starting in 1962. Questionnaires were delivered to municipal offices and disseminated to interview participants. While levirate marriage was practiced in rural areas throughout Japan, this particular research focused on Tochigi Prefecture in the Kantō Region (the central area of Japan). He interviewed widows in a small village (population 7,350 in 1960) consisting of 1,281 households with his actual sample consisting of fifteen households where deaths due to war had occurred. The average age of the wives at the time of the husband's death was 25 to 29 years old and twelve of the fifteen families included children. With only one exception, all the cases of re-marriage in the sample involved the marriage of a widow to a younger brother. The age difference between the older deceased brother and the younger brother ranged from approximately three to four years.

Most of the widows were single for approximately forty-two months, but Anzai (1993) concedes that the time period might have actually been less with eight of the levirate marriages producing

children from the new union. Reasons for levirate marriage in rural areas which emerged out of the research related to four main points:
1. protection of the deceased male's widow and children
2. maintenance of assets (especially land) within the family
3. the utilization of the skilled labor of family members
4. maximization of family stability and laborers through the merging of the deceased husband's family with a younger brother of the family.

All of these reasons involve the inclusion of women and children within the husband's kinship group for tangible purposes related to maintaining property and the retention of family labor (both reproductive and productive) for future generations. In retaining the widow in the husband's family through the custom of the levirate, the interests and advantages of the husband's kin are well-served. A young widow's ability to produce future heirs on behalf of the patrilineal system is also maintained; thus as Stone (2000, pp. 245–247) has argued, a common strategy of the levirate system serves to protect the land and/or asset inheritance base for successors in the patriline. Within the above specific levirate custom scenario not only the widow but also the brother may be forced to marry, so they both can be viewed as tools of the kinship system. Women and men were used due to the pragmatic and cultural demands of keeping farm land intact which affected inheritance by sons (other than the oldest son), as well as daughters who were usually excluded from farmland inheritance. Even with the passage of the new post-war Civil Code, which protected a widow's inheritance allotment, her right to choose a lover or marriage partner freely was sacrificed for the protection and continuation of the system. After the implementation of the new code, a young widow might be persuaded to marry her deceased husband's brother in order to preserve family assets and also to ensure structural fidelity to her first husband in perpetuity. In each case, individual behavior is controlled and manipulated through the mediation of the state for the benefit and protection of the family system.

The Civil Code regarding inheritance also stipulated that wives cannot inherit all of her husband's assets but must share them equally with the children of the deceased. This requirement represents not a choice freely made but a legal mandate. Each child would receive a part of the half portion assigned to the children. More clearly, in the case of two surviving children, they would each receive one-quarter portions each. Thus the law functions to protect children and widows, but also impinges upon the freedom of widows to freely dispose of property, money and assets as she wishes. The ownership of genealogical records, utensils used in religious rituals, land designated for tombs and burial grounds is inherited by the person (almost invariably the widow) who is customarily charged with the management of family graves and performance of memorial ceremonies, reflecting cultural practices and Buddhist influences. Of course, these traditional duties are based on expectations that widows should pray for ancestors and husbands.

Therefore, the custom of levirate marriage was mediated along rural/urban distinctions and was not evenly distributed throughout Japan. Although many impoverished widows hoped to re-marry for economic reasons, levirate marriage was most commonly practiced in rural areas. According to extensive research conducted over fifty years ago in 1950 in a rural village of Gunma prefecture (Tajima, 1951), among a total of sixty-four war widows (age 20 to 45 years old) twenty-two of the total number remarried, but only six of the unions were levirate marriage. Widows who did not re-marry were generally economically independent. Kitagawa (2000, pp. 172–175) states that in another village in Kōchi prefecture in 1948, of sixty-nine war widows interviewed only seventeen of them remarried. Another group of twenty-two widows, but not war widows, also remarried.

One of the faces of the feudal household system demonstrates the domination and subservience of women. However, another argument can be advanced to illustrate that the system also supported many widows and provided economic provisions for upper-middle-class war widows. Additionally, not only men, but women also, accepted the kinship system and relied on its financial support. The navigation of the family system was particularly challenging, as well as financially rewarding, for upper-middle-class war widows who lived on the borderline of life and death as spiritual wives to deceased husbands. However, the case was quite different for widowers in the familial system. It was believed that men represented the 'blood' (*sic*) of the patrilineal based genetic lifeline that connected all the generations; therefore, men could avoid the kind of restrictions and circumscribed lives that widows would be expected to live. Embedded in this patriarchal ideology was the right to freely choose another woman to bear children in order to maintain the bloodline of the kinship group. This practice can be concretely illustrated by the Meiji Civil Code, Article 767, which states that women are legally unable to remarry until after six months have elapsed from a divorce or death of a husband. This prohibition has never been amended, and even today women are required to wait six months after divorce or becoming a widow before they can legally re-marry. Thus patriarchal interests and structural protection of bloodline confirmation are linked and continue to be preserved in modern-day Japan.

While some widows were cared for and supported through the feudal household system, the familial system also benefited from supporting these women as the above reasons indicate. However, contrary to the assumption that most widows (even war widows) were historically supported by family and in-laws as part of the security and benefits of the *ie* system, the idea of feminine modesty was clearly manifested by widows who were independent and able to support themselves without asking for help from family, friends or society (Nolte and Hastings, 1991). In reality, most women found it difficult to obtain a new husband or to receive financial help from relatives or anyone else. Moreover, children of widows were actively discriminated against, since a fatherless boy might be seen as not receiving the kind of moral and strict training that is necessary for a successful company employee. According to Vogel (1963, pp. 17–18), companies in Japan have traditionally worried about whether a 'fatherless son' might succumb to temptations of stealing, fraud, or embezzlement due to the additional economic pressures brought to bear upon such a boy (Aoki, 2003). Therefore, the state of widowhood for both women and children was fraught with contradictions, discriminatory treatment and isolation often accompanied by ongoing poverty.

Economic and social realities

The figures on casualties render a cerebral image, a fixed numerical totality of those who died in war, but the numbers do not convey a feeling of what it was like to actually experience a loved one going off to war never to return home or an official's knock at the door signaling bitter news. One elderly widow, Ms. Aoyama, from Aichi Province provides a narrative window through which we may briefly glimpse a part of the experience of war and loss.

I woke up to the sound of a loud knocking at the door, and a voice broke through the stillness saying that "this is a draft card." I was shocked and seemed to collapse in a chair, as my head was spinning. It was dawn in early August 1937. Although I was only ten years old then, I was filled with worry and a downhearted feeling thinking about my elder brothers and parents. My eldest brother was single when he received his draft card. I remember we only had about a week together before he left home to go to the front. Before he left for war, the three of us talked about taking a souvenir picture and decided to go to the photo shop downtown. We had heard a rumor that when you take a photograph of three people, the person in the middle will certainly die soon. So, perhaps childishly, we carefully placed a doll in the picture with us and then took the picture (See photo 4.3).

The people in our small village decorated the gate to our house with twigs and branches of Japanese cedar trees wrapping them decoratively with bright red and white cloth to celebrate my brother going off to war. He left home walking through that colorful gate, stopping to say a prayer at the local Shrine and going on to the station. People always gathered together at the train station to see off the young men who were drafted. The men got on the train amid the echoes of voices cheering 'banzai.' My brother leaned out of the window in the last train car and waved goodbye to my father, my other brother and me. This is still a painful memory.

Fortunately, my eldest brother was able to return home after two years of fighting, and he got a job working at a company. He studied on his own at night, as he believed that education was very important, and he married a lovely young woman, Tokiko (see Photo 4.4), and they had a son. He was living a happy life, but this peaceful happiness was not to be enjoyed for long. He soon received another draft card in 1941 at the beginning of World War II. My parents and his wife saw him off at the station and were grief-stricken. His wife, Tokiko, had told me that when she went to see him for the last time in Tokyo, he told her that he had asked my other brother to marry her, since he strongly thought he would die on the battlefield. However, this other brother (my second eldest brother) was also sent to the war in 1942 under the mobilization of the student draft (gakuto dōin), and he died on a transport ship stationed off-shore in the Philippines. Then, after all, my eldest brother did die in New Guinea just as he had predicted.

After World War II, whenever I hear the famous song, 'ganpeki no haha' (A mother at the wharf), I always remember my parents who lost

Photo 4.3: On the left hand side of the picture are the two older brothers who will soon be going off to war (and ultimately would die); the older brother is sitting and the younger brother is standing in the middle. On the right hand side is Katsumi-san who wanted to take a picture with her older brothers before they left home.

both their sons and Tokiko, who became a widow so young. I often wonder how she and my parents survived such a deep sadness. Even now, I still pray that we will always have peace.

As mentioned previously in this chapter, after the war, several informants witnessed widows coming from the country to the city carrying vegetables or potatoes to sell in the city. Most of these impoverished widows were working as street vendors and peddlers from early in the morning until late at night. Women picked up their bags, filled them and went to town to sell whatever they could returning to the country to pick up additional supplies moving back and forth between the two venues. Some produce was sold to stores, but the practice was actually part of the black market trade rampant throughout post-war Japan. One woman stated that when she was arrested, the police asked if she was in the black market business, and she told them that she was, but if they gave her husband back, she would stop selling black market produce forever (Suzuki, 1983).

Another informant detailed her story about the realities of widowhood which she experienced after the death of her husband in New Guinea. Ms. Someya was only twenty-four years old at the time of his death. As for financial support from her deceased husband's family, Someya-san explains,

> I had no money, and no help from my natal family. The inheritance was passed from my father to his male children and then to those grandchildren. In those days, you didn't think about your own opinion or what was best for you because parents always talked about duty. I was never envious of women who re-married because if a widow did re-marry, sometimes she would lose her friends. I remember there was one beautiful widow who re-married, but then all of her friends would have nothing to do with her. As for me, I always thought about my son first, and after that my husband's memory.

Widows could be effectively controlled through informal, as well as formal, societal pressures and rigid expectations with punishments meted out for any transgression of rules. All eyes in a small town were watching, aware, evaluating and reflecting upon their own behavior in light of the fate that had befallen a widow numbered among the same group but distinguished as 'the beautiful widow' who remarried and was subsequently shunned by her friends, relatives and neighbors. The monitoring of actions and constriction of choices had a most insidious influence on society as a whole with the effects of punishment rippling throughout communities. As

Photo 4.4: Tokiko-san right before she got married. Soon after her marriage, she would become a war widow herself.

Foucault (1979, p. 105) has shown, the most successful and pervasive disciplinary actions to admonish individuals and control behavior appear invisible, natural, and manifest the idea that 'the power that punishes is hidden.'

Most widows had little time for enjoyment, but focused on saving money, sometimes only a few dollars a month from their meager earnings as peddlers, while other widows sold themselves for sex through prostitution or as a *nigō* (mistress). Even for women who had work experience and abilities, such as making kimonos or working in a restaurant, it was a constant challenge to survive in post-war Japan. A box to bury in memory of a loved one whose body had not been recovered cost 130 yen, which was a small fortune during these lean years. Informants stated that some widows, unable to endure the struggle any longer, committed suicide, and a common place to do so was on the railroad tracks.

Just as tragic as these cases of betrayal of widows and families of the deceased are the cases of widows who suffered the horrendous effects of the atomic bomb. 'The world's a funny old place,' states one widow telling the story of her husband who goes out one day and simply never comes back after the bomb was dropped on Hiroshima. When the atom bomb fell, many people in the city thought it was the end of the world and that the very sun had fallen from the heavens. This widow goes on to relate that the suffering and horrible way her husband died was like all the tortures of this world rolled into one (Kanda, 1989).

Conclusion

As the information and voices relayed in this chapter illustrate, a large number of war widows were not adequately supported by government pensions, members of their own natal families or by the deceased husband's family. Economic support was fragile even for those widows who were willing to live within the traditional bounds of the family system which purportedly cared for all its members. Women were frequently the objects of discrimination, surveillance and control as they struggled to overcome loss and financially support their children.

In rural areas, the family household system added another dimension to society's rigorous control. Due to the fact that the *ie* system in most areas of Japan focused on the male as sole inheritor of the family assets, when one son died, the inheritance was promptly passed on to the next son as the legitimate heir. In the process, any inheritance claims of the deceased son's widow or children were rendered null and void; thus many women and children were legally disinherited (before the passage of the new Civil Code of Japan) through no fault of their own. For widows living in small agrarian villages, life was strictly regimented as these women were viewed like 'outsiders,' since they did not possess the 'blood' of the family. Informants testified to the fact

Photo 4.5: This picture was taken on October 3, 1951. It shows war widows paying their respects to the war dead at Yasukuni Shrine. Tokiko-san is seated in the last row fifth person from the right.

that these widows, 'outsiders,' were incessantly surveilled and forbidden simple liberties and freedoms, such as going to local festivals, meeting friends or walking to town by themselves.

After the war ended, even in the face of society's discrimination and negative portrayals, widows never acquiesced in giving up the political fight to recover their lost pension terminated by America's GHQ. As a result of the synergism of multifaceted political movements, unrelenting action by various individuals and the influence of the popular *Strong Like Weeds Bulletin*, in 1954, the widow's pension was again instituted by the Japanese government along with various other governmental assistance programs, including tax benefits. With these significant successes, the activism of the widow's movement gradually slipped into abeyance.

The violence executed in the war by Japan seeped into society and affected, not surprisingly, widows in both general and diverse ways. Violence inevitably breeds violence and while the war was initially conducted on soil outside of Japan, inside the country violence was mimetically reproduced. We may expand the meaning of violence to include not only the violence which is expressed at the physical level, but violence also includes assaults on the personhood, dignity, sense of worth or value of the victim or victims; according to Scheper-Hughes and Bourgois (2004, pp. 1–31), it is these social and cultural aspects that ultimately give violence its insidious nature. Japanese widows were caught up in the tumultuous wartime state, and it was perhaps predictable that they would become useful tools of, as well as victimized by, the manipulations of the militaristic regime.

State repression is often graphically illustrated, but the *everyday violence* of slow-starvation, despair, hopelessness and humiliation, which destroys those human beings who are already marginalized, may be rendered invisible or unrecognized (Green, 1999). Incidents described in this chapter portraying war widows who were afraid at night and slept with sickles to protect themselves or other women who were ridiculed and isolated on a daily basis illustrate the inextricable relationship between structural, political and social violence.

In the current academic milieu, individuals may be situated as 'empowered' through making their own choices without any contextualized explanation that this range of 'choices' was heavily circumscribed by the realities of Japan's wartime political and social environment. Thus it is not a facile positioning of war widows as victims (of the wars of Imperial Japan) or victimizers (supporters of these wars exercising their own choices), but widows were and are survivors as well.

5 At the Crossroads of Life and Death: Ethnography of ritual and ceremony

The context of this ethnographic event reflects the long history of critical connections between widows, and the development of the Zen Buddhist religion in Japan which was uniquely blended with Confucianism and Taoism imported by Chinese monks. Suzuki (1959, pp. 41–68) and Arai (1999, p. 164) show that financial contributions and land endowments by upper-class widows were important factors in the establishment of Buddhist temples and nunneries throughout Japan. The donation of large tracts of land and money made by wealthy widows provided the necessary linkage to temples and facilitated the responsibility to carry out their duty to pray for the repose of her husband's soul; the stage was set for the role of women in the implementation and transmission of ritual. Thus ceremonial Buddhist services have historically been the responsibility of widows, particularly in upper-middle-class families to commemorate a husband's death and to ensure the smooth rebirth of his spirit, as well as its integration into the family lineage.

However, on another less explicit level, funerary and memorial services involve highly gendered roles enacted predominantly by men but enabled by and embedded in the frequently unseen and largely taken-for-granted work done by women at the informal level (Aoki, 2000). At the time of a husband's death, women may feel invisible as though having brushed too close to death, they themselves become like ghosts and thus widows may seek solace through religious activity. As one 63-year old informant, who lost her husband in a coal-mining accident, commented, 'When I feel alone, I have god to talk to.' This is not an unusual reaction for widows who find themselves suddenly faced with the performance of duties revolving around their role as a personal mediator with the supernatural world. Mystical and ceremonial relationships have appeal for women in particular because many of the more public and esteemed functions have been historically performed by men acting as priests and prophets. Lerner (1993, pp. 71–74) has documented that these types of roles were, and in some cases remain, expressly forbidden to women. For women, entrance into the sacred world of the divine has frequently been part of an intimate relationship with magic, healing and deities. These experiences may also include experiencing dreams filled with signs and visions that seem to suit individuals undergoing loss, misfortune and grief.

Women may also be resisting the general rule in many religions that it is necessary for men to provide mediation between humans and the divine. In these cases, women reach divinity via men, so that they are in fact once removed from the direct relationship with the supernatural (Falk and Gross, 2000). Within anthropological studies, cases are not uncommonly documented where women seek out a religious life through domestic rituals, shamanistic practices and via roles in 'new' religious movements or as members of messianic, male-led religious cults.

In the case of Japan, after a woman's husband died, it was believed that a wife no longer had a clear purpose, position, or function in her husband's family (Cherry, 1987). Widows are thus situated in a condition of ambiguity and 'placelessness,' which in many societies accompanies changes of state in social status or age. This experience of 'placelessness' dovetails with that of the concept of 'liminality' initially formulated by van Gennep (1960, pp. 33, 190) and later refined by Turner (1995 {1969}, pp. 94–96). Although these frameworks have often been used in classic anthropological and symbolic analyses, they have been challenged by Lincoln (1991), who argues that the spatial aspect of van Gennep and Turner's models for ritualized social passage is not applicable to his analysis of women's initiation rituals. He suggests that the concept does not reflect the experiences and symbols used in these initiation rituals as young women are seldom actually separated from their families. Thus Lincoln posits a slightly altered conceptualization of separation-liminality-reincorporation proposed by Turner to an enclosure-metamorphosis-emergence framework advocating that this construction represents the gendered nature of ritual. Crapanzano (2003) also questions van Gennep and Turner's model based on his research of Moroccan rites of circumcision in his detailed ethnography peppered with the psychological and social ramifications of the so-called 'Oedipal desires.' On the basis of this study, he argues that the three-stage structure proposed by van Gennep and Turner 'may reflect less the reality of the ritual than the culture of the anthropologist.' Of course, Western-based interpretations of Oedipal complexes rooted in classical Greek myths, as well as Freudian psycho-social interpretations applied to Moroccan rituals, present an additional set of problematic assumptions which can also be challenged.

However, while the basic concept of liminality may not be universal, it is certainly not static but is clearly linked to the idea of symbolic change, transformation and process highlighting the theme of transition not as a fixed point but rather as a moving continuum. In the case of Japan, a widow becomes a *symbolic* traveler (even though she doesn't *physically* travel) with a shifting ambiguous status and serves as a transitory bridge between the separated, but at times intermingling worlds, of the living and the dead. Turner defines the state of the ritual subject (the 'passenger' or 'liminar') as one of ambiguity 'betwixt-and-between' all prior and fixed points of classification. The liminar passes through a domain which is symbolic in nature and which has few or none of the attributes of the former or future state. This concept is integral to Turner's (1969, pp. 96–97) development of ideas about social inter-relatedness which he designates as 'communitas,' and his conceptualizations regarding the multivocality of symbols themselves.

This liminal period for widows may vary throughout Japan, but generally includes a minimum of one year and often several years. During this time, a widow is usually expected to refrain from attending any community events, celebratory parties or even gift-giving. This is the period during which relatives and friends may not know how to deal with the newly widowed woman. It is a period of both uncertainty and confusion as she is no longer a wife in the physical sense, and yet she is considered by some to be a spiritual wife. She is no longer married, but continues to be part of her deceased husband's family. In cases involving an older widow, she may still be caring for her deceased husband's parents.

The above outlined themes are prevalent in the following ethnography and Turner's model, as explicated above, fits neatly with Japanese ritual and folklore which expresses continuity between the worlds of life and death where the dead do not leave for some far away place, but they are close-by as part of the living world as Hori and Ooms (1986, pp. 9–15) have shown. The deceased are thought to freely visit the living illustrating the relationship between death and life itself as one of circularity and not of absolute opposition in the form of otherness. Yanagita (1986, pp. 136–152) has asserted that it has long been believed in Japan that there is a concealed corridor between the living and dead, i.e., between the 'clear' world and the 'dark' world. This corridor unites the two worlds and facilitates passage completing the ongoing circle of life and death.

Thus we can situate Japanese widows spatially within these clear and dark worlds following the trajectory from entrance into the husband's family until her husband's death. Her initial position at the time of marriage was based on her status as wife to the now deceased husband, so the widow is often positioned as a rather ambiguous figure due to the uncertainty of her new status. Interestingly, Owen (1997, pp. 4–14), states the pattern of loss and lack of clarity in status is the most common inheritance of widows in developed countries, as well as developing nations. However, this particular study of Japanese widows additionally argues that the liminal state of widows is a highly gendered one, which locates women in interlocking positions encompassing both power and vulnerability and arousing fear and pity as well as suspicion from others.

After being touched by death through her husband's demise, a widow is thrown into this other worldly landscape where, particularly in Japan, her behavior is expected to change in tandem with her new situation. A widow falls into the gap between the 'real world' where living breathing human beings hold sway and another world inhabited by frequently hungry ghosts and ancestral spirits. One of the responsibilities of widows illustrating their roles as mediators between these two worlds is to provide a proper location and necessary food for spirits. Neglect of important aspects of death rites and manifesting the proper ritualized behaviors can affect the health and future of the bereaved family as well as their status and reputation within the community. In Japan, deceased spirits are thought to have an intense hunger for water and food. Food may also be used to appease these spirits to prevent them from afflicting family members and friends with illness or death. Japanese folklore reflects these beliefs as Hori and Ooms (1986, p. 115) argue, since evil often comes about from those spirits who do not receive a sufficient food offering; the evil is manifested in poor harvests and plagues of deadly diseases like smallpox and typhus.

With this background firmly in place, the following ethnographic study focuses on an in-depth description, interpretation, and analysis of a special event: a 'behind the curtain view' of a widow and other female family members as they manage and orchestrate the ritual known as *is-shūki no hōyō* (the Buddhist memorial service on the first anniversary of a death).[1] On one level, the ritualized service is held to commemorate a death and to ensure the smooth rebirth of the spirit as well as its integration into the ancestral lineage. However, on another less explicit level, the formal service involves highly gendered roles enacted predominantly by men, but enabled by and embedded in the frequently unseen and largely taken-for-granted work done by women. This chapter includes the perspectives of the individuals involved, analyzes the interactions between women and men as well as those among women, and illustrates how a particular group of women in an upper-class rural family are critically involved in both maintaining and challenging familial practices.

Although there are many thorough explications of Japanese religious rituals and traditions as well as other rites of passage, there are few descriptions of the gendered nature of the labor that supports the enactment of religious ceremonies, since the focus of these studies is frequently on how women are excluded rather than included in such rituals (Martinez, 1995). Additionally, gender roles and the work related to food preparation in the context of religious rituals in Japan are seldom discussed in anthropological literature Metcalf and Huntington (1991, pp. 49–59); however, in anthropological research outside of Japan, there is a richer expression of women's participation in the context of funerals and various types of ritualized feasting as Kahn (1994, pp. 123–158) and Kerns (1997, pp. 127–140) detail. Hence at the theoretical level, this chapter presents an ethnographic study that self-consciously documents and illuminates the so-called ordinary work of women with the same attention to detail and explanation generally given to the religious ritual that such gendered labor supports. The research describes and situates the activities of women on center stage with the ritualized performance itself serving as a backdrop to the important household work that is being done within the ceremonial context – thereby effectively turning the theoretical 'lens' upside down.

Careful examination of the details of so-called mundane labor done in the context of a sacred religious ritual challenges the practice of focusing only on the readily visible performance of the ceremony. Such a focus has dominated analytical discourse, so that the myriad seemingly unimportant details of household work have been consigned to the shadows and periphery of anthropology; historically, domestic labor and the gendered aspects of the household have either been ignored, inadequately interrogated or represented as unimportant as asserted by Bonvillain (2001, pp. 181–184), del Valle (1993, pp. 11–16) and Moore (1988, p. 52). Exclusive focus on the performance of the ritual, which may appear to be of singular importance, obscures other important aspects of the ceremony, i.e., the neglected *underbelly* of the ritual. These aspects include but are certainly not limited to the social interaction among women, the interaction between women and men, the continuity and transformation of the *ie* (family group) system, and the maintenance (as well as the manipulation) of personal and family prestige within the community, which involves considerable status-production work (Papanek, 1990).

The participant-observation based research that follows clearly conveys how the memorial ritual ceremony is actually facilitated, how the performance of vital household labor can be transformed into personal and tangible gain, and how changes taking place in the critical social site of the family have significant ramifications for society. Though this study deals with a particular upper-class rural family located in central Japan and situated in the distinctive cultural milieu of the *ikebana* (flower arrangement) and *chanoyu* (tea ceremony) traditions, the household duties of cooking, cleaning, and other labor performed in the context of memorial rites are not unlike the work that many women do in support of their families throughout Japan. Furthermore, this case study speaks to the more general theme of the multifaceted possibilities of transformation at the personal level as evolving ideas about the meaning of family and the growth of individualism continue to spread throughout Japan (Aoki, 2003; Meguro, 1999).

A second look: Widow's roles in rituals and rites of passage

Examining the lives of widowed women in specific situations sheds light on the hidden politics and agendas within the family as a fundamental social setting, which is manifested cross-culturally as well as in Japan (McGinn, 2008; Lock, 1993). In Japan, a variety of demands are placed on widows – demands that revolve around family service obligations and ritualized religious based duties that are scrutinized and evaluated by surrounding neighbors and community members. On the other hand, widowers do not need to enter the world of Buddhism (*butsumon*) by becoming a Buddhist priest or devoting themselves to religious duties, when a wife passes away. The status of widows in Japan remains somewhat contradictory, however: on the one hand, legends abound that point to the uselessness and burden of caring for older widowed women; on the other hand, many of these stories also argue that aged parents should be revered. In some societies, growth in the authority and power of women accompanies aging in formalized age-hierarchies, but in Japan, reverence and even survival may historically have depended, in part, on whether or not a widow could contribute some kind of labor that was essential to the household, such as caring for young grandchildren according to arguments by Cornell (1991, pp. 71–81) and Dickerson-Putnam (1998, pp. 65–77). This contradiction – and the ambiguity that results there from – continues for many elderly widowed women in Japan even today who may actually prefer to live alone, contrary to popular belief, rather than with family members (Aoki, 2003). Respect for and/or aid to widows cannot be facilely assumed; rather, it is based on the behavior of widowed women as it is observed and critically evaluated. Widows who do not perform familial duties or who take any kind of inappropriate action, as defined by society, may be chastised through discriminatory and institutional practices such as gossip, ridicule, and informal ostracism (Smith and Wiswell, 1982; Hendry, 1998; Hendry, 2010). As illustrated in previous chapters in this work, such punishing behavior can extend to the children in widows' families as well.

Women's support of male-centered, highly visible ritualized performance through their own work, which is characteristically 'unseen,' problematizes classic theoretical foci and orientations, which have frequently used rituals and rites of passage as a preferred vehicle for analyzing, interpreting, and explicating cultural meanings and as reflections of social custom (Rappaport, 1967). Women have historically mediated various rites of passage in key roles, though this participation has often been neglected in anthropological studies (Bonvillain, 2001; Hardacre, 1997; van Bremen, 1995). Widows are also subjected to social, community, and familial expectations as well as sanctions, which make their compliance and participation in such events obligatory. Through participation in funerary and memorial rituals, widowed women are directly engaged in the inevitable confrontation of life with death as the penultimate outcome of the aging process. This ethnographic case study examines the social mechanisms that reinforce and underpin this participation, while exploring the connection between gendered work and the transformation of household practices.

Women's participation in memorial rites

The minimum period of mourning for the death of a spouse, ostensibly for both widows and widowers, is one year, or after the *is-shūki*.[2] However, especially for women, it is actually more ideal to wait until after the *san-kaiki* (although designated as the third ceremony it actually occurs on the second anniversary of a spouse's death) before remarrying or fully re-engaging in societal activities. During the first year of mourning, it is considered inappropriate for the deceased's widow and family to participate in community activities, wear certain clothing, or participate in local Shinto festivals due to the perception that such behavior may bring bad luck or misfortune.

The house in which this memorial ceremony is held is an upper-class one in a rural village located approximately 15 kilometers from Nagoya, or the so-called big country (*ōinaru inaka*), in the heavily industrialized heart of Japan. The family that will hold the memorial service belongs to the Jōdo Shinshū School of Japanese Buddhism and has a tradition of ikebana, which extends back several generations. The deceased, the head of the main house (*honke*), was a highly respected ikebana master in the ikenobō school.[3] The ancestral home of the family over the past generations encompasses three houses: a large, spacious, main house; a smaller house for the practice of ikebana, and an unpretentious but beautifully constructed tea ceremony room and garden area complete with stepping stones, stone water-basin, and lanterns designed to enhance the ritualized communion with nature (Sen, 1979). This is the setting for the memorial ritual in this upper-class traditional family; the Buddhist priest (*obōsan*) will come to this residence to perform the rites, and will be paid a substantial sum of money (approximately 300,000 yen or $3000) in return for his services.

The deceased's wife, the seventy-one year old widow who will orchestrate this particular memorial ceremony, is a teacher of the tea ceremony (*sadō*, or *chanoyu*),[4] in the small, non-commercialized Sekishū School.[5] On this particular day, however, she is the manager and supervisor of all the arrangements for the memorial ritual, freely giving orders to women as well as men. The widow, her only daughter, and the wives (*oyomesan*) of the two sons of this house rise early and begin the cooking and preparing of food as well as organizing the house for the forty-some guests, including family members, who will attend the ceremony at 10:00 a.m. The newly designated head of the *ie*,[6] his wife and two children live in an extended family setting with the widow, while the other son and his wife reside in another large city in Japan. The youngest of the three children, a daughter, and her husband and three children live in Tokyo and arrived the night before.

By 6:00 a.m., the four women have begun cleaning, washing, and preparing the necessary foods, such as *kon'nyaku* (made from arum root, or devil's tongue), adzuki red beans, lotus root (*renkon*), burdock root (*gobō*), shitake mushrooms, and bamboo shoots (*takenoko*).[7] Between 8:15 to 8:30 a.m., two sisters of the deceased and another sister-in-law (the wife of the widow's deceased brother) arrive to help with the cooking. After the various foods are washed, they are slowly simmered in classic Japanese seasonings of sugar (*satō*), Japanese rice wine (*sake*), soy sauce (*shōyu*), sweet sake (*mirin*) and fish broth (*dashi*). Later, miso soup is prepared, along with the ubiquitous steamed white rice.

Although the cooking tasks are shared by the *oyomesan*, in-laws, and aunts in terms of preparing, stirring, and watching the various dishes as they simmer, the widow remains in charge of the overall preparation. Moreover, the combination of the various seasonings to achieve just the right taste, not too strong and not too weak, is a major responsibility that is left completely to her. This delicate balance of seasoning is considered the sine qua non of classic Japanese cooking. In fact, the younger women openly discuss the fact that they do not have the confidence or experience to season such large quantities of food, and the older women fear making a mistake due to the significance of the event and the pressure to produce a perfect meal. Everyone seems relieved when the senior daughter-in-law says, 'Let's leave the seasoning to *Obāsan*!' The experience of the widow and her skill in cooking and preparing food for critical events is well-known, respected and deferred to by even the senior daughter-in-law.

It is clear that an informal hierarchy is operating in this social arena, with the widow clearly in charge of the event but expressing her power in a low-key, friendly way, even though she is in a position of authority in this ceremonial arena. The senior daughter-in-law acts like an assistant coordinator or an extension of the widow, as she frequently (and politely) asks the wife of the other son, the various aunts, and the daughter (who is officially considered a member of her husband's family) to do various cleaning and cooking tasks. However, the intergenerational relationships are not so hierarchically clear-cut, for the senior daughter-in-law does not always unquestioningly obey the widow and seems at times to chafe under the intensity of her mother-in-law's scrutiny of the details of cooking and serving the meals, as well as preparing the house. Although it is never clearly articulated, the senior daughter-in-law is aware of the fact that this ceremony represents the twilight of the widow's power in this traditional family. After the death of a former head of a family, the position of headship of the *ie* is transmitted to his successor, with a parallel passing of the status and duties of manager of the house to the wife of the new head. Historically, as Nakane (1970, pp. 23–26) has stated, the structure of the *ie* household in rural areas has operated to inhibit the initial power of the daughter-in-law. At the point of succession, the daughter-in-law's influence and power increase dramatically, however, and continue to do so as she exercises authority within the household.

Male family members at this ceremonial event remain at a distance from the kitchen and food-preparation area. This is not unusual behavior, for men who attend such ceremonies take center-stage positions, albeit in the passive roles of sitting, listening to, and sometimes chanting but mostly only observing the Buddhist liturgy. However, before the ritual begins, the widow keeps male relatives quite busy. She carefully directs the men, including both her sons, to move tables, place fresh flowers at the Buddhist altar, and arranges the floor cushions (*zabuton*) for sitting in the *butsuma* (a room which houses, in this case, a magnificent gold-inlay *butsudan*, or Buddhist household altar). The altar holds a figure of Buddha and tablets with

Photo 5.1: The picture is taken in front of the Butsudan. There are many flowers placed around the Buddhist altar, and the Buddhist priest can be seen seated in the middle in front of the altar.

the names of deceased family members (*ihai*) where flowers, food, and incense are offered to ancestral spirits.

At about 9:30 a.m., guests begin to arrive and are personally greeted by the widow, with additional female relatives heading toward the kitchen area to extend a helping hand in the preparation of food, while men are shown to the large room (*dei*) in front of the *butsuma*, where they are seated. The closest related male relatives of the deceased are seated in the front row, with the oldest brother of the deceased in the most highly honored position. More distantly related male relatives and family representatives from the surrounding neighborhood are seated behind them, in the second and third rows. In the back of the room, in the last two rows, all the female relatives are seated, including the widow of the deceased. This arrangement seemingly, and perhaps superficially, reinforces the idea that men are the central and most important family members at this ceremony. Such a facile interpretation could easily render, and indeed has often done so, women's roles in the ritual invisible and thus inaccurately perceived as non-existent.

In presenting these observations to the women involved, the explanation given for this seating style was considered a simple matter of practicality. As one female relative patiently explained to me, 'It makes it so much easier in moving back and forth between the kitchen and the ceremony.' Thus rather than accepting the observer's view that women were seated in the back rows because men were so important and women so unimportant, the women I spoke with forcefully resisted this interpretation. They argued that the seating arrangement was not only more convenient but also freed women from the necessity of remaining seated in formal *seiza* position for the entire two-hour ceremony, as well as liberating them from the monotony that memorial services entail. At these ceremonies, the sitting style of *seiza*, where the legs are folded under the body as though in a kneeling position with the back kept perfectly straight, is considered *de rigueur* for women. Understandably, as another woman clearly stated, 'Actually, to tell you the truth, the whole service is rather boring and uncomfortable.' With women sitting in the back rows, they could move freely back and forth between the kitchen and the ceremony, so at times there were as many as eight to ten women working in the kitchen and food-preparation area. The opportunity was also used to chat and exchange information about family members' activities, and the lively conversation facilitated the work.

Guests arriving before 10:00 a.m. are treated to a formal serving of green tea (*maccha*)[8] by the widow. Accompanying the tea is the quintessential Japanese sweet called *manjū* (a bun made of wheat flour, rice flour, or buckwheat flour and stuffed with sweetened white or red bean paste called *ann*). In this particular case due to the fact that the ceremony is held in March, it consists of the pinkish-hued *sakura mochi*, heralding the spring season, prepared the evening before (at the request of the widow) by the two *oyomesan* of this house. As the men quickly eat and obviously enjoy the sticky sweetness of this culinary delicacy, the gendered nature of food, as frequently represented in Japanese culture, is contradicted. As Kondo (1990, p. 244), has argued, sweet foods are usually identified with women, girls, and weak, sick, or tired people, while men are associated with salty, spicy, and heartier fare. These distinctions mirror a gendered division between the stronger tastes, which are thought to reflect the image and personality of men, and soft, sweet tastes that are believed to be more suitable for women. In fact, eating sweets is considered a very feminine characteristic in Japan.

By 10:00 a.m., the softly haunting, rhythmic chanting of '*Namu Amidabutsu*' by the Buddhist priest blends disconcertingly with the dominating sounds emanating from the kitchen in the back of the house. Familiar noises of food bubbling, the clanking of plates being arranged on large serving trays, the distinctive chopping sound of the large kitchen knife (*hōchō*) on the cutting board, and women talking provide a cacophonous accompaniment to the liturgy. In the *butsuma*, all eyes are attentively focused on the front, on the *obosan* and the liturgy, while in the kitchen the widow and other women are busy tasting and checking that the foods have been rendered flavorful. The various dishes are then removed from the heat and placed in large plastic containers on tables. Plates, bowls for miso soup, and the necessary chopsticks (*hashi*) are set up in assembly-line fashion for the *oyomesan*, aunts, in-laws, and female cousins, who carefully arrange the foods in artistically pleasing, symmetrical patterns on each plate to be served to the various guests. A lot of time and care are taken to present seven different foods; if only six foods are served, it would be unlucky, and could bring misfortune or illness to the person receiving such a serving.

In many cultures, sharing and partaking of the same foods is a critical aspect of ritual, signifying that one is member of a social group. Family and friends who eat the same foods at the same time are in a meaningful way transforming their bodies together. More substantively, rituals of eating and drinking create, renew, and enhance social relationships, serving to bind people together in interlocking webs of kinship affiliation. This idea is strikingly illustrated in the painstaking and detailed attention given to food preparation and presentation, which are an important and integral part of Japanese ceremonies.

Widows and other female family members perform an essential role in the mediation of family health and success through their preparation and presentation of food, as well as their arrangement and management of the memorial celebration. Through their efforts, the dead and the living are united in a symbolic and ritualized 'eating.' Thus it is women who provide food, with its believed magical powers as an offering to and appeasement of the dead, and serve as facilitators in bridging the gap between the so-called profane and sacred worlds.

The main meal, gift-exchange, and clean-up

The main meal begins at about noon after the formal ceremony is completed. The individual serving of each of the guests takes about half an hour, with the women alternating in taking out the large serving trays, each of which holds five or six plates. After all the guests are served, the women finally turn to preparing their own plates and settle down to relax and enjoy their dinners. Again, an observer might be tempted to view these women as 'forced' to or resentful of eating last, but this observation is subject to reinterpretation and challenge by those who are actually involved. Bernstein (1983, p. 91) has illustrated that resistance, resentment, and conflict may be expressed in subtler ways by women, but several women who were questioned stated that they did not resent the men eating before they did. It was better to serve men (and children) first, the women said, both because they themselves had already snacked on much of the food as it was being prepared throughout the morning and because, once they had fed the children and men (who are often placed in a single category), they could relax with other women, take their time eating, and enjoy themselves. Thus these women asserted that it is more efficient and actually serves their own interests to get the troublesome chores related to children and men out of the way as soon as possible.

After all the guests have been fed and gradually prepare to leave, they are presented with various gifts of boxed lunches, and common, everyday household items such as sugar, coffee, tea, and sweet beat-paste buns. These gifts are actually, in part, an exchange or return (*okaeshi*)[9] for the money offering received by the widow from each guest who attends the memorial service. This cultural tradition grew out of a practice in which guests gave money as a present to the family of the deceased, to be used as a candle fee for memorial services. At that time, the candle fee was called *obutsuzen*, literally meaning something to place in front of the *hotoke* (the name given to all those spirits who have attained the ideal state of spiritual enlightenment). Guests at memorial services may also bring fruit or other suitable foods.

When gifts are received, the widow carefully records the amount of the gift and from whom it is received in her account ledger (*kakeibo*). In the same way, she notes the contents of the present that she gives to each guest. This is no unimportant transaction, but rather it is part of a complex social phenomenon that lavishes as much detail on the attainment of the perfect exchange as any business or accounting office. It facilitates the easy navigation of individuals through a multi-stranded network of social obligations that situate each other within an intricate pattern of gift giving, status maintenance, and prestige enhancement that cements social ties and kin relationships through feelings of indebtedness and reciprocity. Thus the acceptance and reciprocity of gift giving involves the intertwined aspects of feeling and obligation (Hyde, 1979; Sahlins, 1972; Firth, 1959; Mauss, 1990).

When all the guests have finally gone home, the arduous cleaning up begins with all family members assisting. Men and the older children are again directed by the widow and the senior daughter-in-law to clear off tables, take empty wine and beer bottles to the trash, and retrieve and neatly stack the floor cushions. Asked if she feels a sense of satisfaction at the apparently perfect completion of her duty in orchestrating the memorial service, the widow responds, 'It was really not so special, it's just something I did for my family, because of my family's pride and status in this community.' In true modesty, or perhaps not recognizing her own accomplishments, there is no hint of the weeks of planning, the careful timing and coordination of events, and the purchase and preparation of the essential foods that she has just accomplished. For the widow in this upper-class house, organizing the memorial ritual is just part of her duty on behalf of her family, its standing in the community, and her own personal status in being the proverbial *ii oyomesan*, or 'good wife.'

Resistance through status and ritualized ceremonies

The status of being a 'good wife' is enhanced by the production of and participation in anniversaries of funerals and other annual ceremonies (such as *Obon*). The Bon Festival (known as *Obon*) is another example of a ritualized ceremony within which women have active, albeit not usually formally recognized, roles. This festival is celebrated on an annual basis on July 15 or August 15, depending on the area of Japan and represents one of the most important traditional holiday observances in the country. According to ancient Buddhist belief, ancestral spirits return home to their families every year during this time. Religious services are generally held at all temples, and families pray in front of the Buddhist altar in the home and also at the family grave as they offer flowers, incense, and food to the spirits. After the *Obon* celebration has ended, the souls of the dead are said to return to heaven. Family members travel to their rural homes from densely populated urban areas such as Tokyo and Osaka, and it is through such rites and celebrations that city-dwellers in Japan maintain their connection to family events and their rural hometown (*furusato*)[10] roots. These ceremonies are an important part of status production work, as well as reflecting how people in many different cultures envision themselves as preserving family traditionalism and kin relations, which they define, manipulate and interpret in their own ways.

More pragmatically, status production work and being the constant and faithful *Ioyomesan* (good wife) are not without rewards. The prestige accrued by a woman through her work on behalf of the family can be converted into personal power – namely, the power to claim part of the *ie* assets for herself. This is no easy task because widows, including the one portrayed in this ethnography, are frequently pressured by family members (particularly the successor to the headship) to relinquish inheritance claims in order to prevent the splintering of *ie* assets. Even though a 1947 revision of Japan's Civil Code, Article 900, clearly states that a surviving spouse should inherit 50 percent of the family's assets, and that sons and daughters have equal inheritance rights, this is not usually the case (Aoki, 1997). Noguchi, Uemura, and Kitō (1989, pp. 136–144) have argued that even though widows should legally inherit 50 percent of family assets, with the children (female and male) sharing in the equal division of the remainder, the oldest son or the designated successor continues to receive the lion's share – if not all – of the family property.

When a widow in an upper-class family, where there is so much at stake in terms of assets, challenges the inheritance practices of the *ie* system, even though the law favors her, she must frequently endure the opposition of family members. To dilute this opposition and obtain her fair inheritance, she may call upon her status within the family as the good wife and faithful widow who has done her duty to her family throughout her lifetime. Since the ultimate goal of the *ie* system, especially in rural communities, is to keep the land and financial assets intact for the (usually) eldest son of the next generation, a widow who claims her legal rights effectively challenges and contributes to the dissolution of the very system and assets on which her claim is based. Nakane (1970, pp. 41–81) has shown that as far back as the Tokugawa period, the sole title to the rights and all the assets of the household were not attached to the individual but were held and inherited by the household head, and this has been the fundamental organizing principle of the family system ever since.

The widow's assertion of her individual legal claim to any part of the land and assets directly challenges an extremely old and deeply rooted practice in upper-class rural households. Her assertion of rights is predicated on the fact that she has been the 'ī *oyomesan*,' and an integral part of being the good wife is the management and hosting of memorial ceremonies. The memorial ceremony for her husband is, in essence, the culmination of a lifetime of service and work that she has performed in this house.

A widow's motivation for such a claim may be based on: her need to make sure she will be cared for as she ages, the desire to have financial independence from her son and his wife and to protect herself from the growing power of her daughter-in-law, recognition of the usefulness of a hedge against the vicissitudes of life as an older women in a patriarchal society – or a combination of these reasons. By claiming her legal rights, a widow is in a stronger position to make sure that she is well taken care of by her son and daughter-in-law. She can also enjoy personal financial independence through the control of her own assets and pension, so that if she becomes ill or bedridden in the future and is not cared for in a way that is to her liking, she will have the flexibility and economic power to provide for her own nursing care. Her actions also manifest a lack of trust in the structural base of the *ie* system as providing, without question, for all of her needs as she ages.

The challenge to the head of this family resulted in a partial victory. While not claiming her inherent right to a full 50 percent of the large estate to which she was entitled, this widow did receive approximately 30 percent of the assets, which represented a substantial sum considering the total amount of the inheritance. Significantly, at her insistence, the property and assets were recorded (deeded) in her name. Through her actions, the historical and hegemonic practices of the patriarchal family were interrogated as she forced an economic recognition of her value, rights, and contribution to the household. Her reputation, including her work in managing rituals and ceremonies on behalf of the family, facilitated her resistance to the common practice (especially in rural farm areas among traditional families) of abdicating inheritance and assets to the designated head of the household. Claiming a personal inheritance strikes at the heart of the structural integrity of the *ie* as an entity transcending the provincial interests of individual family members and continuing through the generations with land and assets amassed intact by the head of the family (Fukutake, 1980). Thus while her assertion of individual rights may not be revolutionary in the immediate sense, it nevertheless constitutes resistance to the stated goals and conventional practices of the *ie* system.

The widow is situated within a traditional patriarchal household fundamentally grounded in social control and structural inequalities; however, within this sometimes oppressive arena, on the basis of a good reputation as a wife and work rendered to the household, particularly in memorial ceremonies where status is solidified and enhanced in the community, it is possible for a widowed woman to successfully challenge and transform practices of the feudal-based family system and its centuries old customs regarding apportionment of assets. Concomitantly, women's labor enables the maintenance of the *ie* system and its ongoing traditions, resulting in a complex interplay of transformation and continuity, with gender as a critical mediating force.

Conclusion – Epilogue to the ceremony

The ethnography presented used the context of a particular religious memorial service to capture the hidden dynamics that supported its performance. The focus of the analysis was not the religious ritual itself but the interdependent and interlocking nature of the ritual and the labor that supports it, which was shown through the juxtaposition of these two perspectives. The study also demonstrates the theoretical significance of including gendered aspects of ritual in studies of religious rites to more clearly assess women's participation in, and contribution to, the successful production of such ceremonies. Viewing the ritual from women's point of view reveals the hidden and seldom analyzed worlds of kitchens, cooking, gift exchanges, back room communications and gossip regarding family members and friends, which exist in a parallel fashion with the world of men sitting in the front rows passively observing the ceremony. Through a focus on this dimension of interpretation, the ethnography illustrates the active involvement in, rather than the exclusion of, women in rituals.

Paradoxically, women in upper-class rural families in Japan today can be actively involved in both the maintenance and dissolution of the *ie* system. Analysis of the memorial event described in this chapter, provided the impetus to address frequently posed questions in Japanese studies, such as whether the *ie*, as an important albeit patriarchal foundation of Japanese society, will be subverted by issues of gender equality and the growing individuation of family members as van Bremen (1995, pp. 131–144) has asserted or will it be flexible enough to survive with its structure intact, even though its resources, or economic base, may change (Moore, 1990; Moon, 1990, pp. 117–130). As illustrated throughout this book, the *ie* system is not a static familial institution, but derives its existence, shape and meaning from its past and ongoing, social, historical, and economical constructions. Sievers (1983, p. 111) has noted that this system has been weakened considerably since its legal institutionalization in the Meiji Civil Code. However, while changes are chipping away at its dominance, the flexibility of the *ie* system to accommodate change may well make its complete demise unlikely. Considering the challenges from the inside rather than the pressures applied from the outside, a different question about the survival of the *ie* system can be posed. In fact, a more relevant and ultimately more interesting inquiry might be what the future *ie* will look like. It may well be that the 'new *ie*' will look profoundly different from the patriarchal model as framed in the Meiji Civil Code. Thus the *ie* serves, not only as a hegemonic site for discriminatory practices embedded within its structure, but is also a place for resistance and reformation.

In patriarchal family systems, men are typically placed at the center of the 'action' in many rituals, and there is preferential treatment granted and special focus given to their participation in them, as well as to the linkage among men in intergenerational connections within anthropological studies. However, this chapter clearly illustrated that women involved in organizing and managing religious rituals frequently disagree that this placement of men's roles in such a vaunted position is really warranted. Whether their disagreement is subversive or simply compensatory is a question that can, has, and will be debated, though perhaps there can be no definitive answer. However, the research described here calls attention to the perceptual gap in determining where the important 'action' really occurs in memorial ceremonies, and challenges how relevance and significance are assigned in ritualized contexts within studies of Japanese religious rites. In this study, as Yanagisake and Delaney (1994, p. 14) have suggested, active and meaningful participation has been used as a determinant factor in assigning degrees of importance and unimportance. The present chapter conveys the experiences of an upper-class widow in a particular family and highlights her critical role in maintaining the status and success of that family within a small rural community. It also elucidates the theme of common ground conveyed in this book showing how middle-upper class women can serve as prime movers in challenging and interrogating family practices.

All of these activities were set within the family, a highly politicized social site where status production and service on behalf of family members can be transformed into individual status and enhancement of one's own position within the family and society itself. The widow at this memorial ceremony was fully aware of this political and economic strategy, as she quoted a Japanese saying, 'if you endure, the endurance will pay off in monetary terms,' (*shinbō sureba okane ni naru*). The expression wittily plays on the two meanings of the word, *shinbō*, as 'endurance' and the axle of a wheel, which is a metaphor for the wife as the center of activities in the household. Other women agreed with the widow's point of view, and further stated that they were aware they were tools of the family system (*ie no dōgu*) but expected to receive compensation from the system that they served. Thus, while it has been accurately argued that the prescribed duty for women has been to serve the system, women (particularly in upper-class families) also further personal and economic interests by using their status within that system; they are not only 'acted upon' in a monolithic way but also 'act on' and manipulate the *ie* system in a complex, synergistic relationship. Even though there is no argument made in this study that it is a representative case of all families in Japan, the strategy of women using household resources, status production, service to the family, and domestic labor as leverage to further their own interests, including personal financial gain, is certainly not unusual (Aoki, 1997). On the contrary, this strategy represents an important way that women can actively and knowingly empower themselves within the family setting.

Political and economic maneuverings in families frequently take place in gendered spaces such as the kitchen, serving areas, and back-row seats located far from the easily discernible positions of honorary male guests at funeral and memorial services. These sites seem much less glamorous and interesting than elaborate religious ceremonies and intricate liturgies. Yet it is from these rather mundane locations that the necessary foundation for rituals is provided, and that, at the most fundamental level, the continuity of the tradition is actually maintained. Women, as providers of essential labor within families, are active in constructing and reclaiming their own meanings and interpretations of work, frequently subverting dominant gender ideologies, perspectives, and customs, and ultimately challenging traditional practices within the family itself. As the influence of individualism grows and sometimes conflicts with traditional claims upon widows living in modern-day Japan, tension is created within families and society. In this chapter, another face of widowhood was presented through opening a window upon the life of an upper-class widow and tea ceremony teacher. However, in another world far from this privileged home of an upper-class family, working-class and impoverished widows have distinct challenges and issues of survival; these additional faces of the realities of life for widows will be examined in the following chapter.

6 Life as a Widow

The role of the state, economic issues, historical influences and cultural values contribute to shaping the lives and experiences of widows in multidimensional and complex ways. However, there are areas of common ground for these widows as well. Ideologies regarding suitable gender roles and cultural obligations for widows intersect with societal values about re-marriage, friendships, sexual relationships, work and economic survival. Thus women's collective and individual experiences are affected in both general and highly personal ways.

As illustrated in previous chapters, Japanese women have long had the attention of moralists, politicians, and government policymakers for centuries. Bernstein (1991, p. 14) has aptly demonstrated that women have had gender roles suggested and even prescribed for them through the influence of Confucianism. Along with the construction of disadvantageous legal codes, widows have been forced to endure humiliating jokes and slogans, family pressures and responsibilities of care giving for husbands, children, in-laws and older parents. Widows living within this crucible of persistent and relentless expectations continue to struggle, resist and at times accommodate these pervasive forces. Their lives are additionally complicated by the existence of informal networks, which extend and employ disciplinary mechanisms that function throughout society (Foucault, 1979), including exclusion from group functions and activities, gossip, discrimination and in severe cases the eventual isolation of individuals who do not meet cultural expectations. All of these issues will be explored in this chapter opening another window on the lives of widows in Japan.

This section will also focus on how the feminization of poverty is rapidly escalating within an economic framework of ongoing restructuring of most industries throughout the country, and intensification of job outsourcing to support the global competitive efforts of Japanese companies. These practices have led to the bipolarization of rich and poor, as well as creating a rigidly segmented and gendered labor force of full-time well-paid employees (85.2 percent of these jobs are held by men with only 14.7 percent held by women). At the other end of the spectrum, there exists a low-wage part-time or temporary work-force with 50.7 percent of these irregular employees consisting of women. This illustrates one of the chief causal factors in poverty among households headed by widows (Ministry of Internal Affairs and Communication Employment Status Survey, 2002; OECD Economic Survey of Japan, 2006).[1]

In Japan, a female headed household remains an aberration from the 'normal' male-headed, state-supported family structure, and widows are frequently placed in a group along with other outsiders. This research substantiates the fact that widows and other single-mother families are discriminated against throughout society not only in jobs and hiring, but through active prejudice which creates a disadvantaged environment in general; discrimination may extend to children of these families as well (Aoki and Aoki, 2005). Women who are widowed frequently occupy these marginalized positions, since they are viewed as representing a different state from that which society views as desirable, i.e., being married. Widows stand outside the so-called normative relationship of marriage, but they were once married; they are not divorced but not considered quite the same as single women who have never been married.

'Women alone,' living on the fringe of society are particularly common in societies which have been historically dominated by a system of property and asset transmission that is male-centered (Pallazzi, 1991). Within these systems, women, although widowed, continue to be commonly linked to their husbands depending on the deceased's status, earnings, and assets. Thus widows may have a comfortable financial situation or one that is barely tenable contributing to cumulative advantages or disadvantages. Society still considers it 'natural' that a woman belongs to her husband's household underpinning the fact that a widow's class and financial status are based almost exclusively on that of her husband (Toshitani, 1996). As detailed in this chapter, impoverished women and their husbands frequently share commonalities in holding unstable jobs in day labor, part-time farming, fishing, carpentry and driving taxis. Most of the widows interviewed in this research live in public housing for low-income individuals constituting a 'poor community' of welfare families, older people living on small government pensions and the working poor.[2] The research and interviews presented will demonstrate that all of these groups share similar backgrounds of impoverishment.

Over 65-year old women living alone averaged a yearly income under the $12,000 poverty line set for the country. Among individuals over 65, approximately 37.6 percent of women live alone and 21.5 percent of men live by themselves (Government Cabinet Office Report, 2003). A 68-year old widow brings these abstract figures to life as she explains her experiences as a self-defined 'poor widow.'

> I was 56 years old when my husband died from a stroke. I only get about $10,000 or so per year. After my husband died, I got a job but my health went downhill, and I had to quit after three years. I had trouble sleeping at night, and my kids were on their own; I finally got used to living alone. My kids don't come around much and now is the worst time for me economically. You know, I live like a poor widow. I do miss my husband, and I wouldn't dream of remarrying. It may seem strange, but I got a dog because I felt lonely and that's enough for me.

Many women living on their own simply do not have sufficient support networks comprised of family and friends to meet the formidable tasks and costs involved in caring for children as well as aging parents. Household income differentials have been increasing in Japan which is facilitating an economically polarized society, but there is scant attention given to this trend by the media or state. To the contrary, the argument is often made that Japan has now entered a post-welfare stage of governmental policy due to its unquestioned adoption of a market economy-centered philosophy. The adoption of this ideology has paved the way for a retreat of the state's role in alleviating poverty and led to a more stratified society through a fallback dependence on family-centered resources (Tachibanaki, 1998; Satō, 2000; Hiraoka, 2001; Kariya, 2001; Aoki, 2003; Yamada, 2004; Shirahase, 2005, 2006). Thus we can now speak of the reality of growing class bi-polarization where low-income and even Japan's well-known middle-class households are economically more vulnerable.

Although Japan is frequently cited as the country with the highest rate of savings in the world, over twenty percent of households in the year 2003 actually had no savings (Government Report of the Central Committee of Financial Information, 2003). This fact represents another significant economic and social watershed in a country which has long prided itself on an extraordinarily high savings rate. Throughout the country, lower rates of savings, increasing rates of poverty, the changing labor market structure, curtailment of welfare assistance and weakening of the social safety net are themes that resonate in the following experiences of widows. The narratives highlight the intersection of women's lives with the multiple apparatuses of the state and the challenges of a difficult work and social environment.

Work and survival

Widows struggle with social mores and discrimination, as well as gendered ideologies, which are seamlessly interwoven with aspects of everyday life. One 55-year old informant related the following incident.

> I was working at a local hotel part-time as a maid, and one day one of my male co-workers came into the room that I was cleaning. He made a joke about "a widow who hasn't had the smell of a man around her for a while." I was so embarrassed, I just stormed out of the room immediately; I was humiliated because there were other co-workers around and they all laughed, but I don't want to quit my job.

When confronted with unwelcome sexual 'jokes,' the power of language intersects with gender evoking the humiliation and degradation of the widow targeted. The equating of widows with a vulgar sexuality shatters any image of the workplace as a neutral site illustrating how employment arenas are structured and contoured by gender and class; the sudden eroticization of the work environment exposes blatant harassment and sexual stereotyping. Public comments and actions which cause embarrassment, marginalization and the denial of human dignity are crucial components of the psychological aspects of structural violence which are frequently ignored, but often played out on a daily basis throughout the labor market.[3]

However, this is not to simplistically portray working women as passive victims but within a more subtle line of resistance, the above informant did not quit her job. She returned to work as a maid at the hotel. Even in the face of humiliation and harassment, she tenaciously asserted her right and desire to work by actively showing up the next day...and the day after that. These actions manifest resistance at the level of daily and individual interaction where asserting one's individual rights represent an ongoing challenge. Widows endure not only off-color jokes and harassment but at both the local and national level, it is increasingly difficult to penetrate the rapidly changing labor market as a 42-year widow relates.

> Since my husband died, I've been living in public housing with my two kids. I work part-time at a supermarket as a cashier, but I only make about $800 per month. I get a small pension from my husband's company, but it's not enough to raise and educate my two children. I worry about their future and my own.

While it is well known that during the past ten years the job market has undergone an intensive transformation, what is less recognized is that women have been among the hardest hit groups (Higuchi and Ōta, 2006). This is shown by the fact that regular full-time employment among women has decreased according to a recent report by the OECD (2005), although during the period from 1997 to 2002, regular staff positions have dropped for both sexes. Along with this significant decrease in full-time salaried employment, the percent of individuals involved in irregular work (defined as part-time or temporary) has differentially increased for women and men as shown in Table 6.1.

Although in 2002 women made up 56.8 percent of the total working age population, over half of these jobs consisted of temporary or part-time positions. Examining the above percentages, it is additionally clear that men are also suffering from the general problems of downsizing and restructuring. However, women bear the extra burdens of gender discrimination and a rigid sexual stratification of the dual-track segmented labor market. For example, one of the results of the ongoing restructuring of the Japanese labor market is that many companies prefer to hire women on a part-time basis in order to lower labor costs, and this practice is reflected by the fact that in the year 2002 women's take home pay was only 65 percent of men's (OECD 2005). While women have historically done the bulk of part-time or irregular work, this new trend may be differentiated due to the stated *preference* of companies in hiring

Table 6.1: Percent of irregular employees by sex in the labor force

Year	Female	Male
1987	35.7	8.3
1992	37.4	8.9
1997	42.2	10.1
2002	50.7	14.8
2007	55.2	19.9

Source: Ministry of Internal Affairs and Communications, Bureau of Statistics, Employment Status Survey, 2008.

part-time female workers *instead of* full-time male workers to ease overall business costs.

Several women, who were widowed when they were relatively young (40s and 50s), asserted that they were widows of 'corporate warriors' and that their husbands died as 'salary men soldiers.' One widow in particular stated, 'I want to insist upon the fact that I was the wife of a soldier, a salary-man soldier. He was always working, and I think he actually wanted to die early.' Another widow said, 'My husband was worked to death by his company. He was always afraid he would be fired or given a desk by the window (*madogiwazoku*).' The problem of 'death from over-work' (*karōshi*) is well-known throughout Japan. The most often cited causes of *karōshi* are cerebral hemorrhage, myocardial infarction and acute cardiac insufficiency. The ages of the victims are concentrated in the prime working years of their 40s and 50s with some individuals only in their 30s. Young women, although comprising a much smaller number than male victims, have also been claimed as victims. In the past, it was believed that *karōshi* was predominant among only working class males particularly night shift workers and professional drivers (e.g., taxi and truck drivers). However, recently it has been ascertained that the affliction extends to all kinds of professions including post-war white collar office workers and is fueled by pervasive 'service overtime.' The practice of service overtime means that employees virtually donate overtime to the company by not recording it on their time cards regardless of the hours they have actually worked. Additionally, so-called '*furoshiki*[4] overtime' (work that employees take home so it cannot be documented) is rampant throughout Japan. Phone calls to the '*Karōshi* Hotline' reflect the fact that approximately 55 percent of the calls come from widows who lost their husbands from overwork and wished to have the cause of their husbands' death be made known (Kawahito 1990, 1998, 2006). Closely related to the problem of overwork is male suicide, which has also skyrocketed in Japan, and in 2003 reached a record number of 32,109; most of these men were in the age range of 50 to 54 or in their prime working years (*http://www.mhlw.go.jp*).

Widows demand that the circumstances of these deaths be recognized, and they claim a similar honorary status as 'war widows' and 'wives of the spirits of dead soldiers,' (as discussed in Chapter 3) due to the nature of the sacrifice, i.e., men who died on behalf of the state and for the national good of the country. Viewed in this way, both war widows of military soldiers and corporate warrior widows can be situated in isomorphic positions sharing in and embodying the husband's sacrifice and yet expressing anger at the state and companies which made that sacrifice necessary. Mouer and Kawanishi (2005, p. 74) have documented that annual hours of work in Japan are exceptionally long (over 2,500 hours per year) compared to other industrialized countries. Several widows commented that their husband was at work so many hours they felt like widows long before their husbands actually died.

Connected directly to the overwork of many male employees is the role situating women as part-time workers, and therefore society holds the wives solely responsible for household work and child care. The polarization of the labor market (where short hours are defined as less than 35 hours work per week and long hours defined as 49 hours of work or more per week) is predicated upon the fact that women provide the vast majority, if not all, of reproductive and domestic labor. Not surprisingly, there has been a significant rise from 1997 to 2002 in the ratio of employed men who work long hours and an accompanying increase in the ratio of employed women who work short hours (Employment Status Survey, 2002). Thus widows who must work are ensnared in this labor market restructuring with gendered stratification of full-time jobs (mostly for men) and part-time employment (mostly for women) further attenuated by the overall marketplace shift to low-paid unstable jobs.

The economic strain which some widows endure is illustrated by a portrait of a widowed Japanese mother who became the sole family breadwinner at the age of 49 when her husband died. It was necessary to earn a living for herself and her five children through the performance of odd jobs such as sewing, working in a cannery, and doing laundry for commercial companies (Lebra, 1984). Nolte and Hastings (1991, p. 153) and Hastings (1996, pp. 278–279) have noted that middle-class widows may set up their own businesses, while upper-class widows are frequently able to take over the late husband's position on village councils and in the national government. Some widows become managers of a family-business at the time of the husband's death. However, in many cities of Japan, widows continue to survive on low paying and unstable jobs, but a part-time job is still considered better than unemployment, charity, or, as we shall see in the following pages, receiving stigmatized and paltry government assistance.

Poverty – Welfare assistance

In return for compliance to societal standards, widowed women in Japan may well hope to be respected and cared for in accordance with specific Confucian teachings regarding filial piety as part of the moral base historically incorporated in the *ie* (family) system. Yet, in practice, many widows have struggled and continue to do so in order to financially and emotionally survive while their behavior is closely scrutinized. Widowhood may well represent the most economically and socially vulnerable group within diverse populations, not only in Japan but throughout the world as Owen (1996, pp. 4–5) has stated. In the Japanese media and press, the issue of poverty has always been viewed as a problem of other countries existing in distant places like the United States or in poor developing countries, but recently poverty and its multifarious ramifications have come home to Japan. Still, as a country, poverty is still not viewed nor acknowledged as a serious matter rooted in the fabric of Japanese society as previously argued by Aoki and Aoki (2005, pp. 1–21).

However, this 'secret' and its invisibility are being exposed, as poverty and aging intersect culminating in a crisis situation. It is estimated that by 2020, Japan will have the world's highest percentage of citizens aged 65 or older expanding from the present rate of 15 percent to approximately 25 percent of its overall population. The nation's graying population is exploding while pensions and government benefits are lagging far behind the actual needs of this aging group (*http://www.oecd.org*). The consistent growth in the number of widows rose to almost 8 million by the year 2005, as shown in Table 6.2.

One 79-year old informant discusses the financial problems she faces and situates economic hardship within an inter-generational context;

> My father was a fisherman, and my family just barely made a living. I married a farmer, and we started our life in a small house with no electricity and just a little land. We both also worked as day laborers on construction. We weren't able to pay into the national pension system, especially when the kids were young. When my husband died, I went on public assistance. Even so, I live on less than $10,000 per year. My kids can't help out because they don't have any money either. One of them works as a truck driver and the other is a security guard; both of them dropped out of school.

The reproduction of intergenerational poverty is a phenomenon which clearly accompanies market economies and produces severe inequalities in wealth among families. State polities mediate and reinforce this system through the promotion of 'family values' and fomenting a discourse of mean-spirited 'scare tactics.' Some of the more recent state-sponsored strategies have included the idea of excluding women who do not have children from receiving social welfare services, promulgation of ominous forecasts regarding the impending failure of social services, threatening contractions in the provisions of child care allowances, as well as reducing overall welfare support for single mothers (Aoki and Aoki, 2005). Starkly contrasting with and located far from the much publicized media images of middle and upper-class women with Gucci handbags leisurely shopping along the glitzy streets of Ginza[5] in Tokyo, a 73-year old impoverished widow discusses the difficulties she and her family have encountered throughout her lifetime.

> We lived in Iwate Prefecture, and my parents were poor farmers and made charcoal "sumiyaki." I got married to a carpenter, but he turned out to be an alcoholic. I had to work, so I took a job at an asparagus canning factory. Now I receive a small national pension of $420 plus about $300 per month from my company pension, so it's really a small amount of money. The only extra money I get is from my kids on New Years; I receive $50, which I greatly appreciate.

Life as a Widow 113

Table 6.2: Total number of widows in Japan

Year	Number
1960	4,836,267
1965	4,980,834
1970	5,240,326
1975	5,518,000
1980	5,716,939
1985	6,182,254
1990	6,395,705
1995	6,900,967
2000	7,232,559
2005	7,660,400

Source: Population Census of Japan, 2005.

Another informant, an 82-year old widowed woman, vividly expresses the reality of inter-generational poverty through her own life history.

> I was born in Hokkaido, and my parents worked in a salmon packing factory. I left school after the eighth grade to work as a maid at my cousin's house. He was a principal at one of the local schools. I eventually married a fisherman but gradually fish became more and more scarce, so we couldn't make a living by fishing anymore. We changed our way of life and became farmers, but we had to supplement our income by both of us working as day laborers. When my husband died, I continued to work as a day laborer on farms tying up asparagus and work like that. I get the minimum pension and a small private pension, but my total yearly income is much less than $10,000.

State formation and policy making in Japan has historically inculcated in the Japanese population a mythic sense of familial ideology focusing on hierarchical relationships between parents and children (*oyako*). However, for impoverished families, there is no longer adequate ability to absorb economic shortfalls, and the previous conservative government consistently denied that there was a problem answering *calls for help* with *calls for cutbacks* in welfare and pension benefits.[6]

For wives of coal miners, economic conditions are always difficult, and these difficulties are heightened with the sudden demise of husbands. Four interviews were conducted with widows who lost husbands in coal mining accidents, and not one of them has ever received any assistance from family members or from grown children. All of them currently live in government administered public-housing (previously discussed). A 65-year old widow relates her story of the death of her husband at the young age of 30.

> My husband died after we had only been married 4 years. We had a two-year old child, but I never got any help from my family or from my husband's family. Actually, they couldn't have helped me because they didn't have any money either. Now I live in public-housing, and I get about $13,000 per year. I don't have anything really – no house, no money and I can't rely on my son. I thought about re-marriage years ago, but I decided against it. Even now though, I do get tired of being watched all the time.

Through this narrative window, research themes regarding impoverished individuals, families, and the cycles of disadvantages are clearly drawn, as well as the issue of the 'surrounding eyes' of society monitoring the actions and behavior of widows. The nuclear family now predominates over the extended family which is estimated at only ten percent of all families throughout the country. One result of this change in family structure is that older people are not always able to obtain the help and assistance they require. Families can no longer pool resources from extended kin members and serve as 'shock absorbers' for the restructuring of the economy and ongoing late-capitalist development. Another 72-year old informant comments:

> Since my husband's death years ago, I haven't been able to rely on anyone. Basically, I have nothing but my three children. I have never received support from my family or my husband's family. I can't rely on my kids either, and I only get a small pension of $12,000 per year. My family is poor, so how can they help me – they have no money! The government should do more.

We may view the retreat of the state in providing a hedge against the rampant bipolarization of rich and poor and the concomitant shifting of economic burdens to impoverished families as the 'domestication of responsibility' occurring in tandem with the ongoing feminization of poverty. A young 45-year old widow with two children (eleven and two years old) discusses her work and life experiences.

> My husband died of cancer, and after his death I worked at any job I could get to make some money. I even worked as a caddy at a golf-course for a while and then at a bakery. Finally, I got a job as a part-time cook at a hospital. It's a better job than any of the others, but I still only make about $1000 to $1200 per month. It makes me think sometimes, when the kids are older, I may remarry or maybe have a boyfriend to ease my economic burden.

This widow also receives a child allowance for single mothers of $400 per month but with meager pensions established below the poverty line, most widows receiving governmental assistance and living in public housing cannot afford anything other than the basic necessities of life. At the individual level, they just 'get by' with few options for themselves or their children; at the family level, future possibilities for children are limited due to the costs of competing in Japan's prohibitively expensive education system,[7] and the small market of stable jobs with higher pay are dominated mostly by men.[8] At the local community level, low income single-mother families are situated in public housing with other impoverished individuals who also have disadvantaged and limited choices. Finally, these women are linked to the national level through dependence on government programs and ever-dwindling financial assistance. Due to the inadequate and below-poverty line meager provisions of the government and the ongoing recession, there may not be any long-term solutions forthcoming in the near future.

Natural caregivers?

Widows make up a large percentage of the elderly population and perform the vast majority of the home-management, care-giving, and household labor on behalf of the aged and infirmed. Gaining prestige, control and power in tandem with aging has been reported in other anthropological research by Dickerson-Putnam (1998, pp. 69–72), but this is only one face of widowhood. In the case of Japan, widowed women may be subjected to greater pressure to meet societal standards particularly with regard to providing family-based services.

Caring for the elderly and sick has historically been a highly feminized type of work provided by wives, daughters, and daughters-in-law (particularly those women married to eldest sons). The role of women as family caretakers resonates throughout Japan and is rooted in the anachronistic ideology in which women are portrayed as 'natural' caregivers. Government policies continue to support these roles encouraging and using women in families to furnish care for elderly parents and in-laws, as a way to ameliorate and even avoid government funding and responsibility for the aged as noted by Lock (1996, p. 80) and Long (1996, pp. 156–176).

However, it became clear, rather belatedly, to the Japanese government that women were unable and unwilling to shoulder the entire responsibility of the rapidly aging population. Thus some improvement was implemented in care-giving provisions with the passage in December 1997 of a government proposed bill to create a mandatory insurance system to provide nursing care for the elderly.[9] The new system took effect in April 2000 and provides assistance for elderly households in need of in-home nursing care for ailing relatives with city governments designating organizations to provide nursing services; however, this basic system was revised in April of 2006.

Currently, the government will now pay 90 percent of nursing costs with recipients paying 10 percent of the nursing expenses. Under this revamped system, 40 to 64 year old individuals will pay a long-term care insurance premium included as part of their health insurance. People aged 65 and over pay the insurance premium based on their income. This insurance applies to people aged 65 and over, as well as those individuals 40 to 64, who need care for diseases associated with aging such as dementia. When a municipal government based evaluation committee, along with a doctor, decides that a person needs home care that person or her/his family can choose from a variety of services including: dispatching workers to perform necessary care within the home and to help with household chores, sending nurses to private residences, providing daytime and short-term stays at care facilities and long-term stays at nursing homes.[10]

Of course, insurance benefits are paid to widowed women living on their own through the Widows and Survivors' Benefits Pension, but the income of lone mother families relative to two-parent families has declined since the 1970s dropping from 46.4 percent of the average two-parent family income in 1978 to 45.0 percent in 1983 and just 39.4 percent in 1988. This trend has been attributed to the fact that unlike families of the middle class headed by male breadwinners, widows and other single mothers were unable to take advantage of Japan's 'bubble economy' which occurred between 1976 and 1988. It was during this time span that the average income of two-parent families grew by 63.2 percent, while that of all lone mother families rose by only 29% (Peng, 1997; Yuzawa, 1998). Overall, single mothers in Japan, whether divorced or widowed, are often placed in a fragile economic position relying on a governmental support system that is incomplete and provides inadequate assistance, even with the new governmental assistance regarding care giving duties. In 2004, the average annual income of a single mother household was approximately $22,000 (224.6 man-yen) compared to the overall average household in Japan of $58,000 (579.7 man-yen) for two-parent families with children (Ministry of Health, Labor, and Welfare Annual Report of the Support Policy for Working Single Mothers, 2006 at http://www.mhlw.go.jp/wp/hakusyo/index.html).

Care giving remains an issue of major concern to women and they astutely evaluate relationships, including the consideration of remarriage, in a pragmatic fashion. One widow stated, 'Well, men age faster than women, so if I remarry, I'll have to take care of another man until he dies! I'll never remarry!' Although women are clearly positioned as society's 'natural' caregivers, they are nothing of the kind and if possible attempt to avoid such duties as much as possible. When widows live with their sons or daughters, particularly in middle-class or farm families, there still exists a societal expectation that they will provide care for grandchildren; this is the classic (and mythical) portrayal of the kind and smiling 'obāchan' (a sweet elderly grandmother), who is always ready and available to take care of family needs. However, even in these cases where widows lived with or in close proximity to their children, this study found that the grandchildren in these homes are most often sent to daycare centers rather than to 'grandmother's house.'

Although the role of women in families is in transition, societal perceptions lag far behind the ongoing evolution.

Middle-class widows

Even middle-class widows may be placed in positions of economic vulnerability because, as outlined previously, they receive only half of their husband's estate and pension. Thus many widows struggle to maintain their lifestyle on only one-half of the household resources that they once received. Takata-san, a 67-year-old widow and grandmother, was married to an employee of a large public transportation company. She contributes a personal and historical perspective on the financial hardships of widowhood in the following narrative.

> About sixteen years ago my husband died, and I've lived alone since that time. I have to make do on my husband's pension, and it's not easy. If my husband had lived until he was sixty years old, then I could have received his full-pension, but since he died before reaching sixty, I can only get 50 percent of his pension. It seems to me that I supported him all those years, so it's just not fair that now I only get half. Half of his pension doesn't leave me much money on which to live because I still have most of the same economic responsibilities, such as: paying for heating, electricity, and other living expenses.

For widows like Takata-san, economic realities present serious challenges with little financial help forthcoming from children, other family members, or the government, so they are forced to live on a small national pension or on only half of their husband's company pension. A clearer picture of the financial status of widows and of other single women can be better understood by examining the fact that in the year 2000 the average yearly income for women living alone (including widows, single and divorced women) was 228.9 *man yen* (approximately $23,000 U.S. dollars depending on the current exchange rate). This amount can be directly compared to the average yearly income for men living alone (including widowers, single and divorced men) of 375.3 *man yen (*approximately $38,000) reflecting a significant gap and illustrating the highly gendered financial status of women who are single (National Survey of People's Lifestyle – *Kokumin Seikatsu Kiso Chosa*, 2000).[11]

Although many middle-class widows struggle with serious financial problems, most widows remain deeply opposed to remarriage. Through their resistance to marrying again, widows represent a serious challenge to the family structure. As one forty-seven year old woman living on a yearly income of approximately $30,000 to $40,000 per year, questioned the very basis of societal ideology regarding marriage and remarriage in the following comment.

> I don't think that remarriage would make my life happier; there is really no advantage for me to remarry. Now, I understand that marriage itself is a negative thing.

Another fifty-four year old widow in the $30,000 to $50,000 low middle-income range emphatically agreed with the above informant and remarked,

> You know, I actually didn't have a strong desire to marry before I actually got married. After my husband passed away, I realized that being single and on my own was just as easy as I had originally thought. I was right all along!

Widows have been single, married and then single again providing them with special insights regarding marriage. As the above narratives indicate, their personal experiences and doubts regarding marriage might well give political and social leaders cause for worry regarding the future of the family as will be discussed in the conclusion.[12]

Widow watching: discipline, androgyny and sexuality

Ogino-san, a 53-year-old widow with one child, stated that based on her own personal experiences, 'There is inequality in Japan among women. Specifically, what I mean is that there is inequality among women that are widowed or single and women who are married; in my opinion, it's a serious problem.' Ogino-san has spent most of her adult life supporting herself and her son and related the following story.

> My husband died about twenty years ago, when I was 33 years old, and our son was only 4. My marriage was all arranged when we were children; I didn't even think about love because everything was decided. Anyway, after my husband died, I worked at home making kimonos, and also as a teacher's assistant at the local school. Since 1979, I've had a job at the city community center doing the cleaning, laundry and servicing the boilers. My salary is only $1500 to $1900 per month, and my economic situation is really bad, but even so, I think my biggest problem is the loneliness and that people watch me closely. People always watch widows here. Women are afraid that we'll steal their husbands or boyfriends, so we are discriminated against by other women. If a man is nice to a widow, then women don't want to be her friend or if they are working together, they refuse to help her with the work. So, the treatment of widows and the watching of widows by other women is a major problem that no one talks about much.

The above narrative illustrates the extent to which widowed women may be scrutinized, judged and disciplined by other women; this 'watching' is not casual but is punitive with specific repercussions. Complicated and contradictory emotions regarding death, fear and the stereotypical image of widows as seductive temptresses underpin the foundation of and set the stage for the careful monitoring that many widows experience. The isolation of widows and the resulting loneliness is devastating especially in Japan, where group activities and having friends is considered a necessity as well as a natural and important part of life. It is isolation applied as a disciplinary mechanism and practiced by members of society to enforce compliance with cultural values and norms which impacts not only personal friendships, but discipline is extended spatially to include work places and surrounding neighborhoods. Viewed in this way, as Foucault (1979, pp. 302–303) has argued, prison is only a continuation, albeit of a more extreme nature, of the control of the individual in society. Disciplinary action is inflicted upon widows regardless of age, whether or not they have children or are in positions of lower or middle-class status with punishment subsuming all of these distinctions representing a pervasive practice. Out of the fifty-eight informants surveyed, fifty-two of them when asked if they felt 'watched' by others responded that they did, constituting a nexus of common ground shared by the vast majority of widows represented in this research.

Kohata-san, a 44-year-old widow with two young daughters, relates a similar story of covert 'watching' in the following narrative.

> My husband died four years ago and since that time, I have had to do everything. I met him on a JR train commuting back and forth from work. After he died, I got a job working full-time as a home helper for older people or for the disabled, but it doesn't pay that much. I'm not really interested in marrying again, so I keep busy working, doing the housework and raising my two children. I do think that it's very difficult for widows even now because people watch us, and it can be hard to make friends or keep friends because they worry about husbands or boyfriends. We are suspected of trying to take the man in their life, even if we have no interest in that man or marriage at all.

Instilling societal differences in power and status between women and men and instituting a clear hierarchy among women themselves based upon whether or not they are married, divorced, single, single with children, widowed with children or widowed without children, effectively splinters the experiences of women. It provides a system of reward and punishment meted out along clearly delineated lines dictated by society of appropriate and inappropriate behavior (Palazzi, 1996). This hierarchy exists only for widows; widowers are able to escape the permutations of the stringent nature and intransigence of such a control system. Even if widows comply with these rigorous standards, they are not always able to automatically rely on the support of society members, governmental assistance or family networks.

Unlike the divorced lone mothers with small children who sometimes were able to receive support from the local neighborhood reflected in other research such as Peng (1997, pp. 115–147), the widows in this study were given very little help from the surrounding community members. There are, however, organizations that attempt to help assuage the loneliness and isolation that many women experience in so-called, 'fatherless families.' For example, there is the Y-city Mother and Child Organization (*Y-shi boshi-kai shirayuri kai,* 1992), originally established in 1979 (Showa

54). For a small $2.00 monthly fee, the city provides a multiplicity of activities for widows and children such as: an excursion trip for mother and children in July, a Christmas Party in December, access to counseling in October and opportunities to participate in volunteer work (i.e., caring for the mentally and physically disabled or welfare training as counselors). There is also a journal published, *Mother and Child News* (*Boshi-kai dayori*), which disseminates useful information for fatherless/widowed families such as phone numbers of other widows, welfare department information, and regular announcements of activities.

While widows are judged harshly by surrounding women and men and complain about it vociferously, widows may, paradoxically, judge so-called 'selfish' or 'less deserving women,' defined usually as divorcées. A 43-year old widow discusses her experience of widowhood and distinguishes between herself and 'selfish' women.

> My husband and I worked together in a wholesale business, but after he died my child became unstable, and I began to see ghosts. I became a member of Sōka Gakkai[13] and religion really helped us. There were lots of people who talked about me getting a lot of money, but I'm enjoying life. I'm not like divorced women who just think of themselves as sexual beings – that's selfish. They should think about society more.

Discrimination among women based on marital status is seldom analyzed, but according to the above informant, divorce is sometimes considered an extreme form of selfishness. Another 45-year old widow stated, 'Divorced women are selfish, and people who get divorced sacrifice their children.' Valentine (1990, pp. 36–43) argues that divorced women are frequently classified as outside of society, i.e., in a position of marginality; they also live with the additional stigma of being *batsu ichi* (having one strike out or one strike against them) and present an additional challenge to the state structured traditional family in Japan.

Although an important aspect of control and marginalization of individuals is exclusion from social activities and/or from friendships, this exclusion may not be consistent or permanent since isolation which becomes permanent would mean that one would become a complete outsider (Valentine, 1990). In the case of widows, isolation and marginalization may be sporadic contingent upon behavior. Compliance with societal standards and cultural values often brings emotional rewards of inclusion, rights of participation in group activities and access to precious friendships. Actions interpreted as defiant or in violation of culturally mandated rules of appropriate behavior, may result in isolation and loneliness as a 74-year-old widow in K-city states:

> Life as a widow is difficult. For example, many widows and widowers want to help each other out. Women can help with cooking, and men can help with gardening in a give and take exchange of work. Actually, it's hard to do because everyone in the surrounding neighborhood is watching widows. I couldn't believe it, but people were thinking that such relationships were sexual. Rules are different for widows and widowers, since men are freer to do as they wish, remarry or have a girlfriend, and no one says anything or watches them. Women are not so free, and there's prejudice against us. We have to be more careful and think about our behavior. We have to always think if I do this, will other people judge me harshly or stop talking to me. I have come to understand pretty well what I can do, and what I can't do. Still, I think that we care too much about what other people think, but if you're not careful, you can be isolated. It sounds terrible, but now my husband and his parents are gone and sometimes it's lonely, but my life is peaceful. I want to keep it that way, so I have to live my life carefully.

Throughout this book, it has been documented that in Japanese society women have been expected to exhibit particular behaviors including modesty, faithfulness and obedience in order to maintain their status as 'chaste widows;' thus a widow is expected to enter a state of sexual abstinence lest she be chastised as a licentious woman. As one 76-year old informant commented,

> I felt as a widow that I was a sexless woman, androgynous, neutered – a lot of widows had that feeling. Even so, we still enjoyed life; we wanted to have fun eating and drinking. We worked hard too! We were not like the widows who became Buddhist nuns and renounced worldly desires completely; we wanted to enjoy our lives.

Widows are situated in an ambiguous world of having been married but after entering widowhood, they exist somewhere between the worlds of androgyny and that of eroticism. Although some widows may perceive themselves as sexless and neutered, in present-day society, widows still remain targets in erotica of all persuasions and often appear as sexualized symbols in pornographic magazines, in the media and on adult websites.[14]

Resistance is often romanticized, but the harsh reality requires extraordinary endurance on the part of widows who challenge established images and cultural expectations. In contrast to overt resistance, widows subtly calculate and judge to what extent they should acquiesce in following societal rules, and how far they may go before they are sanctioned by surrounding members of the community. Clearly, as a result of sexualized images of widows, other women fear widows will steal husbands or lovers; however, most widows passionately argue they need not marry again as the following 65-year-old widow explains.

> I think I will never marry again. After my husband died, I found out that I can live for myself. I cook for myself, and I can make the foods that I like without worrying about cooking for anyone else or pleasing someone. I like this way of life, even though it is sometimes lonely.

Rather than desperately looking to remarry, there are underestimated freedoms that women enjoy especially if they feel they have suffered unfairly at the hands of husbands or in-laws. Many women are clearly satisfied and seek to maintain their solitary way of life discovering that they can live on their own and for themselves. Most of the women interviewed represented their widowed lifestyle in positive terms emotionally (though not financially) engaging in activities that they felt they could not have freely enjoyed while they were married. Even the simple pleasures of preparing foods they like, rather than cooking for someone else, were considered positive aspects of being a widow. As reported in previous research, e.g., Lebra (1984, p. 257), many widows felt that they were truly experiencing freedom for the first time and expressed no desire to remarry. Widows discovered new hobbies and developed latent interests playing classical musical instruments, such as the *shamisen* or *koto* (stringed instruments) or attending English classes or cultural events. However, these activities were mediated and predicated on economic status indicating that low-income older women had to be very selective about hobbies due to cost considerations. Lessons to play classic Japanese music or other musical instruments (e.g., piano) are extraordinarily expensive; thus they chose more relatively inexpensive hobbies of drawing, painting or singing karaoke.

The research also elucidates the liberation in spirit that some women experienced after becoming a widow. Women were freed from the responsibilities of cooking, care-taking and cleaning on behalf of husbands. They revealed a high degree of contentment with their present arrangement though they felt that economically they suffered as widows. In Okinawa too, in the southern part of Japan, researchers report a high degree of freedom and autonomy experienced by widows. This freedom has been positively correlated with the longer life expectancy for women many of whom have been widows for an extended period of time. Sered (1999, p. 86) reported that lengthy widowhood was a significant factor contributing to the exceptionally long life for women in Okinawa. Freedom for widows in Japan is a relative concept which may be defined in individual and complex ways with extremely broad applications; however, while the women interviewed are not totally 'free' with respect to societal pressures and expectations, they are free from cooking, caring and cleaning for husbands and frequently for in-laws as well.

Widows in rural areas

Some scholars have questioned the somewhat contradictory status of elderly women particularly in rural Japan, since legends abound regarding the uselessness and burden of caring for widows; yet, many of these stories also argue that aged parents should be revered. Cornell (1991, pp. 71–87) has argued that one important factor in the survival of older widows was whether they could perform labor that was essential to the family such as caring for young grandchildren and doing farm work. If widows could contribute to the household economy in a significant way, then they could greatly enhance their overall longevity and survival prospects. According to other research by Smith and Wiswell (1982, pp. 187–188), in the rural village of *Suye*, widows were frequently impoverished and had a reputation for sexual license along with the freedom to pursue many lovers. These women were also the targets of gossip and isolation with these social practices used as disciplinary mechanisms to regulate behavior, although the widows appeared to resist such methods. This contrasts with widows in Okinawa who may be talked about if they take a lover, but the gossip did not lead to any concrete societal enforcement actions such as ostracism, punishment, accusations of harlotry or witchcraft (Sered, 1999).

Traditions dictated in rural areas required that young brides take care of a husband's family including his sisters and brothers. With the birth of her own children, the wife would be kept busy with child care duties and when that responsibility was completed, she would then care for her aging husband and in-laws. Thus most of a woman's life would be spent in the service of the family providing for inter-generational care-giving.

A 78-year old upper-class widow living in rural Aichi Prefecture in central Honshū shares her story of life as a young bride and then as a widow.

> I got married during the war; I was only 19 and my husband was 23. My marriage was decided between families, between houses, so it was not about whether we were in love. I guess I never really did love him so much, but I had no place to run away to because back then if you left your husband and went back to your parent's house, they were not happy to see you. We were taught to obey, so we couldn't give our own opinions even if we had them. When I first went to my husband's house, it was really terrible; I had to take care of my husband's brothers and sisters. Then, I had to care for my husband's father and for his mother's mother because my husband's mother died early. I've spent most of my life nursing and farming, taking care of family members, and I even cared for my husband for six years before he died. Right now is the happiest time in my life. I always hoped that all of the work I did would pay off economically, and after all it finally did because I could sell off some farmland! This really is the best time of my life!

Farm women are considered important workers in rural areas, and women can still be seen working in the fields wearing large bonnets to shield their faces from the sun, white gloves to protect their hands, towels tied around their necks to soak up the sweat and multi-colored aprons to keep their clothing from getting dirty. While researchers such as Bailey (1991, p. 147), have portrayed wives in northern Honshū as 'under the thumb of a dominating mother-in-law with long hours of work enduring the drudgery of farm life,' women more recently express views that they are partners with their husbands in the farm business. Moreover, upper-class farm women often have concrete plans for future financial rewards. There is great complexity involved in analyzing specifically how women can be empowered through their role in the family, particularly in farm families where work is extremely arduous. Although women have been portrayed as victims, and in some cases indeed they are (as illustrated in this research), in other cases, women assiduously make astute economic judgments and negotiate structural impediments skillfully with close attention paid to the details of farm management and inheritance of land.

For lower-class rural farmers, lack of economic advantages is frequently compounded and transmitted through marriage and family. Impoverished parents do leave something to their children – the innumerable legacies of poverty. Nakamura-san, born in 1935 in a small farming village in Hokkaido, relates her story of an impoverished childhood and the transition to urban life.

> My father was a rice farmer and also raised watermelon; he was a member of the agriculture cooperative. When my mother died, I was only five years old, so my grandmother raised me. I only went to junior high-school because back then children worked on the farm. We had lots of chores to do especially because my mother had died. My father wanted to re-marry because he was only thirty-five years old when he became a widower, but he didn't. However, he played around with women and eventually he sold the farm and spent all that money on women and drinking. After that happened, I moved to the city and became a maid. I just barely got by; I worked for about thirteen different people, and finally I got married at the age of twenty-five. You know, I've learned one important thing in my life and that is having enough money to support yourself is really important. In fact, it is the most important thing especially for women.

Although seldom fully acknowledged, women's role in agriculture has been vitally important in Japan. Women contribute to family farms in various ways. In rural areas, women support their families and farms by working as day laborers, household servants and in factories; additionally, after the exodus of male workers from farms to cities during the industrialization of Japan, women emerged as the real backbone of rural agriculture. Women currently comprise over one-half of Japan's present-day farmers moving into positions once held by men, but the total number of jobs in the agriculture sector has declined by 600,000 during the period from 1997 to 2002 (www.stat.go.jp). Seventy-six year old Mrs. Yoshida relates her story of life on the edge of rural poverty and invisibility.

> After my husband died, I worked at a hospital part-time as a cook, but I got sick and had to quit. I only receive about $600 per month, so I'm not satisfied with my lower-class lifestyle. After my husband died, I felt invisible and still do – no one sees me. I'm ignored because I'm old and poor. At least, I have my religion and that helps me endure life.

Aging and poverty interact in particularly insidious ways that affect individuals not only economically but in body and soul. Feeling invisible and ignored, widows have historically reached out to the spiritual world in order to seek solace as discussed in the preceding pages. Japanese women are drawn into spirituality frequently performing ceremonies on behalf of the dead in a multitude of ways, both formally and informally, such as singing funeral laments and traditional songs at tombs in Okinawa, praying in front of the *butsudan* (Buddhist household altar), regularly offering food to spirits of the deceased and managing funerary and memorial ceremonies as shown in Chapter 5 (Sered, 1999; Aoki, 2000). The fact that women are involved in religious practices is considered culturally appropriate and represents an accepted positive role for widows.

However, economic issues trump other concerns in rural areas as well as in large urban cities. In an impoverished area in Hokkaido, a 73-year old widow starkly illustrates how the government fails to adequately address the urgent needs of all its citizens, particularly elderly women, allowing them to fall through the cracks in the national pension system.

> My husband and I were part-time farmers, so we didn't have the money to pay into the pension system. That's why I only receive a partial pension of $300 plus $400 per month from welfare assistance which I guess you can say makes my life painful and my three kids have also suffered.

Children from lower-class families, as evidenced by a recent OECD (2006) report, do suffer due to the high cost of education and preparation for entrance to the 'best' colleges (i.e., the University of Tokyo or other highly ranked national universities). While upper-class rural farm women calculate and astutely plan how their labor intensive investment will someday pay off, low-income widows in both rural and urban areas realize there are few options regarding future economic rewards for hard work; this acknowledgement shatters once held dreams of equality widely accepted in Japan. State policy continues to inculcate in the Japanese people a mythic sense of family ideology focusing on the relationships between parents and children, which are highly sentimentalized based on an assumed mutual caretaking responsibility including economic support. This is part of the ongoing disingenuous political strategy of the government allowing it to blithely ignore the societal inequalities experienced by poor women and children.

Conclusion

An important finding of the research was that elderly widows and young widows alike did not consider themselves 'natural' caregivers. Having provided nurturing and care for family members for decades, many widows experience feelings of freedom and liberation in only having to care for themselves. This reality stands in contrast to stereotypes of women as natural care-givers who relish the sacrifice of service and time on behalf of families, i.e., women are positioned as more altruistic than men; Folbre (2001, p. 11) argues that this positioning particularly arose within the scope of the growth of capitalism. However, widows speaking for themselves in these narrative interviews did not reflect this altruism but had very pragmatic reasons for caring for sick husbands and bedridden in-laws. In actuality, advanced market economies like Japan are dependent upon women as care givers to bolster and maintain the family which inadequately functions to absorb the financial and emotional shocks inherent in capitalism itself. As detailed in this chapter, elderly women (even widows) can no longer be automatically relied on to care for the needs of families masking the myriad of tasks and hard work under the rubric of '*obāchan.*' Widows in this study made clear that this was a time in their lives that should be lived fully and meaningfully; furthermore, they argued that their work was finished, so why must they continue to do all the care giving work? Care giving duties may be performed out of love or possible future rewards, but the realities of care giving are also about hard work, being on call 24 hours a day, seven days a week and the sacrifice of part of one's life.

The research in this chapter has highlighted the myriad of problems experienced by low-income widows and their children as well as elderly widows throughout Japan. At the same time that economic issues dominated the interviews and the lives of impoverished women and children, the cultural mystique surrounding widows continues to be played out contradictorily. Widows are portrayed as knowledgeable about sex where such knowledge is considered both enticing and dangerous; yet, they also must appear as chaste and honorable. Chastity is therefore constituted as Bourdieu (2001, p. 45) states, 'as a fetishized measure of masculine reputation and therefore of the symbolic capital of the whole family lineage,' and is the basis for the vigilance of society in 'watching' widows.

Closeness to death, the value placed on chastity and paradoxical images of the erotic widow all synergistically combine to create a pervasive societal construction of forbidden and dangerous but still desirable sexuality. Widows represent these images embodying a powerful form of the frequently contradictory nature of gendered meanings and conventions. These contradictions play out not only through individual female bodies but in widow's daily lives intersecting with the labor market, workplace, government policies, care-giving responsibilities and state assistance or more accurately the lack of assistance.

7 Conclusion – The 'New Widows' – Free at Last

Freedom from care giving and time to enjoy the final years of life emerged as critical points for older widows; the word 'free' occurred at least once in every interview conducted. Walking down a country road one morning in rural Aichi-prefecture with an elegant and still spry elderly widow, she explained to me how she accidentally 'discovered' she was free.

> I remember the day my husband died and the wife of the Buddhist priest at the local temple told me, "Now you're actually free at last." Then, it finally hit me that I was in fact free, and I suddenly felt free and light after all these long, long years.

Ideas regarding suitable gender roles and obligations for widows and older women along with care-giving responsibilities, economic provisions, laws governing inheritance and control of property channel the experiences of individuals in both overlapping and personal ways. However, Japanese widows have entered the 21st century, and they are no longer waiting to die. In a sense, they are still viewed as having been 'touched by death,' and are expected to take responsibility for the care of ancestral spirits as the ethnography in Part 5 illustrated. Some widows, especially upper-class women, may still choose to and expect to be rewarded handsomely for fulfilling traditional roles of maintaining the primacy of the family and providing extensive support through managing time-consuming, costly, and labor-intensive tasks of arranging memorial services and performing care-giving duties. The ethnographic examination of the discordant faces of ritual, and the 'behind the scenes' world of inter-family politics and women's strategies to gain access to wealth and property showed that the family, economics, law, and ritual are interwoven. While the economic strategies of the widow may be characterized as covert and subtle, such actions can result in the acquisition of tangible and valuable assets, as well as securing

Photo 7.1: Picture of two widows. To the left is Katsumi-san and to the right is Tokiko-san.

her a pivotal role in decisions regarding future inheritance among children and grandchildren. The ethnography shows specifically how widows may subvert the basis of the patrilineal inheritance system and familial ideology, while also supporting it through the production and management of ritual and paradoxically contributing to the reproduction of the very system they are resisting.

Widows who dedicate themselves to family and find personal fulfillment through hobbies and leisure pursuits receive praise and accolades from society. However, as the above informant comments, most women feel that they are finally able to enjoy a less encumbered lifestyle without being obligated to care for a husband or other family members. They enjoy the simplest of pleasures such as, cooking the foods they like and doing the things they want to do whenever they wish. While some women were apologetic regarding their enjoyment of newfound freedoms, they also rather wistfully and often regretfully expressed the feeling that their lives had improved immensely since the death of their husbands. While they enjoyed visiting grandchildren and children, they preferred to live on their own savoring the luxury of time spent on behalf of oneself. One of the most important findings of the study is that women cannot always be facilely situated as the *sole* care giver for the family. It must be understood that there is great variation among widows; many widows no longer see themselves as representations of '*mibōjin,*' and grandmothers or as the stereotypical *obāchan* (an image involving a taken-for-granted caregiving role). The ramifications of these findings goes well beyond the individual lives of women surveyed and engages broader social and economic issues which challenge the very existence of the current family structure, as it is currently underpinned by gendered ideology.

Challenges for the future in marriage and family

The rejection of total responsibility for caregiving and the overwhelming preference to live alone expressed by widows signals momentous changes in a society where women have born the brunt of household labor and family care responsibilities. These changes can be viewed in both economic and emotional terms, but policies for the future must take contemporary realities into consideration. Rather than promoting an atavistic agenda by cutting benefits to women who don't have children or to impoverished widows on welfare assistance, the government should recognize that women are no longer asking for freedom; they are already taking it. Thus government policies must reward those who perform the arduous work of family care, while at the same time promoting gender equality.

More clearly, women and men should be encouraged to combine paid labor with community activities and family work explicitly drawing men into the world of caregiving. When men discuss the topic of 'family service,' they are generally referring to a Saturday or Sunday when they go shopping or perhaps to a restaurant with their wives and children. Most men still view this so-called family service as a favor to wives, and this service may be and is eliminated if necessary. A *new division of labor* to coincide with the *new realities* of Japanese lifestyles as well as the rapidly aging population is a critical necessity. The present timing is perfect to realign national priorities; corporate downsizing and restructuring is continuing, so men have the opportunity to become involved in family care while more and more women are working outside the home in part-time or temporary jobs to supplement family income.

The 21st century reality not just in Japan, as the most rapidly aging society in the world, but throughout most post-industrialized nations, is that the male breadwinner family model is already evaporating into the mists of history. Even so, as Esping-Anderson (1999, pp. 148–149) argues, the anachronistic gendered character of the marriage arrangement is proving to be quite intransigent, and based on the research of Parreñas (2005, pp. 163–168) the ideology of women's domesticity continues to reconstitute itself on a global transnational basis. The fact that women have historically provided caregiving services has resulted in the saving of many tax dollars and untold public resources which would have been needed if the Japanese government had furnished identical services. The government understands and manipulates this contribution but fails to actually acknowledge it. However, as Part 6 shows, it can no longer be facilely assumed that women, including widows, will automatically provide care for Japan's aging population because there are no *natural* caregivers. Sooner or later, a system similar to Japan's national medical care should be implemented for national caregiving; this system should revolve around eldercare and childcare covering both ends of the life-course care spectrum. This should be done not only on behalf of very young and elderly individuals, but the implementation of such a system would greatly assist adult children and other family members (particularly women).

Throughout this book, widows have been situated at the center, a nuclear nexus around which history, politics, laws, social customs and ideologies revolve, collide, and sometimes fuse almost seamlessly with their lives. In Parts II and III, the historical and cross-cultural connections between nascent nation building and family formation were developed illustrating a fusion of the state and family in order to augment solidarity among diverse groups. Changes in language were also analyzed and through the analysis we are alerted to the idea that the strongest form of power may well be the ability to define social reality and to impose visions of the world on others; these notions of reality are solidified and inscribed through language. The genesis and progression of the powerful family system (*ie seido*) was traced as a specific outgrowth of Confucian familial ideology which was incorporated initially in feudal warrior households. This reorganization of the family was set against the background of the early formation of the Japanese state. The merging of law, policy, and family ideology became the basis of state development with the emerging state functioning in a patriarchal role assuming the mantle of power, yet leaving the legal control of the family to male household heads. New social policies emerged not only within a specific time and cultural context but also reflecting change in how social values are constructed and reconstructed (Goodman, 2002). These historical and ideological shifts placed legal and behavioral restrictions upon the conduct of widows.

The political and ideological positioning of widowed women as 'wives of spirits' (*eirei no tsuma*) of deceased soldiers was fostered and manipulated by Japanese state hegemony through the official cemetery for the war-dead located in Tokyo and known as Yasukuni Shrine. This was accomplished through the power of the state apparatus as regular visits by widows to the shrine were mandatory and enforced by the government. Full media coverage and reporters were pre-arranged for these events. In this way, mythic images related to the honor of 'fallen heroes' and their virtuous widows were constructed. The focus of the analysis exposes the role of the wartime state in creating and maintaining expectations of the continued chastity and honor of wives, which was specifically aimed to reassure professional soldiers as well as reluctant draftees. With the collapse of Japan's imperial wartime government and American Occupational Forces (GHQ) suspension of state pensions for bereaved families, widows experienced a parallel loss of position and status in Japanese society.

In contemporary Japan, we may describe the current situation between the state, widows and families as more collision than fusion. The Japanese family is in crisis and as if to validate this statement, younger widows in the research almost unanimously rejected marriage, at least until their children were grown, and most of them stated they would never dream of remarrying. The number of single, widowed and divorced women living alone is steadily increasing and represents a significant challenge to the current structure of the family. The media in Japan bombards women with questions regarding, 'Why don't women want to marry;' however, a better question would be to ask, 'Why should they want to marry?' In other words, what does marriage offer to contemporary women in Japan?

While women may have once married for economic security, most women no longer need to consider marriage as a financial necessity. In present-day Japan, marriage is an option, a choice and will remain so in the future, and this reality drives the conclusion that marriage itself must be reconstituted to present a more attractive choice for women. This will involve nothing more than a revolution, in which women are already taking the lead by delaying or rejecting marriage and not having children. Another factor as to why younger people are postponing marriage is that the polarized dual-system labor market of regular employees and part-time, low-paid employees has made it much more difficult to consider the prospects of marriage and family. Part 6 also illustrates how women's traditional responsibility for child-rearing and care of the elderly shapes their choices of work, and generally disadvantages women in Japan's highly competitive segmented labor force. Employers anticipate marriage and expect that primary domestic and child-care duties will affect women's commitment to employment, education and training.

This book has depicted how widows are placed in positions of extreme vulnerability after the death of a husband, and the same degree of vulnerability obtains for women (particularly women with children) who are separated or divorced which signals a precipitous drop in the standard of living resulting in some cases of outright destitution. Marriage continues to be embedded in societal structures including sex-segmented labor markets, the gendered division of unpaid labor and social welfare policies structured on preconceived notions of gender roles and expectations. The legacy of the sexualized widow is still prevalent and inevitably accompanies widows to the workplace, affects making and maintaining friendships and permeates society at every level. As women face challenges and difficulties in the gendered terrain of widowhood, they are expected to conform to traditional ideologies of women especially to those for older women. In effect, even after the death of her husband, a widow continues to be defined by her relationship to him in terms of how she conducts herself in the community and through the economic legacy of asset inheritance and the amount of pension received.

As mentioned above, women are taking the lead in putting pressure on society to reconstitute marriage in a more 'female friendly' way. Yet, society and the government have not yet 'connected the dots' with respect to women's reluctance to marry. Japan's notoriously low birth rate (Japan registered a record low 1.15 million births in 2002) shows that the patriarchal family structure clearly is being challenged. However, there are some signs that the government is starting to react but in an ironic twist, it is fomenting a 'backlash' to ideas regarding gender equality. For example, in the summer of 2005, the Tokyo Board of Education asked public schools to desist from using terms like 'gender free' because the word ignored the biological differences between girls and boys. Tokyo Governor Ishihara Shintarō has on many occasions publicly denounced any notions of gender-free language or gender equality and dismantled the Women's Foundation that operated the Tokyo Women's Plaza in Aoyama. Fortunately, the foundation was subsequently taken over by the local municipality. Additionally, in another disturbing development, Japan's Liberal Democratic Party (LDP) has advocated revisions to Article 24 of the Constitution which established equality and human dignity as the basis of marriage and guarantees the rights of women to inherit 50 percent of all assets.

The future of impoverished widows

Throughout this book from historical, political, legal and personal perspectives, the ways that society punishes, encourages, and rewards women to act in accordance with its dictates and how violations of prescribed gender roles are punished in informal and formalized ways has been portrayed. It has also been shown how women actively resist, acquiesce to and challenge the application of disciplinary and controlling mechanisms. From poor widows gleaning rice fields in the Kamakura Period to destitute war widows and including contemporary impoverished and welfare widows living on pensions, poverty has been an abiding legacy of women living on their own. This was also shown in the cross-cultural studies presented in the first chapter and represents a significant nexus of common ground detailed through the analysis. Japan can also be placed within this historical and comparative arena with its long history of a particular patriarchal society in which the poorest of the poor have been and continue to be widows with children and other female-headed households.

Looking through the lens of widowhood, this book peals away the façade of equality which has obfuscated the fact that inequality and poverty are Japan's 'invisible secrets,' and reflects a clear perspective regarding the accelerating problem of the feminization of poverty. The legacy of single female-headed household poverty still shadows and continues to structure the lives of widows whether reflected in the workplace, through welfare assistance policies, or in the meager pensions doled out to aging women through governmental assistance. In a dangerous new trend, due to the relentless economic bipolarization of rich and poor in Japan and the wholesale acceptance of neo-liberalism with small government, and the privatization and outsourcing of jobs, poverty is not only continuing but increasing.

Based on a news headline in *The Japan Times* on July 21, 2006, (OECD, Japanese relatively poor), relative poverty suddenly became the hottest topic of conversation among not only academics but also on television talk and news shows as well. Suddenly, it seems, everyone is talking about skyrocketing poverty in Japan. The article pinpointed the fact that the portion of the population living in poverty (defined as less than one-half of the median household income) was 13.5 percent in Japan in 2000. This percentage places Japan in the second-highest position among all OECD members following 13.7 percent in the U.S.

To date, there has been little concrete response from the government, even regarding the above cited newspaper article. In fact, in 2006, payments for elderly welfare recipients were cut by $150 per month, and assistance for single mother welfare recipients was also reduced. Research currently begun will target how these cutbacks are significantly and negatively impacting elderly widows, as well as younger widows and single mothers. If these policies are continued, widowed women as heads of 'fragile families,' and elderly women living on their own will experience serious problems in balancing the enjoyment of 'freedom' with severe economic constraints.

Some tentative suggestions have been offered in this conclusion, but these important questions will continue to be the subject of future research and critical analysis in order to further illuminate the lives of widows and the aging population in Japan. While this work is by no means perfectly constructed, it is hoped that the book will contribute to the historical deconstructions of long-held myths and prejudices, as well as open a window on the current realities of the lives of widows.

Endnotes

Part 1

1. I thank Dr. Rhacel Salazar Parreñas, University of California, Davis, for suggesting and clarifying this point.
2. Although various claims are made that Japan's economy is recovering, the current economic climate is in a state of recession witnessed by record numbers of debt-ridden Japanese falling prey to loan sharks, who operate a booming business of illegal lending (usually associated with organized crime), charging exorbitant interest rates of 1800 percent per year and threatening borrowers with violence in order to extort payments from the hapless victims. Individual bankruptcies rose fivefold over the last five years to more than 214,600 in 2002, up 34 percent from the previous year. This total may be compared to 1990 where individual bankruptcies numbered approximately 10,000 per year. While legal lenders may charge up to 29 percent interest rates, racket lenders (yami-kinyū) charge as much as 50 percent interest for a 10-day loan. The ongoing cycles of corporate restructuring and downsizing have led to the development of a 'suicide economy,' where record numbers commit suicide to extricate themselves from the dire situation. See Osamu Aoki, ed., *Gendai nihon no mienai hinkon* (Akashi Shoten, 2003).
3. Sapporo's large urban population of 1,822,368 ranks it is as the largest city on the island. However, this figure does not include the suburbs and outlying areas. If these areas are included, the metropolis encompasses over 2.5 million people, and thus Sapporo is actually classified as an urban city-state with the authority to carry out welfare and urban planning on behalf of the Hokkaido Prefecture Government. The city ranks as the eighth most concentrated populated area in Japan employing about 50 percent of the population of Hokkaido. However, not surprisingly, even in this urban state, available employment is based on service-oriented sectors with little manufacturing or other industries.
4. The term ie connotes a family group, as well as a household that is carried forth in perpetuity based on the intergenerational transmission of property and assets. It includes both ancestors and descendants, and represents a conceptual and abstract family that continues even when all existing family members are deceased. In Nakane Chie's classic work, *The Structure of the Japanese Family* (*Kazoku no kōzō*), (University of Tokyo Press, 1970), she points out the problems of translating and using the concept of family cross-culturally. For example, she argues that the term 'stem family' is used most accurately in the case of a family, which consists of at least two couples living in the same household with the relationship of parent and child. However, in Japan, the 'stem family' (chokkei kazoku)

has typically included three generations (e.g., grandparents, their oldest son and his wife, and their grandchildren), and more clearly reflects the concept of lineality; thus it is more accurately used in the case of Japan. Even now, the influence of the ie system remains in rural areas throughout Japan, where an older son is considered the successor in the generational line, and is entitled to sole inheritance of family assets and wealth. Many women consider this traditional practice a considerable impediment to their economic equality.

5. The concept of patriarchy in this study is employed to illuminate and explain relevant aspects of widow's lives, as related to society and historical transformations. As the concept developed, it was used as an analytical device to identify the nature of political, hierarchical and power relations between women, older men, and younger men arguing that the root of the domination of women was patriarchal ideology, which exaggerates and polarizes biological differences between men and women. Later, ground-breaking works in anthropology, e.g., Michele Zimbalist Rosaldo and Louise Lamphere, eds., Woman, *Culture & Society* (Stanford University Press, 1974) and Rayna R. Reiter, ed., *Toward an Anthropology of Women* (Monthly Review Press, 1975), reflected the influence of these arguments, as anthropologists attempted to refine and explicate questions related to the comparative status of women in diverse societies. Further developments of the concept of patriarchy continued among scholars including the contribution of T.S. Lebra in *Japanese Women: Constraint and Fulfillment* (University of Hawaii Press, 1984), who argued that aspects of the Japanese patriarchy co-exist along with the wife's monopoly of household rights and duties. Bina Agarwal, ed., *Structures of Patriarchy: The State, the Community and the Household in Modernising Asia* (Zed Books, 1988) extended the argument to include not only patriarchal ideology but patriarchal structures positing that the state, policies regarding households (whether envisioned as a site of conflicting or convergent interests) and the accepted roles of women and men in the family represent interacting structures, which causes pulls and pressures at specific times and in various cultural contexts; space is created by these push and pull forces and within these spaces, the development of resistance is possible. The concept that unites all the structures is that they are dominated by patriarchal interests and more often than not, the contradictions produced in society have tended to work to women's detriment. Maria Mies argued in *Patriarchy and Accumulation on a World Scale: Women in the International Division of Labor* (Zed Books, 1986) that while the term patriarchy literally means the rule of fathers, it denotes the totality of exploitative relations which affect women and is useful as a struggle concept. In analyzing patriarchy, there is not simply one universal system, but each patriarchy is constructed in 'particular times, by particular peoples and in particular geographical locations.' In this way, the criticism that the concept of patriarchy was too broad, and even worse, that the term effaced women's agency, was challenged. Finally, Sylvia Walby, *Theorizing Patriarchy* (Blackwell, 1990) concluded that patriarchy is not effectively employed as a totalizing concept, but rather, as a particularized one encompassed by the term patriarchies, which are not monolithic or unchanging.

6. Chizuko Ueno in *Nationalism and Gender* (Trans Pacific Press, 2004) suggests that recent trends in academia have rendered cultural analysis bereft except for the binary positioning of 'self and other,' and the privileging of ethnicity in a totalizing and essentialist manner. As Jack Goody, *The East in the West* (Cambridge University Press, 1996), argues, the construction of 'others' as a framework for self-understanding and critique is hardly new or unique to the West and reflects yet another distinct and problematic polarization of 'East' and 'West,' which is an inaccurate dichotomy yet to be resolved.
7. It is often overlooked that over one-hundred years ago, Franz Boas (1896, p. 92) argued that placing events in local and historical context is critical, and asserted that the important function of the historical method was to compare the processes (emphasis mine) of growth, not the results of growth alone, by studying cultures in smaller geographical areas. He also discussed the limits of the comparative method for anthropology and the concept of cultural relativism (e.g., for an extensive debate regarding the much derided and much praised conceptualization of cultural relativism refer to: Clifford Geertz, Distinguished Lecture: Anti-Anti Relativism in *American Anthropologist*, 1984, pp. 263–278; and Melford E. Spiro in *Cultural Relativism and the Future of Anthropology in Cultural Anthropology*, 1986, pp. 259–268). Contextually, Boas was reacting to the overuse of comparative studies particularly to those involving static comparisons reflecting evolutionary scenarios of the development of societies attaching labels of superior.

Part 2

1. According to S.J. Tambiah, From Varna to Caste through Mixed Unions, in *The Character of Kinship*, ed., Jack Goody (Cambridge University Press, 1973, pp. 191–229), Manu is one of the classical writers in India who gives the most detailed discussion of, and defines the laws of, the caste system including those related to marriage and inheritance.
2. Widows could not enjoy any luxuries of life, but were required to dress only in white and partake of a strict vegetarian diet.
3. Such customs have been documented in Fiji where widows were strangled or buried alive at the funeral of their husbands. By sacrificing themselves, widows were assured of maintaining a cherished and high-ranking status as favorite wife and companion in the hereafter. According to Bendann in *Death Customs: An analytical study of burial rites*, pp. 198–199, (Knopf Publishing, 1930) wives accompanied the spirits of their husbands into death and their bodies were laid at the bottom of the grave for the deceased to lie upon. In Indonesia, 18th century engravings remain, which illustrates a wife purportedly choosing to be buried with her deceased husband. On the island of Bali in Indonesia, the last account of two women of the royal family accompanying their 'deceased master to his celestial abode' in 1903 is still widely disseminated among the Balinese people (see Weinberger-Thomas, *Ashes of Immortality: Widow-burning in India* (University of Chicago Press, 1999, pp. 11–13).
4. Rural widows in England could hold a legal interest in the house and land, but in many villages women controlled the holdings only until the male

heir came of age (usually at twenty-one). Widows of merchant families in urban areas might be able to take over the family craft or trade, although many women were unable to do so. In some cases, widows kept a family business operating for the sake of the children, but other widows actually took over the work themselves.
5. Brynhild was a queen in ancient Germanic legends. The basis of the myths appeared in the Volsunga Saga (The Story of the Volsungs), which was written in the Old Norse language in the thirteenth century by an unknown author though the material originated in older works. *The Story of the Volsungs* was translated by William Morris and Eirikr Magnusson and published in 1888 by Walter Scott Press, London. In Chapter XXXII entitled, Of the Ending of Brynhild, it states that Brynhild first stabbed herself and, 'then died Brynhild, who was burned there by the side of Sigurd and thus their life-days ended.'
6. The play The Seven Against Thebes was written in 467 B.C.E. by Aeschylus. It is based on the ancient Greek legend of seven heroes who made war on Eteocles, King of Thebes. This was related to the legacy of Oedipus, who was banished, while his sons Eteocles and Polynices agreed to share in ruling the kingdom in alternating years. However, Eteocles refused to yield the throne after his year was finished, and thus Polynices organized the doomed expedition, which came to be called The Seven Against Thebes. The relevant point is that one of these seven heroes, Capaneus, was killed as he was climbing the walls of Thebes; his wife, Evadne, threw herself on his funeral pyre and was burned with him.
7. For example, Martha C. Nussbaum argues in *Women and Human Development: The capabilities approach* (Cambridge University Press, 2000) that India is one of the most diverse countries in the world, and has encompassed matrilineal, not only patrilineal systems; however, even in this case, women eventually lost their rights to own land, even though they had held that right for hundreds of years.

Part 3

1. In this section detailing historical developments, I am greatly indebted to the volumes in Japanese of *The Comparative Family History Encyclopedia*, 1995, published by Kōbun-dō. Much of the detailed linguistic analysis of the roots of the four words surveyed can be found in these volumes. We highly recommend these historical references to persons who are interested in further details regarding the documentation of the connections between Japanese linguistic, familial, and historical developments.
2. The word yamome is a word, which is read as kafu according to the Chinese (kun) reading, and most likely indicates the Chinese origin of this word for widows. Both terms use 'ka,' differentiated by gender and refer to individuals living alone with the implication that they need assistance. Nowadays, yamome is still used to designate widowers (otoko yamome), but is not usually used with reference to women. This fact indicates an interesting point that widowers have always been referred to by the same term throughout most of Japanese history. However, designations for woman have depended on changing historical periods and their shifting status; thus the larger number of terms to designate widows.

3. The practice of women changing surnames upon marriage to that of her husband's family name was not practiced before, nor during, the Kamakura Period. Inheritance practices during these time periods included the legal transmission of assets from parents to daughters, as well as to sons. These indigenous inheritance practices would change drastically with the institutionalization and adoption of Confucian familial ideology, which emphasized women's subservient position vis-à-vis men.
4. Unlike informal nuns, formal nuns (bikuni) lived in convents and practiced a strict Buddhist monastic lifestyle involving not only celibacy but daily regimentation: rising before dawn, sitting for hours in the kneeling position called seiza (knees are folded gracefully under the body with the back straight) and studying in the pursuit of wisdom, compassion and enlightenment. Although informal, widowed nuns continued to live in the secular world and did not have to follow such an ascetic lifestyle, they strictly practiced sexual abstinence, devoted themselves to religious rites for the salvation of husbands' souls, and kept the five important commandments of Buddhism (gokai) against murder, lust, theft, lying and intemperance. Even if widows did not become nuns, either informally or formally, widows in upper-class samurai families were expected to hold Buddhist memorials at proscribed intervals. Within this religious and symbolic context, a woman became the living spiritual wife of the deceased husband and remained in this state until she died. For more details regarding women's historical participation as nuns and in the founding of Buddhism in Japan, see Paula Kane Robinson Arai, *Women Living Zen: Japanese Sōtō Buddhist Nuns* (Oxford University Press, 1999).
5. In many societies, poor peasant farmers and widows traditionally could scavenge food left over after the harvesting of fields. This was also the case in Japan where it was customary for widows to pick-up leftover grains of rice or other foods when the harvest was completed. Later, after rice harvesters (senba koki) came to be used, widows could no longer count on this work. The rice harvesters were sometimes called 'goke daoshi,' as it was jokingly said that the introduction of these machines took the jobs of widows; thus widows were forced to 'fall down.' These jokes also conveyed a sexual nuance in widows 'falling down.'
6. In recent historical time lines reflecting greater accuracy, the year 1603 is used as the time of the institutionalization of the Tokugawa shogunate government (bakufu) by Tokugawa Ieyasu; Tokugawa Yoshinobu returned governmental authority to the Emperor formally in 1867. However, the traditional timeline of 1600–1868 used to designate the Edo Period is retained in this work in order to prevent confusion.
7. Martha C. Tocco, Norms and Texts for Women's Education in Tokugawa, Japan, in *Women and Confucian Cultures in Premodern China, Korea, and Japan*, eds., Dorothy Ko, JaHyun Kim Haboush and Joan R. Piggott (University of California Press, 2003) makes the assertion regarding women's education in the Edo Period that 'in the absence of systematic study, many scholars of Japanese women's history continue to view Japan's versions of Neo-Confucianism in totalizing ways. It is still widely believed that the impact of Neo-Confucian thought on the status of Tokugawa women was devastating, as Confucian tenets confined women within the family, subordinated their interests there and proscribed their public

participation in the political realm.' Tocca argues that there was variation in thinking on women's education with several philosophers arguing for more education for women, not less. Yet, the question should not be posed simplistically in terms of more or less education, but also consideration should be given to what was taught. A truly relational analysis of aspects of domination between men and women should be approached as it establishes itself not only in the family but also in the world of education, the labor market, law, and state politics. Women were educated in order to inculcate Confucian-based moral and ethical codes; education was one way to promulgate the newest propaganda. Thus the educational process itself cannot be separated from the content of that education.

8. As noted by Laurel Rasplica Rodd in Yosano Akiko and the Taisho Debate over the 'New Woman,' *Recreating Japanese Women, 1600–1945*, ed., Gail Bernstein (University of California Press, 1991), influence from Western countries through literature and plays like Henrik Ibsen's A Doll's House, swept through Tokyo in 1911 evoking reactions from playwrights and critics regarding the themes of challenging male authority, marriage as an uncontested, sacrosanct terrain, and reconsideration of women's roles as wives and mothers. Japanese feminists and socialist activists attacked the Japanese marriage system due to its foundation based on making connections and gaining power, rather than romantic love. Debates raged regarding the proper societal roles for women influenced by the importation of the work of Western feminist scholars. In the literary field too, women were exploring and exchanging views in the magazine Seitō (Bluestocking) in which women discussed the current issues of the day such as abortion, prostitution, state protection of mothers and children and motherhood itself. Sharon Sievers argues in *Flowers in Salt: The Beginnings of Feminist Consciousness in Modern Japan* (Stanford University Press, 1991) that while the culturally fashionable 'modern girls,' served as cultural icons of the 1920s, some Japanese feminists challenged the societal control of women's bodies in general. They argued that chastity was a luxury that poor women could ill-afford, and women need not worry about such an archaic notion, since there was an obvious double-standard at work with men never reproached for not protecting their own chastity. Other feminists argued women's chastity was precious and should be protected, as part of the 'good wives and wise mothers' traditional view. For a more detailed explication of Japanese women's history, see the excellent work, *Recreating Japanese Women, 1600–1945*, ed., Gail Bernstein.

Part 4

1. The Manchurian Incident at Rokōkyō involved the explosion of a bridge by Japanese soldiers.
2. In Hiroshima and Nagasaki, victims ran through the streets of fire, their bodies covered with thermal burns escaping as far away as they could from the all-engulfing destruction occurring in the two cities on August 6th (Hiroshima) and August 9th (Nagasaki). These are the only known cases of the use of atomic bombs by any country in the world. Citizens of Hiroshima and Nagasaki continue to observe yearly anniversaries of the

horrific bombings and harbor lingering indignation and anger about the use of atomic weapons, which is directed not only at the U.S. but at the Japanese government as well. Ishikawa, E. and D. Swain, *Hiroshima and Nagasaki: The physical, medical and social effects of the atomic bombings* (Basic Books, 1981).
3. Sasaki, Junnoske, et.al., reports in *Introduction to the History of Japan* (Gairon nihon rekishi) (Yoshikawa Kōbunkan, 2000, pp. 263–264) that the ratio of food expenditures to total income for the average citizen's budget before the war was about 30 percent, but just after the war, this expenditure increased to 60 percent. Before World War II and during the war as well, Japan had been importing rice and other food supplies from its wartime colonies of Korea and Taiwan. The country had relied on the importation of food (22 percent of all rice, 72 percent of soybeans and 82 percent of sugar) from foreign countries. Jerome B. Cohen, *Japanese Economy in War and Reconstruction* (Senji sengo no nihon keizai, (Iwanami shoten, 1948), argues that this dependence on foreign imports and the lack of fertilizer available for farmers became primary causes of the drastic drop in farm yields. Japan's mountainous terrain and its outdated feudal-based landowner system were also obstacles to more efficient farm production. Thus when imports were cut-off from occupied countries at the end of the war, famine quickly emerged throughout Japan.
4. It is estimated that with various additions to the diet, the average intake of calories may have risen to 1,400. In 1944, it was calculated that the average Japanese consumed approximately 1900 calories, while before the war an individual would have taken in about 2265 calories. Additionally, there was a considerable drop in the total amount of food consumption by Japanese compared to people in other countries. Even in Germany, comparing the level of calorie consumption before the war, estimated at 2907, and in 1944, at 2941 calories, there was an actual increase in the amount of food consumed by the German population.
5. The meaning of 'takenoko seikatsu' is based on stripping or peeling away the layers of bamboo one by one. However, at least these individuals had something to sell; others much less fortunate had lost their homes and all their possessions leaving them nothing to sell for food.
6. It must be remembered that most houses in Japan, unlike those in European countries, were made of wood due to the important cultural aesthetic placed on the use of natural wood products in housing construction, which has a long heritage in Japan. Thus the urban cities and its surroundings were rapidly turned into incendiary areas. The targeted areas which suffered most extensively from the fire-bombings were as follows in order of overall damage incurred: (1) Tokyo, (2) Osaka, (3) Hyogo Area (Kobe), (4) Aichi Prefecture (Nagoya), (5) Kanagawa Prefecture, and (6) Shizuoka (Nakamura and Miyazaki, 1995). As previously noted, the cities of Hiroshima and Nagasaki where the first (and to-date the only) atomic bombs were dropped are placed in a separate category.
7. The damage to Japan's total national wealth included: a loss of 34 percent of homes and buildings, 27 percent loss of money, jewelry and other assets, 12 percent loss in machinery and 11 percent in ships. However, these numbers do not take into account the actual loss of war-related equipment and machinery, including weaponry, ships, airplanes, etc.

8. Suzuki Itsuko is a long-time activist who has written several books and historical records of widow's activism in the Pacific War and after the end of the war. In an interview with Ms. Suzuki in March 2004 conducted in Tokyo, she stated that 'Nobody was doing anything about recording what was happening, so it became my mission. Women, including widows, were doing everything in the war – working as drivers, doing factory work, any kind of work.'
9. This name is given additional emphasis due to the meaning of the kanji characters used to write the word. The meaning is a play on the Japanese word for reed 'ashi' and the kanji denoting beauty 'mi.'
10. Yasukuni Shrine was constructed in June 1869, as Japan implemented Shintō as the state religion with the emperor as divine, to honor soldiers who died the year before in the Meiji Restoration that marked the start of modernization. In 1978, fourteen Class-A war criminals were secretly enshrined, including General Hideki Tojo, the prime minister who ordered the attack on Pearl Harbor and was hanged for war crimes by the U.S.-led tribunal. The shrine lists the names of 2,466,532 'spirits' – mostly soldiers, but also nurses, bureaucrats and firefighters – killed in eleven wars, two of them domestic, and the others with Russia, China, Korea, Taiwan, and the Allies. Yasukuni Shrine has become a controversial place due to the visits of Japanese government officials, including Prime Minister Junichiro Koizumi, who has made repeated trips to the shrine in 2002, 2003, 2004 and 2005; he visited the shrine again on August 15th of 2006. The governments of South Korea and China have strenuously objected to these actions interpreting them as condoning war and past Japanese military aggressions, due to the internment of high ranking military leaders convicted of war crimes and executed. Mr. Koizumi counters that he visits the shrine in order to pray for peace and the spirits of the dead.

    The name of the Shrine, Yasukuni, which was adopted in 1879, is based on classical Chinese literature and means 'to bring peace to the nation.'
11. The name kasutori used to designate this genre of magazines literally means a cheap, usually illegally brewed, low-quality rice or sweet potato wine (sake). The images in these magazines were generally pornographic in nature portraying women in degrading and humiliating ways. Many of these same images are still actively promoted on the internet continuing to present widows in sexualized situations and reflecting society's stereotypical negative views of widowed women. However, it is important to note that the informants in this research clearly did not view themselves in this way and continue to actively reject such meanings engaging in the struggle that widows after the Pacific War began.

Part 5

1. Parts of this chapter originally appeared as a previous article in U.S. Japan Women's Journal: A Journal for the International Exchange of Gender Studies, Number 18, 2000 and are included with the written permission of the publisher, the Center for Inter-Cultural Studies and Education, Jōsai University and Purdue University; the chapter presented in this work has been substantially updated with fresh insights enhanced by additional information. I would also like to thank family members and others for

their forbearance in allowing me to ask questions, work alongside them, and take notes during ritualized ceremonies. Such an opportunity to closely observe and interview women so intimately involved in memorial service arrangements is not usually open to researchers and provided a rare opportunity for insight. In keeping with anthropological convention and in adhering to the wishes of the family members observed, all names, locations, and relationships have been changed to protect their privacy.
2. It is commonly known, though not officially recognized, that widowers may re-marry or enter into affairs much sooner than women without societal condemnation. The number of memorial services varies depending on the religious sect within Buddhism and also with respect to region. In this particular area and within the Jōdo Shinshū tradition, the is-shūki begins a series of memorial services performed on the anniversary of a death to ensure good treatment for the deceased in the afterlife and to appease the spirits. Memorial services continue with the san-kaiki (designated as the third anniversary of death, but the ceremony actually occurs on the second anniversary). Following the san-kaiki, there are services held in the seventh, thirteenth, seventeenth, twenty-third, twenty-seventh, thirty-third, thirty-seventh, forty-third, and forty-seventh years. The last ceremony is performed on the fiftieth anniversary of a death. Widows are frequently involved in the preparation and management of memorial ceremonies in the Nagoya region, though the extent of such involvement varies from family to family.
3. The Ikenobō School dates from the work of Ikenobō Senno in the mid-sixteenth century. As Kudō Masanobu states in *The History of Ikebana* (Weatherhill, 1986, p. 17), the philosophical premise of this school is that it is most important to create arrangements that reveal the basic characteristics of the tree or plant as it exists in nature itself.
4. Several scholars have noted that the translation of chanoyu as 'tea ceremony' is a clumsy one and imparts nothing of the 'wabi-naturalistic' art of the tea service, which is a ritual of communion with the art and soul of Japanese aesthetics: for example, Iguchi Kaisen, *The Tea Ceremony* (Hoikusha Publishing, 1975, p. 22); A.L. Sadler, *Cha-no-yu: The Japanese Tea Ceremony* (Charles E. Tuttle, 1962); and Okakura Kakuzo, *The Book of Tea* (Dover Publications 1964, 1906). However, a more appropriate translation has yet to be offered. Some practitioners lament the loss of the wabi-sabi aesthetic paradigm, which, they argue, has been pervasively commercialized into a slick, saccharine, corporate style of beauty. See Leonard Koren, *Wabi-Sabi for Artists, Designers, Poets, and Philosophers* (Stone Bridge Press, 1994, pp. 7–11).
5. The Sekishū Ryu founder was Sekishū Katagiri, who was born in 1605 in Osaka. He was born into a samurai family, and upon the death of his father, he became a feudal lord. He was a tea ceremony master in the early years of the Edo Period and became very famous due to the fact that he was the teacher of the Tokugawa Family. Thus the Sekishū School's historical roots lie in its focus on teaching students from aristocratic families and in its philosophy that beauty is to be found in poverty and simplicity. This school has yet to be fully commercialized. Though some practitioners have argued that the small Sekishū School has almost ceased to exist, present adherents of this school state that this is not the case. They argue that

the school retains isits elite status and historical emphasis on simplicity and elegance, which differentiates it from the more commercialized and larger branches of the Ura-senke and Omote-senke Schools. Thus this particular chanoyu teacher accepts no money for lessons and receives or rejects potential students as she wishes.
6. The terms 'designated head' is used because in reality this particular son is the younger of the two sons in the family. The second son was chosen by his father as the successor because the eldest son did not want to take over the headship of the family and the responsibilities involved. Additionally, the eldest son had no interest in the art of ikebana or in farming. Hence, the younger son was elevated to the position of headship.
7. According to Higuchi Kiyoyuki in *Nihon Shokumotsu-shi* (Shibata Shoten 1987, 1959, pp. 239–240), such foods are part of a tradition known as temple cooking, or 'cooking for Buddhist priests' (shōjin ryōri) developed during the Edo Period. All the foods served at the memorial service should be indigenous to Japan and represent the same type of menu established at such ceremonies in the Edo Period. In keeping with this traditional Buddhist memorial service, there is no kind of meat or fish served at the ceremony.
8. This tea is commonly known as hikicha, which is the finest quality green tea, made from the youngest leaves of old tea shrubs. The tender leaves are ground into a fine light green powder, and the powdered tea is then whipped to a delicate froth in hot water. The resulting flavor is mild and fragrant when the tea leaves are brewed in water at a temperature of about 60 degrees Centigrade.
9. The more formal term for okaeshi is kōdengaeshi, but according to etiquette, this term is properly used only at the actual funeral.
10. The term furusato is commonly translated to refer to one's hometown; however, the term has highly evocative cultural resonance in Japan. As Tamanoi argues, the term can also apply to an individual or a collective group of Japanese expressing a range of historical and public meanings that are highly sentimentalized; see Tamanoi Mariko Asano, Under the Shadow of Nationalism: Politics and Poetics of Rural Japanese Women (University of Hawai'i Press, 1998, pp. 194–197). Also see Eyal Ben-Ari, 'Contested Identities and Models of Action in Japanese Discourses of Place-Making: An Interpretive Study,' in Joy Hendry, ed., *Interpreting Japanese Society*, pp. 68–87, and Millie Creighton, 'Consuming Rural Japan: The Marketing of Tradition in the Japanese Travel Industry,' *Ethnology* 36, 3 (Summer 1997, pp. 239–254).

Part 6

1. Growing poverty among elderly and single mother families and the bipolarization of rich and poor in Japan are never addressed by the conservative Liberal Democratic Party (LDP) government headed by Prime Minister Koizumi; poverty and inequality are still not viewed nor acknowledged as serious societal issues.
2. Public housing refers to apartments or small, detached houses for low-income households, which are administered by the municipality.

Occupation of these government-funded housing programs is based on annual income.
3. There are quite different portrayals of women in the Japanese workplace including: Glenda S. Roberts, *Staying on the Line: blue-collar women in contemporary Japan* (University of Hawaii Press, 1994), Dorinne Kondo, *Crafting Selves: power, gender, and discourses of identity in a Japanese workplace* (University of Chicago Press, 1990), Alice Cook and Hiroko Hayashi, *Working Women in Japan: Discrimination, resistance and reform* (Cornell University Press, 1980).
4. A furoshiki is a scarf-like cloth (square or oblong shaped) usually made of silk, cotton or even polyester. It is often used to wrap and carry things and when not in use is folded into a small square. Many of these cloths are beautifully made, etched with artistic pictures of flowers, trees, scenery or even more modern symbols have come into use recently. The word furoshiki literally means a 'bath cloth,' since it was originally used to wrap clothes in a public bath or to sit on after taking a bath. When used in the phrase furoshiki overtime, it indicates overtime that is hidden from view and thus not compensated.
5. Ginza is located in the district of Chūō Ward of Tokyo, east of Yūrakuchō and Uchisaiwaichō and north of Shinbashi. Ginza derives its name from the silver coin mint that was established there during the Edo Period when the Tokugawa bakufu (the military feudal government administered by the shōgun in the Kamakura, Muromachi and Edo Periods) set up the facilities to coin silver in 1612. It is now well-known as the premier upscale shopping area of Tokyo with an abundance of famous name brand shops (e.g., Chanel, Hermes, Burberry, Prada), various boutiques and department stores. The area is also famous for excellent restaurants, cafes, tea houses, and coffee shops.
6. According to Japan's Ministry of Finance, the recently submitted budget of 79.69 trillion yen for the fiscal year beginning in April 2006 represents the first budget since 1998/99 that is less than 80 trillion yen. However, this budget reflects the influence of Prime Minister Junichiro Koizumi's fiscal reform efforts, including a downsizing of the nation's medical care system and significant cuts in social programs (*The Japan Times*, December 20, 2005).
7. Expenses for children's education vary depending upon whether or not the school is private or public. In junior high school, costs of public schools are estimated at a minimum of $1700 per year with this expense including school supplies, travel fees, money for school trips, but not including special 'cram school' (juku) fees (expensive cram schools offer private lessons and tutorials to enter a prestigious university or school). Private junior high schools are much more costly, running approximately $10,000 per year, while public high school costs escalate to $3500 per year. Impoverished parents must either save the money or borrow it through a government-sponsored or private institution loan program; however, most single mother families are unable to obtain a loan. Thus disadvantages are linked and passed down from poor parents to their children.
8. The most recent figures on Japan's unemployment rate show an increase to 4.5 percent in October 2005 suggesting a slowdown in the creation of

new jobs despite marked improvements in corporate profits. Japan may be entering a period, much like the U.S., of a jobless recovery.
9. The government's official stance has been that care of the aged is the family's responsibility and social welfare assistance would be extended only in cases where circumstances and economic conditions made it impossible for families to fulfill that responsibility. An analysis of GDP indicators comparing the amount of money spent on human services illustrates that the financial burden imposed upon the family is substantial in Japan compared to other countries. For example, Japan spends approximately 14.7 percent of its total GDP on public social expenditures compared to the European Average of 24.5 percent with Sweden (31.0 percent) at the top (Operation for Economic Co-operation and Development, 1980–1998). A more shocking fact is that Japan, as a percent of social security transfers to total GDP, is listed at 10.3 percent meaning it is more miserly than the U.S. at 11.3 percent (OECD Observer-Supplement, 2003; Aoki and Aoki, 2005). Local governments do provide retirement homes and 'home helpers,' but there is a shortage of such services even though they are in constant demand. People who need nursing care, but do not qualify for government assistance are often hospitalized by their families for long periods, so that family members may receive the proper attention. However, this practice simply shifts the burden from the family caregivers (almost always women) to the national medical insurance system.
10. The system also has some problems. For example, if someone can walk 10 meters without assistance, that person will probably be classified as self-reliant. However, the same person may need help if they are required to carry something, as is frequently the case in doing shopping or errands.
11. While the poverty line in Japan is roughly estimated at $10,000 to $13,000 for one person per annum, it is also the case that many younger unmarried women and men (known as 'parasite singles') live with parents in order to defray expenses and thus have ample money to spend on travel, brand-name goods, and expensive designer clothes, feeding the stereotypical image of 'wealthy Japanese.' Of course, there are no such luxuries for widowed women working to support their families.
12. A recent development tentatively indicates that widows may be more apt to remarry than previously thought;however, it remains to be seen as to whether or not this tendency will develop into a significant trend or not.
13. Most of the successful new religions of Japan began as offshoots of the main religious organizations involving Shintō or Buddhism. In the case of Sōka Gakkai, the group is a derivative of the Nichiren sect of Buddhism and has more than seventeen million members nationally. More interestingly, this new religion formed in 1930 is connected to the Kōmeitō, a conservative political party. The cult that is notorious throughout the world is Ōmu Shinrikyo (Supreme Truth) whose followers were responsible for a series of kidnappings and murders that culminated in the sarin gas attack on a Tokyo subway in 1995, which killed twelve people and injured over 5000. The cult's notorious leader,

Matsumoto Chizuo, has been sentenced to death, but his attorneys are appealing the decision.
14. There are many adult websites in Japanese which feature introductions and 'parties' to meet available widows; pornographic pictures are frequently accompanied by stories reminiscent of the kasutori zasshi of old.

References

Abrahams, R. G., 1973. Some aspects of levirate. In: Jack Goody ed. *The Character of Kinship*. Cambridge: Cambridge University Press, pp. 163–174.
Agarwal, Bina, ed., 1988. Patriarchy and the 'modernising' state: an introduction. In: *Structures of Patriarchy: the state, the community and the household in modernising Asia*, London: Zed Books, pp. 1–28.
Agnes, Flavia, 1999. *Law and Gender Inequality: the politics of women's rights in India*. New Delhi: Oxford University Press.
Althusser, Louis, 2001. *Lenin and Philosophy and Other Essays*. New York: Monthly Review Press.
Anderson, Bonnie S. & Zinsser, Judith P., eds, 1988. *A History of their Own: women in Europe from prehistory to the present*, Volume II. New York: Harper Perennial.
Anderson, Perry, 1998. *The Origins of Postmodernity*. London: Verso.
Anzai, Ikuo, 1993. A case study of levirate marriage (Kyōdai gata keishō kon (gyaku-en kon) no jirei kenkyū). In: *Josai Bunka Kenkyū-jo Kiyō* 2, pp. 147–159.
Aoki, Deborah McDowell, 1997. Gender, class, and age in the microcosm of the family: the household division of labor in Hokkaido Japan. *U.S.–Japan Women's Journal: A Journal for the International Exchange of Gender Studies*, 13, pp. 87–104.
Aoki, Deborah McDowell, 2000. Widow's rites in Japan: an interpretive study of women's participation in memorial rituals and the transformation of family practices. *U.S.–Japan Women's Journal: A Journal for the International Exchange of Gender Studies*, 18, pp.84–106.
Aoki, Osamu & Aoki McDowell, Deborah, 2005. Invisible poverty in Japan: case studies and realities of single mothers. *Journal of Poverty: Innovations on Social, Political & Economic Inequalities*, 9, (1): pp. 1–21.
Aoki, Osamu, ed., 2003. *Invisible Poverty in Japan (Gendai nihon no mienai hinkon)*. Tokyo: Akashi Shoten.
Arai, Paula Kane Robinson, 1999. *Women Living Zen: Japanese Soto Buddhist nuns*. New York: Oxford University Press USA.
Bailey, Jackson H., 1991. *Ordinary People, Extraordinary Lives: political and economic change in a Tohoku village*. Honolulu: University of Hawai'i Press.
Basu, Monmayee, 2004. Hindu women and marriage law: from sacrament to contract. *Women and Law in India*. New Delhi: Oxford University Press, pp. 1–153
Benedict, Ruth, 1989a {1934}. *Patterns of Culture*. Boston: Houghton Mifflin Co.
Benedict, Ruth, 1989b {1946}. *The Chrysanthemum and the Sword: patterns of Japanese culture*. Boston: Houghton Mifflin Co.

Bendann, E., 1930. *Death Customs: an analytical study of burial rites.* New York: Knopf Publishing.
Bernstein, Gail Lee, ed., 1991. *Recreating Japanese Women, 1600–1945.* Berkeley and Los Angeles: University of California Press.
Bernstein, Gail Lee, ed., 1983. *Haruko's World: a Japanese farm woman and her community.* Stanford: Stanford University Press.
Bestor, Theodore C., 1989. *Neighborhood Tokyo,* p.167. Palo Alta: Stanford University Press.
Blount, Ben G., 1995. *Language, Culture, and Society: a book of readings.* Long Grove: Waveland Press.
Boas, Franz, ed., 1911. Introduction. In: *Handbook of American Indian Languages.* Bureau of American Ethnology Bulletin, 40, pp.1–83.
Bingham, Marjorie Wall & Hills Gross, Susan, eds, 1987. *Women in* Japan. St. Louis Park: Glenhurst Publications.
Bonvillain, N., 2001. *Women and Men: cultural constructs of gender.* Upper Saddle River: Prentice-Hall.
Bourdieu, Pierre, 1991. *Language & Symbolic Power.* John B Thompson, ed.; Translated by Gino Raymond & Matthew Adamson. Cambridge: Harvard University Press.
Bourdieu, Pierre, [1998] 2001. *Masculine Domination.* Translated by Richard Nice. Cambridge: Cambridge University Press.
Bremmer, Jan & Van Den Bosch, Lourens. eds, 1995. *Between Poverty and the Pyre: moments in the history of widowhood.* London: Routledge.
Brettell, Caroline B. & Sargent, Carolyn F. eds, 2001. *Gender in Cross-cultural Perspective.* Upper Saddle River: Prentice-Hall, Inc.
Brown, J.K., Subbaiah, P. & Sarah, T. 1998. Being in charge: older women and their younger female kin. In: J. Dickerson-Putnam & J. Brown, eds, *Women among Women: anthropological perspectives on female age hierarchies,* Chicago: University of Chicago Press, pp. 100–123.
Buckley, Sandra, 1997. *Broken Silence.* Berkeley: University of California Press.
Buitelaar, J., 1995. Widows' Worlds: representations and realities. *Between Poverty and the Pyre: moments in the history of widowhood.* London, pp. 1–18.
Butler, Judith, 2004a. *Undoing Gender.* New York and London: Routledge.
Butler, Judith, 2004b. *Precious Life: the powers of mourning and violence.* London and New York: Verso.
Casagrande, Carla, 1992. The protected woman. In: Christiane Klapisch-Zuber, ed., *A History of Women: silences of the Middle Ages,* Cambridge: Harvard University Press, pp.70–104.
Chandra, Sudhir, 2004. Enslaved daughters: colonialism, law and women's rights. In: Flavia Agnes, Sudhir Chandra & Monmayee Basu, eds, *Women and Law in India,* New Delhi: Oxford University Press, pp. 1–188.
Cherry, K., 1987. *Womansword: what Japanese words say about women.* Tokyo: Kodansha International.
Chesler, Phyllis, 2005. *The Death of Feminism: what's next in the struggle for women's freedom.* New York: Palgrave Macmillan, pp. 1–38.
Christie, Christine, 2001. *Gender and Language.* Edinburgh: Edinburgh University Press.

Clifford, James & Marcus, George E. eds, 1986. *Writing Culture: the poetics and politics of ethnography*. Berkeley: University of California Press.
Cohen, Jerome B., 1948. *Japanese Economy in War and Reconstruction (Senji sengo no nihon keizai)*. Tokyo: Iwanami Shoten.
Cook, H. K. & Cook, T., 1992. *Japan at War: an oral history*. New York: The New Press.
Cornell, Laurel, 1991. The deaths of old women. In: Gail Bernstein, ed., *Recreating Japanese Women, 1600–1945*, Berkeley: University of California Press, pp. 71–87.
Cressy, David, 1997. *Birth, Marriage & Death: ritual, religion, and the lifecycle in Tudor and Stuart England*. Oxford: Oxford University Press.
Crapanzano, Vincent, 2003. *Imaginative Horizons: an essay in literary-philosophical anthropology*. Chicago: University of Chicago Press.
Culter, Suzanne, 1999. *Managing Decline: Japan's coal industry restructuring and community response*. Honolulu: University of Hawai'i Press.
Cumings, Bruce, 1997. *Korea's Place in the Sun: a modern history*. New York: W.W. Norton & Company.
Dahlberg, Frances, ed., 1981. Introduction. *Woman the Gatherer*. New Haven and London: Yale University Press, pp. 1–33.
del Valle, Teresa, 1993. *Gendered Anthropology*. London: Routledge Press.
Deuchler, Martina, 2003. Propagating female virtues in Chosŏn Korea. In: Dorothy Ko, Jahyun Kim Haboush & Joan R. Piggott, eds, *Women and Confucian Cultures in Premodern China, Korea, and Japan*, Berkeley: University of California Press, pp. 142–169.
Dickerson-Putnam, J., 1998. Old women at the top: an exploration of age stratification among Bena Bena women. In: J. Dickerson-Putnam & J. Brown, eds, *Women among Women: anthropological perspectives on female age hierarchies*, Chicago: University of Chicago Press, pp. 65–77.
Douglas, Mary, 1966. *Purity and Danger: an analysis of concepts of pollution and taboo*. London: Routledge and Keegan Paul Ltd.
Dower, John W., 1999. *Embracing Defeat: Japan in the wake of World War II*. New York: The New Press.
Draper, Patricia., 1975. !Kung women: contrasts in sexual egalitarianism in foraging and sedentary contexts. *In:* Rayna R. Reiter, ed., *Toward an Anthropology of Women*. New York: Monthly Review Press, pp. 77–109.
Dube, S.C., 1963. Men's and women's roles in India: a sociological review. In: B. Ward, ed., *Women in New Asia*, Paris, pp. 174–203.
Duranti, Alessandro, 2001. Linguistic anthropology: history, ideas, and issues. In: Alessandro Duranti, ed., *Linguistic Anthropology: a reader*, Malden: Blackwell Publishing Ltd, pp. 1–41.
Ebrey, Patricia Buckley, 2003. *Women and the Family in Chinese History*. London and New York: Routledge.
Ehrenreich, Barbara & English, Deirdre, 1973. *Witches, Midwives, and Nurses: a history of women healers*. New York: The Feminist Press at the City University of New York.
Elman, Benjamin, Duncan, John B. & Ooms, Herman, eds, 2003. Introduction. *Rethinking Confucianism: past and present in China, Japan, Korea, and Vietnam*. Los Angeles: University of California, pp. 1–29.
Endo, O., 1995. Aspects of sexism in language. In: K. Fujimura-Fanselow &

A. Kameda, eds, *Japanese Women: new feminist perspectives on the past, present, and future*. New York: City University of New York, pp. 29–42.
Engels, Friedrich, 1972 {1884}. *The Origin of the Family, Private Property, and the State*. London.
Esping-Anderson, Gosta, 1999. *Social Foundations of Postindustrial Economies*. Oxford: Oxford University Press.
Evans-Pritchard, E.E., 1956. *Nuer Religion*. Oxford: Oxford University Press.
Falk, Nancy Auer & Gross, Rita M., 2000. *Unspoken Worlds: women's religious lives*. Florence: Wadsworth Publishing.
Faithorn, Elizabeth, 1975. The concept of pollution among the Káfe of the Papua New Guinea Highlands. In: Rayna R. Reiter, ed., *Toward an Anthropology of Women*, New York: Monthly Review Press, pp. 127–140.
Family Registration Law, 1947. *EHS law bulletin series*, Volume II. Tokyo, Eibun-Hōreisha.
Farmer, Paul, 2003. *Pathologies of Power: health, human rights, and the new war on the poor*. Berkeley: University of California Press.
Firth, Raymond, 1959. *Economics of the New Zealand Maori*. New York: W.W. Norton.
Folbre, Nancy, 2001. *The Invisible Heart: economics and family values*. New York: The New Press.
Forbes, Geraldine, 1996. *The New Cambridge History of India IV.2: women in modern India*. Cambridge: Cambridge University Press.
Foucault, Michel, 1979. *Discipline and Punish: the birth of the prison*. New York: Vintage Books.
Fraser, Nancy, 1997. *Justice Interruptus: critical reflections on the 'postsocialist' condition*. New York: Routledge.
Frugoni, Chiara, 1992. The imagined woman. In: Christiane Klapisch-Zuber, ed., *A History of Women: silences of the Middle Ages*, Cambridge: Harvard University Press, pp. 336–422.
Fuess, Harald, 2004. *Divorce in Japan: family, gender, and the state, 1600–2000*. Stanford: Stanford University Press.
Fukasawa, Shichirō, 1964. *Thoughts about the Folklore of Narayama (Narayama Bushikō)*. Tokyo: Shinchōsha.
Fukuta, Shigejirou, 1903. Family counselor (Katei komon). In: Mutsuhiko Yuzawa ed., *A Collection of Materials on Japanese Women's Problems (Nihon fujin mondai shiryō shūsei dai go kan – kazoku seido)*, Tokyo: Domesu Publishing.
Fukutake, Tadashi, 1980. *Rural Society in Japan*. Tokyo: University of Tokyo Press.
Fuma, Susumu, 1993. The custom of forced remarriage and the position of widows in Ming and Quing China (Chūgoku min-shin jidai ni okeru kafu no chii to kyōsei saikon no fūshū) In: Katuya Maekawa, ed., *Kazoku-Setai-Kamon – kōgyōka izen no sekai kara*. Kyoto: Minerva Shobō.
Futabatei, Shimei, 1906 {1962}. Widows and humanity (*Jogaku zasshi*). In: Tsubouchi Shōyō & Futabatei Shimei, *Nihon gendai bungaku zenshū No. 4*, Tokyo: Kōdansha Publishing.
Gal, Susan, 2001. Language, gender, and power; an anthropological review. In: Duranti Alessandro Malden, ed., *Linguistic Anthropology: a reader*, Blackwell Publishing Ltd, pp. 420–430.

Galvin, Kathey-Lee, 2001. Schneider Revisited: sharing and ratification in the construction of kinship. In: Linda Stone, ed., *New Directions in Anthropological Kinship*, Lanham: Rowman & Littlefield Publishers, Inc, pp. 109–124.
Gelb, Joyce, 2003. *Gender Policies in Japan and the United States*. New York: Palgrave Macmillan.
Geertz, Clifford, 1973. *The Interpretation of Cultures*. New York: Basic Books, Inc.
Geertz, Clifford, 1984. Distinguished lecture: anti-anti relativism. *American Anthropologist*, American Anthropological Association, pp. 263–278.
Geertz, Clifford, 2000. *Available Light: anthropological reflections on philosophical topics*. Princeton: Princeton University Press.
Gingrich, Andre & Fox, Richard G., eds, 2002. *Anthropology by Comparison*. London and New York: Routledge.
Goodall, H.L., Jr., 2000. *Writing the New Ethnography*. Lanham: AltaMira Press.
Goodman, Roger, ed., 2002. *Family and Social Policy in Japan*. Cambridge: Cambridge University Press.
Goodenough, Ward H., 1957. Cultural Anthropology and Linguistics. *Georgetown University Series on Language and Linguistics*, No. 9, pp. 167–173.
Goody, Jack, 1973. Polygyny, economy and the role of women. In: Jack Goody, ed., *The Character of Kinship*. London: Cambridge University Press.
Goody, Jack, ed., 1983. *The Development of the Family and Marriage in Europe*. Cambridge: Cambridge University Press.
Goody, Jack, ed., 1996. *The East in the West*. Cambridge: Cambridge University Press.
Gordon, A., 2003. *A Modern History of Japan: from Tokugawa times to the present*. New York: Oxford University Press.
Gottlieb, Nanette, 2005. *Language and Society in Japan*. Cambridge: Cambridge Uni-versity Press.
Gough, Kathleen, 1975. The origin of the family. In: Rayna R. Reiter, ed., *Toward an Anthropology of Women*, New York: Monthly Review Press, pp. 51–76.
Green, Linda, 1999. *Fear as a Way of Life: Mayan widows in rural Guatemala*. New York: Columbia University Press.
Gubbins, J. H., 1897. *The Civil Code of Japan*, Vol. II, Tokyo, p. 11.
Gunji, Atsushi, 2003. *The Society of Military Assistance (Gunji engo no sekai)*. Tokyo: Dōseisha.
Hardacre, Helen, 1997. *Marketing the Menacing Fetus in Japan*, Berkeley: University of California Press, pp. 12–13.
Harris, Colette, 2004. *Control and Subversion: gender relations in Tajikistan*. London: Pluto Press.
Hashimoto, Kenji, 2003. *Class Structure in Contemporary Japan*. Melbourne: Trans Pacific Press.
Hashimoto, Noriko & Henmi, Masaaki, eds, 2003. *Gender and the History of Education (Jendā to kyōiku no rekishi)*. Tokyo: Kawashima Shoten.
Hastings, Sally A., 1996. Women legislators in the postwar diet. In: A. Imamura, ed., *Re-imaging Japanese Women*, Berkeley: University of California Press, pp. 278–279.

Hendry, Joy, 1981. *Marriage in Changing Japan*. Rutland.
Hendry, Joy, 2010. *Marriage in Changing Japan: community & society*. London: Routledge Press.
Henmi, Masaaki, 2003. The history of special training schools for war widows: eyes on war widows and their economic independence (Senbotsusha kafu tokusetsu kyōin yōseisho shi: sensō mibōjin heno manazashi to jiritsu to). In: *The History of Gender and Education (Jendā to kyōiku no rekishi)*. Tokyo: Kawashima Shoten.
Higuchi, Yoshio, Ōta, Kiyoshi & the Research Group on Economic Planning, 2006. *The Lives of Women in the Heisei Era Depression Surveys (Josei tachi no heisei fukyō)*. Tokyo: Nihon Keizai Shinbunsha.
Hiraoka, Kōichi, ed., 2001. *Social Inequality among Elderly People in Japan (Korei ki to shakaiteki fubyōdō)*. Tokyo: Tokyo University Press.
Hoare, Quintin & Smith, Geoffrey Nowell, eds and translated, 1971. *Selections from the Prison Notebooks of Antonio Gramsci*. New York: International Publishers.
Hoffman, Michael, 2002. City or sticks? It's what you make of it. *The Japan Times*, 14 April, p. 12.
Hong, Fan, 1997. *Footbinding, Feminism, and Freedom: the liberation of women's bodies in modern China*. London: Frank Cass & Co. Ltd.
Hori, Ichirō & Ooms, H., 1986. Yanagita Kunio and about our Ancestors. In: Ichirō Hori & H. Ooms, ed., *The Yanagita Guide to the Japanese Folktale*. Bloomington: Indiana University Press, pp. 1–18, 115.
Hufton, Olwen, 1995. *The Prospect Before Her: a history of women in Western Europe 1500–1800*. New York: Vintage Books.
Hyde, Lewis, 1979. *The Gift: Imagination and the Erotic Life of Property*, New York: Vintage Books, pp. 56–58.
Hymes, Dell H., 1959. Fieldwork in linguistics and anthropology. *Studies in Linguistics*, No. 14, pp. 82–91.
Ichibangase, Yasuko, 1978. The activist movements of widows after World War II (Sengo mibōjin undō). In: Yasuko Ichibangase, ed., *Collected Information about Japanese Women's Issues: health and welfare (Nihon fujin mondai shiryō shūsei dai-rokkan: hoken to fukushi)*. Tokyo: Domesu Publishing.
Ichinose, Toshiya, 2005. *Social History on the Home Front: the fallen soldiers and the bereaved families (Jūgo no shakai shi: senshisha to izoku)*. Tokyo: Yosikawa Kōbunkan.
Imamura, Anne E., ed., 1996. *Re-imaging Japanese Women*. Berkeley: University of California Press.
Inuma, Kenji, 1992. The power of widows: formation and role (goke no chikara). In: Sumio Minegishi, ed., *The Family and Women (Kazoku to josei)*, Tokyo: Iwanami Shoten.
Isamu, K., 1990. Toward a new perspective on aging society – quality of life approach. *The Journal of Social Security Research (Kikan Shakai Hoshō Kenkyū)* 26(3), pp. 255–269.
Ishikawa, E. & Swain, D., eds and translated, 1981. *Hiroshima and Nagasaki: the physical, medical and social effects of the atomic bombings* (The committee for the compilation of materials on damage caused by the atomic bombs in Hiroshima and Nagasaki.) New York: Basic Books.
Iwao, S., 1993. *The Japanese Woman: traditional image and changing reality*. Cambridge: Cambridge University Press.

Iwasaka, M. & Toelken, B., 1994. *Ghosts and the Japanese: cultural experience in Japanese death legends*. Logan: Utah State University Press.
Jayawardena, Kumari, 1986. *Feminism and Nationalism in the Third World*. London: Zed Books.
Johnson, Chalmers A., 2004. *The Sorrows of Empire: militarism, secrecy, and the end of the republic*. New York: Holt Paperbacks.
Kageyama, Yuri, 2003. Loan sharks feasting on ballooning number of people deep in debt. *The Japan Times*, 15 February p. 3.
Kahn, Miriam, 1994. *Always Hungry, Never Greedy: food and the expression of gender in a Melanesian society*. Long Grove: Waveland Press.
Kanda, Mikio, 1989. *Widows of Hiroshima: the life stories of nineteen peasant wives*. New York: St. Martin's Press.
Kano, Masanao, ed., 1984. A war widow: *Asahi journal*. In: *Women's History after World War II (Onna no sengo shi)*. Asahi Shinbun Publishing.
Kariya, Takehiko, 2001. *Educational Crisis in Stratified Japan: formation of an incentive divided society through the reproduction of inequality (Kaisōka nihon to kyōiku kiki: fubyōdō saiseisan kara Iyoku kakusa shakai he)*. Tokyo: Yūshindō Kōbunsha Publishing.
Kawaguchi, E., 1999. The War Widows of World War II in the Occupation. *Nihon Joshi Daigaku Ningen Shakai Kenkyū-ka Kiyō*, No. 7, Tokyo, pp. 191–206.
Kawaguchi, E., 2001. Miyake Yasuko's opinions on widows. *Nihon Joshi Daigaku Ningen Shakai Kenkyū-ka Kiyō*, No. 8, pp. 163–176.
Kawaguchi, E., 2003. *The War Widows: between victim and perpetrator (Sensō Mibōjin: Higai to kagai no hazama de)*. Tokyo: Domesu Publishing.
Kawahito, Hiroshi, 1990. Karōshi and its background: from the 'Karōshi hotline' program. In: Hiroshi Kawahito, *Karōshi: When the 'corporate warrior' dies*. Tokyo: Madosha.
Kawahito, Hiroshi, 1998. Suicide by Karō. *(Karō jisatsu)*. Tokyo: Iwanami Shoten.
Kawahito, Hiroshi, 2006. The Collective Responsibility of Company's for Suicide by Overwork *(Karō jisatsu to kigyō no sekinin)*. Tokyo: Junpōsha.
Kawanishi, Y., 1997. An aging society needs new structures. *The Japan Times*, 22 November p. 21.
Kerns, Virginia, 1997. *Women and the Ancestors: Black carib kinship and ritual*. Urbana: University of Illinois Press.
Kikuchi, Keiichi & Omura, Ryō, 1964. That Person didn't Come Home *(Ano hito wa, kaette konakatta)*, Tokyo: Iwanami Shoten, pp. 2–21,161–163.
Kim, Y-C., 1976. *Women of Korea: a history from ancient times to 1945*, Seoul, pp. 97–99.
Kitagawa, Kenzō, 2000. *The Beginning of Japan's Postwar: regional community enlightenment, youth groups and war widows (Sengo no shuppatsu)*, Tokyo: Aoki Shoten, pp. 141–205.
Kitagawa, Kenzō, 2005. War widows and deceased family group (Sensō mibōjin to izokukai: mibōjinkai). In: Noriyo Hayakawa, ed., *War, Violence and Women: colonies and war responsibility (Sensō bōryoku to josei: Shokuminchi to sensō sekinin)*, Tokyo: Yoshikawa Kōbunkan.
Kitahara, Itoko, 1995. *The Social History of Urban Poverty (Toshi to hinkon no shakai shi)*. Tokyo: Yoshikawa Kōbunkan.

Kitamura, Riko, 2005. Men, women and family during wartime (Senji ka no dansei, josei, kazoku). In: Noriyo Hayakawa. ed., *War, Violence and Women 2: women in the militaristic state (Gunkoku no onna tachi)*, Tokyo: Yoshikawa Kōbunkan.

Klein, J.L., 1992. *Daughters, Wives, and Widows: writings by men about women and marriage in England, 1500–1640*. Urbana-Champaign: University of Illinois Press.

Knauft, Bruce M., 1996. *Genealogies for the Present in Cultural Anthropology*. New York and London: Routledge.

Ko, Dorothy, 2001. *Every step a lotus: shoes for bound feet*. Berkeley: University of California Press.

Ko, Dorothy, JaHyun Kim Haboush, and Joan R. Piggott, eds, 2004. *Women and Confucian Cultures in Premodern China, Korea, and Japan*. Berkeley: University of California Press.

Koibuchi, Kaneko, 2000. *The Path to the Establishment of Welfare for Widows and Children (Boshi fukushi no michi hitosuji ni)*. Tokyo: Domesu Publishing.

Kondo, Dorinne. K., 1990. *Crafting Selves: power, gender, and discourses of identity in a Japanese* workplace. Chicago: University of Chicago Press, p. 244.

Kondō, Katsunori, 2005. *Inequalities in Health: what is destroying our health? (Kenkō kakusa shakai: nani ga kennkō o mushibamunoka?)*. Tokyo: Igaku Shoin.

Koyama, Sizuko, 1999. *The Formation of Home and the Nationalization of Women (Katei no seisei to josei no kokuminka)*. Tokyo: Keisō Shobō.

Kulick, Don, 1992. *Language Shift and Cultural Reproduction: socialization, self, and syncretism in a Papua New Guinean village*. Cambridge UK: Cambridge University Press.

Kurushima, Noriko, 1989. The study of words used for widows (Goke to yamome). *A cultural history of words (Kotoba no bunka-shi)*, Volume III: Tokyo: Heibonsha, pp. 163–195.

Lamphere, Louise, 2001. Whatever happened to kinship studies: reflections of a feminist anthropologist. *In:* Linda Stone, ed., *New Directions in Anthropological Kinship,* Lanham: Rowman & Littlefield Publishers, Inc, pp. 21–47.

Lamphere, Ragone, Louise, H. & Zavella, P., 1997. *Situated Lives: gender and culture in everyday life*. New York: Routledge.

Laungani, Pittu, 1997. Death in a Hindu family. In: Colin Murray Parkes, Pittu Laungani & Bill Young, eds, *Death and Bereavement across Cultures*, London: Blackwell Publishing, pp. 52–72.

Lebra, T.S., 1984. *Japanese Women: constraint and fulfillment*. Honolulu: University of Hawaii Press.

Lee, Hai-soon, 2003. Representation of females in twelfth-century Korean historiography. In: Dorothy Ko, Jahyun Kim Haboush & Joan R. Piggott, eds, *Women and Confucian Cultures in Premodern China, Korea, and Japan*, Berkeley: University of California Press, pp. 75–96.

Lee, Richard B. & DeVore, Irven, 1968. *Man the Hunter: the first intensive survey of a single, crucial stage of human development*. Piscataway: Aldine Publishing.

Lerner, Gerda, 1986. *The Creation of Patriarchy*. Oxford: Oxford University Press.
Lerner, Gerda, 1993. *The Creation of a Feminist Consciousness: from the Middle Ages to eighteen-seventy*. Oxford: Oxford University Press.
Lincoln, Bruce, 1991. *Emerging from the Chrysalis: rituals of women's initiation*. New York: Oxford Press USA.
Liu, Xin, 2000. *In one's own Shadow: an ethnographic account of the condition of post-reform rural China*. Berkeley: University of California Press.
Lo, Jeannie, 1990. *Office Ladies, Factory Women: life and work at a Japanese company*. New York: M.E. Sharpe.
Lock, Margaret, 1993. *Encounters with Aging: mythologies of menopause in Japan and North America*. Berkeley: University of California Press.
Lock, Margaret, 1996. Centering the household: the re-making of female maturity in Japan. In: Imamura, A., ed., *Re-imaging Japanese women*, Berkeley: University of California Press, pp. 73–103.
Long, Susan O., 1996. Nurturing and femininity: the ideal of care giving in postwar Japan. In: A. Imamura, ed., *Re-imaging Japanese Women*, Berkeley: University of California Press, pp. 156–176.
Lopata, H.Z., 1987. *Widows, Volume I, the Middle East, Asia and the Pacific*. Durham: Duke University Press.
Lopata, H.Z., 1996. *Current Widowhood: myths & realities*, Thousand Oaks: Sage Press, pp. 21–26.
Mackie,Vera, 2003. *Feminism in Modern Japan*. Cambridge: Cambridge University Press.
Marcus, George E. & Fischer, Michael M. J., 1986. *Anthropology as Cultural Critique: an experimental moment in the human sciences*. Chicago: The University of Chicago Press.
Marcus, George E, 1998. *Ethnography through Thick and Thin*. Princeton: Princeton University Press, pp. 182–183.
Martinez, Dolores P., 1995. Women and ritual. In: D. Martinez, ed., *Ceremony and Ritual in Japan: religious practices in an industrialized society*. Cambridge: Cambridge University Press, pp. 183–200.
Martin, Terry L. & Dola, Kenneth J., 2000. *Men don't Cry...Women do*, Philadelphia: Brunner/Mazel, pp. 113–121.
Mascia-Lees, Francis E. & Black, Nancy Johnson, 2000. *Gender and Anthropology*. Prospect Heights: Waveland Press.
Mauss, Marcel, 1990{1950}. *The Gift*. New York: W.W. Norton.
McAnally, D.R., 1996. *Irish Wonders: Popular tales of ghosts, giants, leprechauns, banshees, fairies, witches, and other marvels of the Emerald Isle*, New York: Gramercy Books, pp. 189–218.
McGinn, Thomas A.J., 2008. *Widows and Patriarchy: ancient and modern*. London: Gerald Duckworth & Co. Ltd.
Mead, Margaret, 1935. *Sex and Temperament in Three Primitive societies*, New York: Columbia University Press, pp. 100–106, 223–229.
Meguro, Yoriko, 1999. An outline: modern characteristics of the Japanese family. In: Yoriko Meguro & Hideki Watanabe, eds, *Sociology Series 2: the family*, Tokyo: Tokyo University Press.
Mendelson, Sara & Crawford, Patricia, 1998. *Women in Early Modern England 1550–1720*. Oxford: Clarendon Press.

Metcalf, P. & Huntington, R., 1991. *Celebrations of Death: the anthropology of mortuary of ritual*. Cambridge: Cambridge University Press, pp. 49–50.
Mies, Maria, 1986. *Patriarchy and Accumulation on a World Scale: Women in the international division of labor*. London: Zed Books.
Mies, Maria, Bennholdt-Thomsen, Veronika & Von Werlhof, Claudia, 1988. *Women: the last colony*. London: Zed Books.
Miyake, Y., 1991. Doubling expectations: motherhood and women's factory work under state management in Japan in the 1930s and 1940s. In: Gail Bernstein, ed., *Recreating Japanese Women, 1600–1945*. Berkeley: University of California Press, p. 267.
Moon, Okpyo, 1990. Is the *ie* disappearing in rural Japan? The impact of tourism on a traditional Japanese village. In: Joy Hendry, ed., *Interpreting Japanese Society*. London: Routledge, pp. 117–130.
Moore, Henrietta L., 1988. *Feminism and Anthropology*. Minneapolis: University of Minnesota Press.
Moore, Henrietta L., 1994. *A Passion for Difference*. Cambridge: Polity Press.
Moore, Henrietta L., 1999. *Anthropological Theory Today*. Cambridge: Polity Press.
Moore, Richard H., 1989. *Japanese Agriculture: patterns of rural development*. Boulder: Westview Press.
Mouer, Ross & Kawanishi, Hirosuke, 2005. *A Sociology of Work in Japan*. Cambridge: Cambridge University Press.
Mullings, Leigh, 1997. *On Our Own Terms: race, class and gender in the lives of African-American women*, New York, p. 96.
Muta, Kazue, 1996. *The Family as Strategy (Senryaku toshite no kazoku)*. Tokyo: Shinyōsha.
Nagano, Hiroko, 2006. *Learning Gender History (Jendā-shi o manabu)*. Tokyo: Yosikawa Kōbunkan.
Nakamura, Kiiko, 1966. *Woman and the Sword (Onna to katana)*. Tokyo: Domesu Publishing.
Nakamura, Takafusa & Miyazaki, Masayasu, eds, 1995. *Report on Damage and Causalities in Japan Caused by World War II (Shiryō taiheiyō sensō higai chōsa hōkoku)*. Tokyo: University of Tokyo Press.
Nakane, Chie, 1970. *The Structure of the Family (Kazoku no kōzō)*, Tokyo: University of Tokyo Press, pp. 34–35.
Namihira, Emiko, 2004. *The Japanese Way of Thinking about Death: from formal traditions to Yasukuni Shrine (Nihonjin no shi no katachi: dentō girei kara yasukuni made)*. Tokyo: Asahi Newspaper Publishing.
Nishikawa, Yūko, 2000. *Modern State and Family Model (Kindai kokka to kazoku moderu)*. Tokyo: Yoshikawa Kōbunkan.
Noguchi, Yukio, Uemura, Kyōko & Kitō, Yumiko, 1989. Structure of the intergenerational transmission of inheritance (Sōzoku ni yoru sedai-kan shisan iten no kōzō: shutoken ni okeru jittai chōsa kekka). *The Quarterly of Social Security Research (Kikan shakai hoshō kenkyū)* 25(2), pp.136–144.
Nolte, Sharon H. & Hastings, Sally A., 1991. The Meiji state's policy toward women. In: Gail Bernstein, ed., *Recreating Japanese Women, 1600–1945*. Berkeley: University of California Press, pp. 153–172.

Nomura, Yasuyo, 1992. Inheritance of widows in the Middle Ages (Chūsei ni okeru goke sōzoku). *Research on Comparative Family History (Hikakukazoku shi kenkyū)*, No. 6, pp. 43–53.
Norton, M.B., 1996. *Founding Mothers and Fathers: gendered power and the forming of American society*, New York, pp. 147–165, 394–395.
Nussbaum, Martha C., 2000. *Women and Human Development: the capabilities approach.* Cambridge: Cambridge University Press.
Ogasawara, Yūko, 1998. *Office Ladies and Salaried Men: power, gender, and work in Japanese companies.* Berkeley and Los Angeles: University of California Press.
Ōhama, Tetsuya, 2003. *The Japan–Quing War and the Japan–Russia War from the Viewpoint of the Japanese people (Shomin no mita nisshin-nichiro sensō)*. Tokyo: Tōsui Publishing.
Okada, Hiroki, 2007. Widows outside of the family system: gaps in the images of widows in Confucianism and globalization (Ie no soto ni sarasareru kafu: Jukyōteki kafu zō to gurōbaru ka no hazama de). In: Wakana Sīna, ed., *Lives of Widows: cultural anthropology of widows (Yamome gurashi; jendā no bunka jinruigaku)*, Tokyo: Akashi Shoten.
Ōkubo, Kenji, 1999. The rise and fall of widows in novels during the Japan–Russia war (Bungaku no yukue – nichiro sensō ni okeru [mibōjin shōsetsu] no shōchō) *Studies of the Modern Literature of Japan (Nihon kindai bungaku)*, 60, pp. 41–55.
Ong, Aihwa, 1987. *Spirits of Resistance and Capitalist Discipline: factory women in Malaysia*. Albany: State University of New York.
Organization for Economic Co-operation and Development, 2005. OECD Economic Surveys 2005 Japan. OECD Publishing.
Organization for economic Co-operation and Development, 2006. OECD Economic Surveys 2006 Japan. OECD Publishing.
Owen, Margaret, 1997. *A World of Widows*. London: Zed Books.
Pallazzi, M., 1991. Work and residence of 'women alone' in the context of a patrilineal system (eighteenth and nineteenth-century northern Italy). In: Mary Jo Maynes, et al., eds, *Gender, Kinship, Power: a comparative and interdisciplinary history*, New York: CUNY Press, pp. 215–230.
Papanek, Hanna, 1990. Family status-production work: women's contribution to social mobility and class differentiation. In: Maithreyi Krishnaraj & Karuna Chanana, eds, *Gender and the Household Domain: social and cultural dimensions*. Thousand Oaks: Sage Publications USA, pp. 97–116.
Parkin, Robert, 2004. *Kinship and Family: an anthropological reader*, Robert Parkin & Linda Stone, eds, Hoboken: Wiley-Blackwell Publishers.
Parrenas, Rhacel, 2005. *Children of Global Migration: transnational families and gendered woes.* Stanford: Stanford University Press.
Peng, I., 1997. Single mothers in Japan: unsupported mothers who work. In: S. Duncan & R. Edwards, eds, *Single Mothers in an International Context: mothers or workers*. London: Blackwell Publishing, pp. 115–147.
Perl, L., 2001. *Dying to Know: about death, funeral customs, and final resting places*. Brookfield: Twenty-First Century Books, pp. 38–39.
Pesek, William Jr., 2003. 'Suicide economy' thinning Japan's ranks. *The Japan Times*, 18 March p.13.

Potash, Betty, ed., 1986. *Widows in African Societies: choices and constraints.* Stanford University Press.
Pratt, Mary Louise, 1986. Fieldwork in common places. In: James Clifford & George E Marcus, eds, *Writing Culture: the poetics and politics of ethnography,* Berkeley: University of California Press, pp. 27–50.
Puckle, B. S., 1926. *Funeral Customs: their origin and development.* London: T. Werner Laudir, Ltd.
Rappaport, Roy A., 1967. *Pigs for the Ancestors: Ritual in the ecology of a New Guinea people.* New Haven: Yale University Press.
Reiter, Rayna R., ed., 1975. Introduction. *Toward an Anthropology of Women,* New York: Monthly Review Press, pp. 11–19.
Rifkin, Jeremy, 2009. *The Empathic Civilization: the race to global consciousness in a world in crisis.* New York: Penguin Group USA.
Roberts, Glenda S., 1994. *Staying on the Line: blue-collar women in contemporary Japan.* Honolulu: University of Hawai'i Press.
Roberts, Glenda S., 2002. Aging Japan's urban landscape. In: Roger Goodman, ed., *Family and Social Policy in Japan: anthropological approaches,* Cambridge: Cambridge University Press, pp. 54–88.
Robertson, J., 1991. The Shingaku woman. In: Gail Bernstein, ed., *Recreating Japanese Women, 1600–1945,* Berkeley: University of California Press, pp. 94–120.
Rodd, Laura Rasplica, 1991. Yosano Akiko and the Taisho debate over the 'new woman.' In: Gail Bernstein, ed., *Recreating Japanese Women, 1600–1945,* Berkeley: University of California Press, pp. 175–198.
Rosaldo, Michelle Zimbalist, 1974. Woman, Culture, and Society: A theoretical overview. In: Michelle Zimbalist Rosaldo & Louise Lamphere, eds, *Woman, Culture & Society.,* Stanford: Stanford University Press, pp. 17–42.
Rosenberger, Nancy Ross, 2001. *Gambling with Virtue: Japanese women and the search for self in a changing nation.* Honolulu: University of Hawai'i Press.
Saku, Takashi, 1962. Widows in historical context (Goke to yamome). *Local Historical Research (Chihōshi kenkyū),* Volume 12–6.
Sahlins, Marshall D., 1972. *Stone Age Economics.* Piscataway: Aldine Transaction Publishing.
Sapir, Edward, 1933. Language. *Encyclopedia of the Social Sciences,* 9. New York: Taylor & Francis. pp. 155–169.
Sasaki, Junoske, et.al., 2000. *Introduction to the History of Japan (Gairon nihon rekishi),* Tokyo: Yoshikawa Kōbunkan, pp. 263–264.
Sato, Barbara, 2003. *The New Japanese Women: modernity, media, and women in interwar Japan.* Durham and London: Duke University Press.
Satō, Toshiki, 2000. *Inequalities in Japanese Society (Fubyōdō shakai nihon).* Tokyo: Chūō Kōron Shinsha.
Scheper-Hughes, Nancy & Bourgois, Philippe, eds, 2004. Introduction: making sense of violence. *Violence in War and Peace: An anthology.* Oxford: Blackwell Publishing Ltd.
Schneider, David, 1984. *A Critique of the Study of Kinship.* Ann Arbor: University of Michigan Press.
Scott, James C., 1985. *Weapons of the Weak: everyday forms of peasant resistance.* Yale University Press.

Seijiyama, Kaku, 1996. *Patriarchy in East Asia: comparative sociology of gender (Higashi ajia no kafujyosei: Jendā no shakaigaku)*. Tokyo: Keisō Shobō.
Sekiguchi, Hiroko, 2003. The patriarchal family paradigm in eighth-century Japan. In: Dorothy Ko, Jahyun Kim Haboush & Joan R. Piggott, eds, *Women and Confucian Cultures in Premodern China, Korea, and Japan*, Berkeley: University of California Press, pp. 27–46.
Sen XV, Sōshitsu, 1979. *Chadō: the Japanese way of tea*. Boston: Weatherhill Press.
Sered, Susan, 1999. *Women of the Sacred Groves*. Oxford: Oxford University Press.
Shirahase, Sawako, 2005. *The Unseen Gaps in an Aging Society: locating gender, generations, and class in Japan (Shōshi kōrei shakai no mienai kakusa: jendā, sedai, kaisō no yukue)*. Tokyo: University of Tokyo Press.
Shirahase, Sawako, 2006. *Inequality in a Changing Society: Hidden disparities behind the demographic shift in Japan (Henka suru shakai no fubyōdō: shōshi kōreika ni hisomu kakusa)*. Tokyo: University of Tokyo Press.
Shirōzu, Noriko, 2000. The Position of Widows in Modern and Present-day China (Kin gendai Chūgoku ni okeru kafu nochii: chūsetsu to saikon o megutte), *The Journal of the Institute for Advanced Studies on Asia (Tōyō Bunka Kenkyū-sho Kiyō)*, No. 140, pp. 372–414.
Shirōzu, Noriko, 2001. *Chinese Women in the Twentieth Century: a study of a modern patriarchy system (Chūgoku josei no nijuu seiki)*. Tokyo: Akashi Shoten.
Shostak, Marjorie, 1981. *Nisa: the life and words of a !Kung woman*, New York, pp. 203, 325.
Shostak, Marjorie, 2000. *Return to Nisa*. Cambridge: Harvard University Press.
Sievers, L. Sharon, 1983. *Flowers in Salt: the beginnings of feminist consciousness in modern Japan*. Stanford: Stanford University Press.
Sloan, Christopher, 2002. *Bury the Dead: tombs, corpses, mummies, skeletons, and rituals*, Washington D.C.: Smithsonian Institute, p. 18.
Skeggs, B., 1994. Situating the production of feminist ethnography. In: Mary Maynard & June Purvis, eds, *Researching Women's Lives from a Feminist Perspective*. London: Taylor & Francis, pp. 72–92.
Smith, Robert J., 1984. Japanese religious attitudes from the standpoint of the comparative study of civilization. *Senri Ethnological Studies*, 16, pp. 99–104.
Smith, Robert J. & Wiswell, E., 1982. *The Women of Suye Mura*. Chicago: University of Chicago Press.
Sōgō, Masaaki & Hida, Yoshihumi, 1986. Widow (*Mibōjin*). *The Encyclopedia of Language in the Meiji Period (Meiji no kotoba jiten)*. Tokyo: Tokyōdō Publishing, pp. 485–486.
Spiro, Melford E., 1986. Cultural Relativism and the Future of Anthropology. *Cultural Anthropology* 1(3), August. American Anthropological Association.
Squad, 2005. *Burned Alive: a survivor of an 'honor killing' speaks out*. New York: Warner Books.
Stacey, J., 1988. Can there be a feminist ethnography? *Women's Studies International Forum*, 11(1), pp. 21–27.

Stone, Linda, 2000. *Kinship and Gender.* Boulder: Westview Press.
Stone, Linda, ed., 2001. Introduction: theoretical implications of new directions in anthropological kinship. In: *New Directions in Anthropological Kinship.* Lanham: Rowman & Littlefield Publishers, Inc.
Stone, Linda & James, Caroline, 2001. Dowry, bride-burning, and female power in India. In: Caroline B. Brettell & Carolyn F Sargent, eds, *Gender in Cross-cultural Perspective,* Upper Saddle River: Prentice-Hall, Inc, pp. 307–316.
Strathern, Marilyn, 2005. *Partial Connections.* Walnut Creek: AltaMira Press.
Sugano, Noriko, 2003. State indoctrination of filial piety in Tokugawa Japan: sons and daughters in the official records of filial piety. In: Dorothy Ko, Jahyun Kim Haboush & Joan R. Piggott, eds, *Women and Confucian Cultures in Premodern China, Korea, and Japan,* Berkeley: University of California Press, pp. 170–189.
Suzuki, Daisetz T., 1959. *Zen and Japanese Culture.* Princeton: Princeton University Press.
Suzuki, Itsuko, 1998. *Living as an Activist Leader for Social Welfare for Widows (Fukushi ni ikiru: Yamataka Shigeri).* Tokyo: Ōzorasha.
Suzuki, Itsuko, 1983. The *History of Post-war Widows,* Volumes I, II, III *(Mibōjin-tachi no sengo-shi).* Tokyo: Tsukuba Shorin.
Tachibanaki, Toshiaki, 1998. *Economic Difference in Japan (Nihon no keizai kakusa).* Tokyo: Iwanami Shoten.
Tajima, Ichirō, 1951. War widows in rural areas (Nōson mibōjin no jittai: shu toshite sensō mibōjin ni tuite). *Social Work (Shakai jigyō),* 34 (9), pp. 58–85.
Takagi, Yutaka, 1982. Women as wives, widows, and nuns in the Middle-Ages of Japan (Chūsei no saijo to goke to goke-ni). *Monthly Encyclopedia (Gekkan Hyakka),* 240, pp. 9–18.
Tambiah, S. J., 1973. From Varna to caste through mixed unions. In: Jack Goody ed., *The Character of Kinship,* Cambridge: Cambridge University Press, pp. 191–229.
Tamanoi, Mariko, 1998. *Under the Shadow of Nationalism: politics and poetics of rural Japanese women.* Honolulu: University of Hawai'i Press.
Tanaka, Yuki, 2002. *Japan's Comfort Women: sexual slavery and prostitution during World War II and the U.S. occupation.* London: Routledge.
Tarukawa, Noriko, 2002. The birth of widows (Mibōjin no tanjō). *Research on mothers and children (Boshi kenkyū),* 22, pp.1–20.
Terai, Minako, 1982. The consciousness of widows regarding the family system (Mibōjin to ie ishiki). *Monthly Encyclopedia (Gekkan Hyakka),* 240, pp. 23–26.
The Civil Code of Japan, 1947. *EHS Law Bulletin Series,* Volume II. Tokyo: Eibun-Hōreisha.
Thomasset, Claude, 1992. The nature of woman. In: Christiane Klapisch-Zuber, ed., *A History of Women: silences of the Middle Ages,* Cambridge: Harvard University Press, pp. 43–69.
Thompson, E., 1928. *Suttee: a historical and philosophical enquiry into the Hindu rite of widow-burning.* London: George Allen & Unwin Ltd.
Tocco, Martha C., 2003. Norms and texts for women's education in Tokugawa Japan. In: Dorothy Ko, Jahyun Kim Haboush & Joan R., Piggott, eds,

Women and Confucian Cultures in Premodern China, Korea, and Japan, Berkeley: University of California Press, pp. 193–218.
Toland, J., 1970. *The Rising Sun: the decline and fall of the Japanese empire, 1936–1945*. New York: The Modern Library Press.
Toshitani, Nobuyoshi, 1996. *Family Law (Kazoku no hō)*. Tokyo: Yūhikaku Publishing.
Traphagan, John W., 2004. *The Practice of Concern: ritual, well-being, and aging in rural Japan*. Durham: Carolina Academic Press.
Turner, Victor, 1995 {1969}. *The Ritual Process: structure and anti-structure*. New York: Aldine De Gruyter.
Tsunoda, Ryusaku, DeBary, Wm. Theodore & Keene, Donald, 1958. *Sources of Japanese Tradition*, Volume 1. New York: Columbia University Press.
Ueno, Chizuko, 2004. *Nationalism and Gender*. Melbourne: Trans Pacific Press.
Ueno, Chizuko, 1994. *The Foundation of the Modern Family and its Demise (Kindai kazoku no seiritsu to shūen)*. Tokyo: Iwanami Shoten.
Uno, Katherine S., 1999. *Passages to Modernity: Motherhood, childhood, and social reform in early twentieth century Japan*. Honolulu: University of Hawai'i Press.
Valentine, James, 1990. On the borderlines: the significance of marginality in Japanese society. In: Eyal Ben-Ari, Brian Moeran & James Valentine, eds, *Unwrapping Japan: society and culture in anthropological perspectives*, Honolulu: University of Hawai'i Press, pp. 36–43.
VanGennep, A., 1960{1908}. *The Rites of Passage* (Translated by M. Vicedom & S. Kimball). Chicago: University of Chicago Press.
Vecchio, Silvana, 1992. The good wife. In: Christiane Klapisch-Zuber, ed., *A History of Women: silences of the Middle Ages*, Cambridge: Harvard University Press, pp. 105–135.
Vogel, E. F., 1963. *Japan's New Middle Class*. Berkeley and Los Angeles: University of California Press.
Wakita, H., Hayashi, R. & Nagahara, K., 1987. *Women's History in Japan (Nihon josei-shi)*. Yoshikawa Kōbunkan.
Walby, Sylvia, 1990. *Theorizing Patriarchy*. Oxford and Cambridge: Blackwell.
Walthall, Anne, 1991. The life cycle of farm women in Tokugawa Japan. In: Gail Lee Bernstein, ed., *Recreating Japanese Women, 1600–1945*, Berkeley and Los Angeles: University of California Press, pp. 42–70.
Waltner, Ann, ed., 1996. *Gender, Kinship and Power: a comparative and interdisciplinary history*. London: Routledge.
Webster, Paula, 1975. Matriarchy: a vision of power. In: Rayna R. Reiter, ed., *Toward an Anthropology of Women*. New York: Monthly Review Press, pp. 141–156.
Weinberger-Thomas, Catherine, 1999. *Ashes of Immortality: Widow-burning in India*. Chicago: University of Chicago Press.
Weiner, Annette B., 1988. *The Trobrianders of Papua New Guinea*. New York: Holt, Rinehart and Winston.
Wiesner, Merry E., 2000. *Women and Gender in Early Modern Europe*. Cambridge: Cambridge University Press.
Yalam, Marilyn, 2001. *A History of the Wife*, HarperCollins, New York, p. 208.

Yamada, Masahiro, 2004. *Hope-polarized Society: hopeless feelings of losers tear-up Japanese society* (*Kibō kakusa shakai: make gumi no zetsubō kan ga nihon o hikisaku*). Tokyo: Chikuma Shobō.

Yamamoto, Akira, 1976. *Research on the History of Symbols in Kasutori Magazines* (*Kasutori zassi kenkyū: shinboru ni miru fūzoku-shi*). Tokyo: News-sha.

Yamataka, Shigeri, 2001 {1977}. Shigeri Yamataka: Forty Years of Social Welfare for Single-mother Families (*Yamataka Shigeri: boshi fukushi yonjū nen*). Tokyo: Nihon Tosho Center.

Yanagisako, Sylvia & Delaney, Carol, eds, 1994. *Naturalizing Power: Essays in feminist cultural analysis*. London: Routledge.

Yanagita, Kunio, 1986. *The Yanagita Kunio Guide to the Japanese Folktale*, Bloomington: Indiana University, pp. 136–147.

Young, Iris Marion, 1997. *Intersecting Voices: dilemmas of gender, political philosophy, and policy*. Princeton: Princeton University Press.

Yuzawa, Yasuhiko, 1998. A new system for delineating the rights and obligations of divorced couples is necessary (Kyōgi rikon ni hitsuyō na kakunin seido). *Asahi Newspaper*, 3 March.

Index

activism and Identity 49, 51, 53, 55, 57, 59, 61, 63, 65, 67, 69, 71, 73, 75, 77, 79
ages 5, 12, 29, 35, 37, 48, 53–4, 64–5, 74, 84, 99, 109–10, 117, 120, 127, 142
aging 4, 89, 115–16, 128
agriculture 64, 127
Aichi Prefecture 5–6, 12, 53, 145
Akita Prefecture 56–7
Allied Powers 58–9
ambiguity 84–5, 89
American soldiers 59
ancestors 74, 139
anniversary 87, 90, 97, 147
anthropologists 16–18, 85, 140
anthropology 34, 88, 140–1
Arapesh widows 18
arrangements 91, 93, 95, 125, 147
assertion, widow's 99
assets 2, 6, 17, 21–2, 32, 37–40, 51, 71–4, 98–100, 105, 132, 137, 139, 143, 145
atomic bombs 49, 80, 144–5
aunts 91–2, 95
authority 20, 36–7, 40–1, 57, 89, 92, 139
 ruling 25–6

bankruptcies, individual 139
Beautiful Reeds Association 61
beauty 65, 146–7
behavior 47, 56, 69, 78, 86, 89–90, 92, 111, 121, 123, 126

behavior of widows 8, 30, 56, 114
bereaved families 56–7, 59, 63, 86, 135
bodies 13–14, 19, 21–2, 43, 45, 80, 94–5, 128, 141, 143–4
 women's 16, 25, 27, 29, 144
boyfriends 115, 120–1
brides, young 126
brothers 18, 26, 49, 53, 63, 65, 71, 73, 76, 93, 126
 eldest 76
 older 77
Brynhild 142
Buddhism 23, 25–6, 89, 143, 147, 150
Buddhist altar 92–3, 97
Buddhist priest 89, 91, 93, 131
buke class 11, 36
butsuma 89, 92–3, 95

calories 51, 145
candle fee 96
capitalism 46, 129
care 12, 14, 32, 41, 49, 53, 69, 95, 99, 104, 116–17, 123, 126, 129–34, 136, 150
care givers 14, 129, 133
ceremony 4, 13, 17, 41, 83, 85, 88–94, 97–101, 106, 116, 122, 125, 129, 147–8
charcoal 61, 68–70, 112
chaste 19–20, 25–6, 38–9, 67, 130
chastity 11, 20, 23, 25, 27–8, 45, 57, 130, 135, 144

children 37–8, 48–50, 52–4,
    59–60, 63–5, 70–5, 80, 91,
    96, 104–6, 112–15, 117–18,
    120–2, 129–30, 132–3,
    135–7
  adult 134
  male 78
  married 19
  older 97
  small 121
  surviving 74
  young 53
China 5, 9, 11, 23–7, 30, 32, 36,
    68, 146
Chinese 23, 35–6, 142
choices 11, 27, 53, 73, 78, 82,
    135–6
cities 40, 49–53, 58, 60, 78,
    111, 122, 127, 144–5
Civil Code of Japan 71
class 11, 22, 27, 30, 36, 47, 64,
    105, 107
commitment, women's to
    employment 136
community 3, 7–9, 11, 13, 21,
    29, 33, 42, 45, 56, 72, 78,
    86, 88, 90, 97
companies 75–6, 108–10
company pension, husband's
    118
Confucian ideology 23, 26–8,
    36, 39, 48
Confucian image of widows
    28
Confucianism 23–4, 28, 36, 39,
    47, 83, 104
Contemporary Japan 15, 135
continental brides 51
contribution, women's 37,
    99–100, 134, 140

control 8, 21, 26, 29–30, 32,
    43–4, 47, 80, 99, 115, 120,
    122, 131
cooking 88, 91–2, 100, 123–5,
    132, 141
cultures 9–10, 17–19, 30–1, 34,
    71, 85, 95, 141
customs 16–18, 26, 47, 103,
    141

daughter-in-law 92, 99
daughters 32, 69, 73, 91–2, 98,
    116–17, 143
day laborers 2, 50, 64, 112–13,
    127
dead soldiers, spirits of 43, 53,
    57, 110
death 1, 7, 14, 19–20, 44–7, 68,
    70–2, 74–5, 78, 83, 85–7,
    90–3, 109–10, 114–15, 136,
    147
debt, husband's 22
deceased husbands 4, 17–18,
    23, 26–30, 37–9, 42, 47, 55,
    62, 64, 71, 74, 86, 141, 143
discipline 119–20
discrimination 35, 80, 104–5,
    107, 122, 149
divorce 11, 26, 32, 42, 75, 122
dowry 21–2
duties 20, 35–6, 38, 44, 46, 78,
    83, 92, 97–8, 117, 140

eating 95–6
economic co-operation 150
economics 131
economy 51, 114
Edo, city of 40
Edo Period 36, 39–41, 71, 143,
    147–9

education 54, 76, 129, 136–7, 144, 146, 149
eirei 43–4, 53, 135
emperor 11–12, 33, 43–5, 47, 143, 146
employees 3, 105, 109, 118
employment 5–6, 57, 60, 136, 139
employment status survey 109–10
equality 26, 129, 137
eroticism 66, 124
eroticized images of war widows 65
eroticized widow stealing 8
ethnography 6, 9, 13, 84, 98, 100–1, 131–2
Europe 20, 27, 30, 145
exclusion 101, 104, 122
expectations, societal 17, 31, 117
experiences 7, 9, 12, 35, 68, 75, 84, 91–2, 102, 104, 106, 121–2, 138
  personal 51–2, 119

familial system 74–5
family honor 1, 16, 22, 27–8, 64
family household system 41, 72, 80
family members 3, 18, 38, 40, 42, 44, 67, 73, 89, 91, 93–4, 97–8, 101–2, 114, 118, 146–7
family services 41, 133
family system 34, 42–4, 46, 71, 73–4, 80, 99, 102, 134
  patriarchal 32, 34, 41–2, 101
farm women 126

upper-class 127
upper-class rural 129
farmers 49–51, 112–13, 145
farms 50, 53, 113, 127, 145
father 24, 41, 44, 63, 68, 76, 78, 112, 127, 140, 147–8
  husband's 126
father-in-law 69
fatherless/widowed families 122
fetishism 1, 11, 16, 21–2, 27
feudal household system 74–5
filial piety 11, 24, 28, 41
financial support 44, 54, 59, 63–4, 74, 78
flowers 41, 62, 93, 98, 144, 149
foods 48–51, 53, 86–7, 91, 93–8, 124, 128, 132, 143, 145, 148
  preparing 91–2, 124
forced marriage 23
foreign countries 45, 51, 145
forfeiture of inheritance 38
freedom 15, 20, 43, 46–7, 74, 81, 124–5, 129, 131, 133, 138
front 76, 93, 95–7, 128

GDP, total 150
gender 1, 16–17, 31, 33–5, 45, 48, 100, 107, 141–2, 149
gender roles 16–17, 87, 104, 131, 136
General Headquarters (GHQ) 58–9, 63, 135
generations 6, 41, 46, 73–4, 90, 98, 100, 140
gifts 21, 38, 96–7
Ginza, city of 112, 149

goke 34–8, 40, 45
gossip 8, 71, 89, 100, 104, 125–6
government 2, 10, 24, 26–7, 35, 50–2, 54, 56–7, 114–16, 118, 128–9, 133–6, 138, 146, 148, 150
government policies 11, 116, 130, 133
grandchildren 78, 89, 117, 125, 132, 140
grandmother 117–18, 127, 133
grave 27, 34, 45, 47, 141
groups 7, 16, 28, 56, 61–2, 74, 78, 105, 108, 150
growth 88–9, 112, 129, 141
guests 91, 93–7

harassment 107–8
heads of families 39, 42, 56, 90, 92, 98–100, 138, 148
health 86
heirs, male 18, 22
Hindu Succession Act 19
Hindu Widow-Remarriage Act 19
Hindu widows 20
Hindu women 19
Hiroshima and Nagasaki 49, 144–5
historical legacies 10, 12
historical periods 10, 23, 34–5, 47
Hokkaido 5–6, 50–1, 58, 113, 127–8
Hokkaido Prefectures 4–5
Hokkaido Region 5–6
homes 12, 18, 21, 39, 45–6, 57, 59, 64, 97, 108–9, 111, 116–17, 120, 133, 145

honor 20–1, 25, 28, 39, 45, 54, 57, 59, 62–3, 135
  collective 29
  husband's 25, 70
  women's 29
hours
  long 110, 127
  short 110
house 24, 40, 50, 52, 68–70, 76, 90–2, 94–5, 99, 114, 118, 126, 141
  husband's 126
household 5–6, 41, 72, 88–9, 92, 99–100, 102, 105–6, 139
  average size 5–6
  husband's 105
household work 87–8, 110
housing, public 105, 108, 115, 148
humiliation 82, 107
husbands 18–22, 24–7, 32, 34, 36–8, 43–5, 50–7, 68–71, 73–5, 78, 80, 104–6, 108–10, 112–15, 118–28, 131–2
  aging 126
  fallen 54
  innocent 8
  lost 2, 114
  new 19, 27, 44, 75
  resident 41
  sick 129
  soldier 51
  steal 124
  support 59
  virile 70
  woman's 84
husband's absence 57
husband's assets 22, 73
husband's brothers 68, 126
  deceased 72–3

husband's death 20, 22, 27–8, 47, 61, 68, 72, 83, 86, 111
husband's estate 71, 118
husband's family 22, 25, 37, 44–6, 53, 68, 73, 84, 86, 92, 114, 126
  deceased 32, 73, 78, 80, 85
husband's family name 143
husband's kin 73
husband's kin-group 30
husband's parents 44–5
  deceased 85
husband's position, late 111

Ibaraki Prefecture 61
ideologies 11, 17, 24–5, 28, 33, 42–3, 46–7, 71, 104, 106, 134
  societal 38, 119
ikebana 6, 88, 90, 147–8
images 12, 14, 36–7, 40, 46, 53, 55, 62, 65, 94, 107, 124, 130, 133, 146
images of widows 40–1, 65
importation of food 145
impoverished families 113–14
Impoverished rural women 67
in-laws 20, 32, 45, 75, 91, 95, 104, 116, 124–6
income 3, 30, 113, 116–17, 149
India 19–20, 27, 30, 141–2
individuals 11, 20, 25, 31, 35, 41, 50, 81–2, 84, 87, 97, 104, 106, 108–9, 116, 122
Indonesia 141
inequality 9, 11, 31, 33, 112, 119, 137, 148
informants 5, 7, 35, 50, 58, 78, 80, 107, 113, 119–20, 122, 146

inheritance 11, 16, 21, 26, 37–8, 44, 56, 71, 73, 78, 80, 99, 131–2, 140–1
inheritance rights 26, 28, 30, 33, 40
initiation rituals, women's 84
institutionalization 9, 11, 56, 143
intense bombings 52
interviews 1, 3–4, 6–7, 65, 67–8, 105, 114, 130–1, 145–6
  personal 1, 4, 60
isolation 31, 75, 104, 120–3, 125

Japan
  modern-day 75, 103
  post-war 10, 52, 71, 78, 80
  present-day 5, 8, 10, 135
Japan-Quing War 34
Japan Widow's Group Association 61, 63
Japanese ceremonies 13, 95
Japanese culture 4, 7, 11, 62, 94
Japanese families 14, 30, 43, 46, 135
Japanese feminists 144
Japanese folklore 86
Japanese government 14, 57–60, 81, 116, 134, 145
Japanese government officials 41, 146
Japanese imperialism 52
Japanese labor market 108
Japanese language 34
Japanese marriage system 144
Japanese military government 55
Japanese society 33, 41–2, 46, 53, 67, 101, 111, 123, 135

Japanese state hegemony 135
Japanese village society 37
Japanese war propaganda 12
Japanese war-regime 57
Japanese widows 13, 34, 60, 82, 86, 131
Japanese women 2, 7, 32–3, 40, 47, 58, 104, 128
Japanese women's history 143–4
Japan's aging population 134
Japan's Child Welfare Ministry Report 64
Japan's economy 139
Japan's imperial wars 11, 34, 63
Japan's imperial wartime government 135
Japan's League of War Bereaved 63
Japan's mountainous terrain 145
Japan's post-welfare state 14

kafu 34–6, 45, 142
karōshi 109
kasutori magazines 65–6
kids 106, 108, 112, 114–15, 128
Kingdom of Silla 25–6
kinship 14, 23–5, 141
kinship groups 18, 23, 25, 29, 40, 42, 75
 husband's 18, 29–30, 73
kinship systems 1, 16–17, 36, 73–4
kitchen 92, 94–5, 100, 103

labor 87–9, 100, 103, 109, 117, 125, 129, 133, 140
 women's 100

labor market 3, 107, 110, 130, 144
land 6, 25, 29, 38, 48, 51, 72–4, 83, 98–100, 112, 141–2
language 7, 11, 33–5, 45, 47, 134
laws 1, 6–7, 11, 16, 22, 27–8, 38, 42, 71, 127, 131, 134, 141, 144
LDP (Liberal Democratic Party) 65, 137, 148
leaders 41, 58–9, 61
legacy 52, 136–7, 142
legislation 19–20, 64
levirate 18, 29, 73
levirate marriage 18, 29–30, 71–4
 revival of 71
Liberal Democratic Party (LDP) 65, 137, 148
lifestyle, widowed 124
lilies, white 35, 53, 62, 64–5
liminality 84–5
liminar 85
local communities 8, 25, 37, 39
lone mother families 117
loneliness 70, 120–1, 123
love 20, 46, 66, 120, 126, 130
lovers 73, 124–6
loyalty 24–5, 33, 41

magazines 65, 67, 146
maids 2, 49, 64, 107, 113, 127
maintenance 17, 73, 88, 100–1
managers 91–2, 111
manufacturing jobs 5–6
marginalization 107, 122–3
marriage 18, 21–2, 37–9, 42, 44, 46, 53, 71–2, 79, 86,

105, 119–21, 126–7, 133, 135–7, 143–4
  regarding 64, 119
marry 19, 39, 49, 51, 73, 76, 119, 124, 135–6
marrying 27, 119, 121
meals 92, 96
Meiji Civil Code 11, 42, 71, 75, 101
Meiji Era 30, 34, 41–3, 45
Meiji Period 40–4, 46–7
memorial ceremonies 13, 74, 90, 99–100, 102, 128, 147
memorial services 83, 90, 94, 96–7, 103, 131, 147–8
men 24, 97
mibōjin 34–5, 41, 43, 45, 61–2, 133
Middle Ages 36
military government 56–8
Ministry of Justice 56–7
money 37, 50, 69, 74, 78, 83, 91, 96, 112, 114–15, 118, 122, 127–8, 145, 148–50
mothers 41, 67, 122, 144
mourning 17–18, 38, 90
movement, widow's 64, 81

Nagoya 6, 90, 145
natal family 32, 37, 47, 78, 80
nationalism 6, 43, 48, 141, 148
natural caregivers 115–17, 129
New Guinea 18
New Widows 14, 131, 133, 135, 137
nuns 25, 143
  widowed 143

obligations 17, 20, 25, 36–7, 97, 131

Okinawa 49, 125–6, 128
older women 19, 99, 125, 131, 136
organization
  political 7–8
  widow's 64
outsiders 80–1, 105
overwork 110
ownership 20–1, 74
oyomesan 91, 94–5, 97–9

Pacific War 2, 8, 49, 64, 71, 146
parents 32, 37, 39, 44, 70, 76–8, 112–13, 123, 129, 139, 143, 150
part-time work 108, 133, 136
participation, women's 87, 90, 100
passage, rites of 13, 87–9
patriarchal family 30–1, 39, 41, 99
patriarchal ideology 74, 140
patriarchy 9, 140
peddlers 53, 78–9
pensions 4, 8, 59–60, 99, 111, 118, 136–7
  husband's 118
poor urban widows 65
poverty 3–4, 14–15, 21, 44, 49, 51, 53–5, 57, 59–61, 63, 65, 75, 105–7, 111, 137–8, 147–8
poverty line 3, 115, 150
pressures, societal 27, 38–9, 76, 78, 125
property 2, 20–1, 32, 38, 74, 99, 105, 131, 139
  husband's 45
prostitution 59, 65, 79, 144

protection 21, 44, 73
provisions 12, 51–2, 112
public assistance 56, 60, 112

re-marriage 17, 27, 45, 48, 70, 72, 104
re-marry 17–19, 26, 29, 38, 48, 54, 60, 64–5, 74, 78, 127, 147
reeds, beautiful 35, 53, 61, 64–5
relatives, male 92–3
religions, new 150
religious rituals 12, 74, 87, 100
remarriage 7, 20–1, 24, 30, 38, 42, 54, 56, 117, 119
 widow 24
remarriage of widows 19, 25–6, 56
remarry 19–23, 26–7, 38–9, 42, 74–5, 115, 117, 119, 123–4, 150
resistance 7, 9, 14, 30, 52, 62, 96–7, 100–1, 107, 119, 124, 140
resources 32, 60–1, 101
responsibility 17, 37, 58, 83, 86, 91, 104, 115–16, 125–6, 131, 148, 150
 care-giving 130–1
rice 50, 59, 143, 145
rice harvesters 143
rights
 husband's 36
 legal 42, 44, 98–9
 widow's 21
rites 19, 28–9, 91, 98
 memorial 13, 88, 90
ritualized performance 87, 89

rituals 13, 17, 19, 83–5, 87–8, 92–3, 95, 100–1, 103, 131–2, 147
 memorial 90–1, 97
 widow's 20
roles 2–3, 11–12, 14, 19, 21, 25, 27, 31, 33, 38, 42, 46–7, 83–4, 86, 95, 97
 widows 16, 18
 women's 14, 55, 93, 127, 140, 144
rural areas 24, 40, 49, 67, 71–4, 80, 92, 125–8, 140
rural widows in England 141
rural women 68, 70

sacrifice 20, 29, 34, 36, 44–5, 56, 59, 64, 110, 129–30
 husband's 110
salaries 5, 120
san-kaiki 90, 147
Sapporo 4–5, 58, 139
savings 106–7
scholars 12–13, 23, 28, 33, 40, 64, 125, 140, 143, 147
school 54, 112, 147–9
seasonings, classic Japanese 91
seido 6, 41–2, 46, 134
service overtime 109
services 12, 91, 94, 99, 102, 116, 126, 129, 133, 147, 150
sex 67, 69, 79, 130
sexuality 1, 22, 44–5, 119, 130
 women's 24
shira ume 61–2
shrine 43, 55–6, 64, 135, 146
single mothers 3, 54, 58–60, 64, 112, 115, 117, 138
Sino-Japanese War 49
sisters 19, 29, 65, 91, 126

societal condemnation 8, 147
societal issues 14, 148
societal taboos 24, 27
society 10–12, 14, 22–3, 26, 29–31, 33–6, 40–1, 57, 64–5, 67, 80–1, 88–9, 102–5, 120–2, 132–3, 140–1
  aging 1, 134
  diverse 30–1, 140
  members of 20, 120–1
  present-day 16, 124
soldiers 12, 44–5, 49–51, 56–9, 63, 109, 146
  professional 43, 45, 135
  widows of 56, 58
sons 22, 24, 27, 37, 44, 52, 63, 68–70, 72–3, 76–8, 80, 91–2, 98–9, 114, 120, 148
  eldest 6, 38, 98, 116, 148
souls 17, 37–9, 53, 98, 128, 143, 147
  husband's 83
spirits 53, 70, 86, 96, 98, 128, 141, 146–7
spiritual wives 44, 74
spouse 35, 71–2, 90
standards, societal 111, 116, 123
stem family 139
stories 12, 26, 29, 51, 67–8, 78, 80, 89, 114, 121, 125–8, 142
stories of war widows 66
structural impediments 7–9, 127
successors 36, 71, 73, 92, 98, 140, 148
suicide 27–9, 139
supplies 51–2, 78
survival 48, 52–3, 60, 63, 70, 101, 103, 107, 125

suttee 19
symbols 59, 62, 66, 84–5
system 3, 6, 23–4, 26, 33, 36, 41, 46, 73–5, 80, 88, 98–102, 105, 111–12, 121, 134

tea 94, 96, 147–8
tea ceremony 6, 88, 91, 147
teachers 54–5, 57, 91, 147
term mibōjin 43–4, 46–7
term patriarchy 140
term yamome 35–6
themes 1, 13, 17–20, 28–9, 48, 85, 88, 102, 107, 144
  cross-cultural 27–8
Tokyo 4–6, 40, 49–50, 58, 60, 63, 76, 91, 98, 112, 135, 144–6, 149
towns 6, 39, 70, 78, 81
traditions 6, 87–8, 90, 100, 103, 126, 148
transformations 9, 11, 16, 23, 33, 36, 41, 47, 53, 65, 85, 88, 90, 100
tsuma 44, 53, 135
Turner's models 84–5
two-parent families 117

United States 50, 52, 111
upper-class families 6, 12, 23, 37–8, 98, 102–3
upper-class widows 22, 25, 27–8, 39, 83, 102–3, 111
upper-class widows in Korea 27
urban areas 51–2, 129, 142
urban cities, large 4, 6, 60, 128
usage 34, 36, 40, 43, 45

Van Gennep 13, 84–5

Index

victims 12, 58, 63, 82, 109, 127, 144
village 6, 19, 24, 33, 39, 70, 72, 74, 76
violence 29, 81–2, 139
Volsungs 142

wabi-sabi 147
war 1, 12, 28, 34, 43, 45, 48–55, 57–60, 62–5, 68, 70–2, 75–8, 81–2, 126, 142, 145–6
war efforts 52, 54–5
war stories 12
war widows 11–12, 34, 43, 45, 48–9, 51, 53–63, 65–7, 69–71, 73–5, 77, 79–82, 110
  dangerous 65
  destitute 137
  monitored 56
  upper-middle-class 74
  young 67
warriors 25, 36
wartime 8, 52
wealthy Japanese 150
welfare 113, 139
widow-burning 20
widow-concubine 18
widow sacrifice 20, 28–9, 39
widow-suicide 27
widow surveillance 8
widowed women 1–2, 8, 18, 20, 32, 47, 62, 85, 88–90, 100, 111, 113, 116–17, 120, 135, 138
widowers 2, 6, 17, 20, 39–41, 74, 89–90, 118, 121, 123, 127, 142, 147
widowhood 9, 12, 14–15, 23–4, 35, 75, 78, 103, 111, 115, 118, 122, 124–5, 136–7

widows
  affluent 3
  corporate warrior 110
  deceased son's 80
  destitute 39, 60
  elderly 14, 75, 129–31, 138
  erotic 130
  faithful 98
  grieving 26
  integrative role of 16, 22
  low-income 3, 129–30
  lower-class 22, 48
  middle-class 111, 118
  middle-upper-class 67
  old 18, 21, 62, 85, 91, 106, 112, 114–15, 119, 122, 125, 128, 131
  poor 21, 30, 39, 47, 53, 60, 65, 74, 78, 103, 106, 133, 137
  present-day 14
  self-sacrificing 25
  sexualized 136
  training 57
  upper class 38
  virtuous 11, 135
  watching 123, 130
  wealthy 37, 83
  women fear 124
  young 73, 129
  young urban 60
  younger 135, 138
  youthful 45
Widows' Association 61
widow's inheritance allotment 73
widow's motivation 99
widows of merchant families 142
widow's pension 64, 81
widow's roles 88

widow's sentiments 14
widow's status 46
wife 11, 24–5, 29, 40, 44–5, 69, 76, 84–6, 89, 91–2, 99–100, 102, 109, 126, 131, 140–2
 good 97–9
wives 2, 12, 20, 22, 36, 45–6, 53, 57, 59, 65, 67, 72–3, 91, 110, 113, 133
women
 aging 12, 138
 destitute 60, 63
 divorced 8, 118, 122, 135
 educated 68
 elderly 125, 128–9, 138
 employed 110
 impoverished 14, 47, 105, 130
 less deserving 122
 married 8, 70
 middle-class 47
 middle-upper class 102
 nationalization of 58
 old 106
 poor 129, 144
 regarding 39, 143
 rights of 10, 137
 role of 83, 116, 118
 single 3, 35, 54, 105, 118
 slave 28
 unmarried 150
 upper class 47
 wealthy 25
 young 51, 64, 67, 84, 91, 109
women, upper-class 11, 64, 112, 131
women activists 65
women alone 54
women of wealth 32
women's chastity 144
women's detriment 140

women's domesticity 134
women's education 143–4
women's movements 8
women's positions 9, 36
women's power 32
women's reluctance to marry 136
women's status 16, 33, 40
wood houses 145
workplace 14, 107, 130, 136, 138
World War II 35, 43, 50, 76, 145

yamome 34–6, 40–1, 142
Yasukuni Shrine 53–4, 56, 58–9, 63, 81, 135, 146
yearly income 106, 118–19
yen 80, 91, 118, 149
young middle-class women 46
younger brother 72–3, 77

www.ingramcontent.com/pod-product-compliance
Lightning Source LLC
Chambersburg PA
CBHW071439080526
44587CB00014B/1908